[illegible] Dragon (reissued [illegible]

1935: The Old Man's Place, Albert & Charles Boni (reissued [illegible] by Permabooks 1957 as [illegible] by Signet)

1939: Seventy Times Seven, Knopf (reissued 1954 & 1957 as Make My Bed in Hell by Avon)

1943: The People from Heaven, Harcourt Brace (reissued 1995 by University of Illinois)

1951: A Man Without Shoes, Plantin (reissued 1982 by Black Sparrow)

1953: The Land that Touches Mine, Doubleday & Jonathan Cape

1964: Every Island Fled Away, Norton

1967: The $300 Man, Prentice-Hall

1976: Adirondack Stories, Capra

CREATIVE INTERPRETATIONS OF HISTORY

1975: A More Goodly Country, Horizon

1977: View from This Wilderness, Capra

1980: To Feed Their Hopes, University of Illinois (reissued 1995 as A Book of American Women by University of Illinois)

1984: The Winters of That Country, Black Sparrow

1997: Intruders in Paradise, University of Illinois

AUTOBIOGRAPHY AND MEMOIR

1984: William Carlos Williams/John Sanford: A Correspondence, [illegible]

1985: The Color of the Air, Black Sparrow

1986: The Waters of Darkness, Black Sparrow

1987: A Very Good Land to Fall With, Black Sparrow

1989: A Walk in the Fire, Black Sparrow

1991: The Season, It Was Winter, Black Sparrow

1993: Maggie: A Love Story, Barricade

1994: View from Mt. Morris, Barricade

1995: We Have a Little Sister, Capra

2003: A Palace of Silver, Capra

BOOKS BY JOHN SANFORD

Novels and Stories

1933: *The Water Wheel* (as Julian L. Shapiro), Dragon (reissued 2020 by Tough Poets)
1935: *The Old Man's Place*, Albert & Charles Boni (reissued 1953 by Permabooks; 1957 as *The Hard Guys* by Signet)
1939: *Seventy Times Seven*, Knopf (reissued 1954 & 1957 as *Make My Bed in Hell* by Avon)
1943: *The People from Heaven*, Harcourt, Brace (reissued 1995 by University of Illinois)
1951: *A Man Without Shoes,* Plantin (reissued 1982 by Black Sparrow)
1953: *The Land that Touches Mine*, Doubleday & Jonathan Cape
1964: *Every Island Fled Away*, Norton
1967: *The $300 Man*, Prentice-Hall
1976: *Adirondack Stories*, Capra

Creative Interpretations of History

1975: *A More Goodly Country*, Horizon
1977: *View from this Wilderness*, Capra
1980: *To Feed Their Hopes*, University of Illinois (reissued 1995 as *A Book of American Women* by University of Illinois)
1984: *The Winters of that Country*, Black Sparrow
1997: *Intruders in Paradise*, University of Illinois

Autobiography and Memoir

1984: *William Carlos Williams/John Sanford: A Correspondence*, Oyster
1985: *The Color of the Air*, Black Sparrow
1986: *The Waters of Darkness*, Black Sparrow
1987: *A Very Good Land to Fall With*, Black Sparrow
1989: *A Walk in the Fire*, Black Sparrow
1991: *The Season, It Was Winter*, Black Sparrow
1993: *Maggie: A Love Story*, Barricade
1994: *The View from Mt. Morris*, Barricade
1995: *We Have a Little Sister*, Capra
2003: *A Palace of Silver*, Capra

SPEAKING IN AN EMPTY ROOM

SPEAKING IN AN EMPTY ROOM

The Selected Letters of John Sanford

❧

Edited and with an introduction by Dan Giancola

Afterword by Jack Mearns

Tough Poets Press
Arlington, Massachusetts

Back cover photo by Dan Giancola

ISBN 978-0-578-77472-5

Tough Poets Press
Arlington, Massachusetts 02476
U.S.A.

www.toughpoets.com

For Maggie & The Governor
As Always . . .

TABLE OF CONTENTS

INTRODUCTION

What might readers glean from a volume of letters written by an author who published a five-volume autobiography? Everything. The John Sanford Archive at Boston University's Howard Gottlieb Archival Research Center contains seventy-two years of letters to family members, editors, publishers, friends, fans, and other writers. These letters begin in 1931 and end less than two weeks before Sanford's death in 2003, almost three months shy of his ninety-ninth birthday. The letters comprise a fascinating addendum to the autobiography because they reveal the artist and man behind the creation of the autobiographical mask, and they are written, like most letters, in the first person, a departure from the second person voice Sanford adopted in the writing that comprises the latter half of his writing life.

These letters reveal Julian Shapiro—Sanford's birth name—rather than Sanford the literary construct. The letters mirror Sanford's stylistic evolution; the letters written in the 1930s, for example, reveal a young writer's influences and his struggles to arrive at a voice at once experimental *and* clear.

More than anything else, however, these letters illustrate a writer's life. In selecting from thousands of pages contained in the archive, I've tried to show an American writer at work—his ambition and self-consciousness, his self-promotion and unflagging attempts to publish and the attendant feelings associated with the failure to publish, his perfecting his blend of style and content, his thoughts about writing, and his support of other writers.

As a by-product of this attempt, a man emerges, full of warts and blemishes but balanced by confidence and integrity. Sanford had a reputation in publishing circles—especially within the East Coast publishing establishment—as a writer with whom it was difficult to work. This reputation arose from Sanford's insistent belief in the efficacy of his modernist, *sui generis* approach to making books; beginning with *Seventy Times Seven*, his third novel, published in 1939, he begins interlacing his poems concerning American history with his fiction to give readers "the color of the air" as a way of providing readers with an historical background to help explain his characters' motivations and actions. Sanford's view of American history is neither kind nor patriotic; to perhaps oversimplify, Sanford believed all of America's problems—income and civil rights inequality in particular—resulted from the evils of capitalism, which necessitates a perpetual underclass. Publishers, therefore, didn't quite know what to do with Sanford's work. They often objected to both the message and the expression of this message. In a letter (#154 in this volume) to Norwegian novelist Per Petterson, Sanford writes "People on my side of the fence don't get awards from the Establishment for trying to pull the Establishment down; they get what we call a swift kick in the ass." In a later letter (#202), Sanford writes "I'm against the establishment, and of course it's against me. At no time in my career did I expect to be put forward by the very thing I was out to put down."

But as a younger man Sanford *did* expect to be put forward by the establishment. He feverishly tried to place his work and was often stung by publishers refusing it as the letters show. In a letter from New York to his wife, Maggie, awaiting his triumphant return to California, Sanford bemoans "the malignancy of ambition" after his attempts to publish *A Man Without Shoes* (the only one of his books he would ultimately self-publish) met with rejection after rejection. Sanford makes clear in many letters that he would happily revise manuscripts and conform to the wishes of his editors by editing out superfluous or ineffective writing, but he adamantly refused to tone down his rhetoric or remove the poems, which remained a point of contention when he tried to publish fiction and which may have ultimately led to Sanford creating his own brand of nonfiction beginning in the 1970s. This is why, in a letter to me dated October 23, 1995, Lyle Stuart, publisher of Barricade Books, which had published Sanford's *Maggie: A Love Story* and *A View from Mt. Morris*, writes, "He's a crank and a pest and it's become quite clear why no major publisher ever did a second book with him."

It's easy for readers of this volume to ascertain the partial truth of this. Sanford could be acerbic, vituperative, and excoriating. He did not suffer fools gladly and is particularly scathing toward anyone who treated him—and especially Maggie—shabbily. For instance, he never moved a step closer to compassion in assessing those who took part in the House Un-American Activities Committee, which blacklisted the Sanfords from 1951–1960, revoking the couple's passports and depriving Maggie of her livelihood as a Hollywood screenwriter. As a result, Sanford could write forty-six years later (letter #198) about Elia Kazan that he took "the pose of having chosen loyalty to his country over loyalty to his friends. The pose is fake: the fink never lived who didn't invoke the flag."

Readers of these letters will learn something else about Sanford that doesn't appear in his autobiography—he seems to relish any opportunity to debate those who criticize his writing. Editors, fans, and fellow writers received carefully constructed, counterpointed arguments to letters they'd written hoping to help Sanford improve upon his work. If Sanford liked you (see letter #73 to fellow writer and communist Albert Maltz), Sanford's tone could be respectful, and if he didn't like you the tone could be withering; whatever the tone, Sanford tries to convince his epistolary challengers to alter their thinking about his work. Readers must decide, finally, if this is healthy self-confidence or arrogant bitchiness, but Sanford, trained at Fordham Law School and admitted to the New York State Bar on May 1, 1929, reveals in these letters the rhetorical tenacity of a crackerjack trial attorney. To call him argumentative is an understatement.

By this time, anyone unfamiliar with Sanford's work might write him off as just another curmudgeon. But these letters also present a softer, more jocular, and somewhat less abrasive Sanford. For example, the autobiography never reveals Sanford's helpfulness toward other writers. While it's true that the letters show Sanford often criticizing other writers' work, he could also praise effusively, particularly in the case of younger writers. He *always* found *something* to praise. One exception is to be found in the letters to his longtime friend Eli Jaffe, whose work Sanford lambasted. The problems Sanford has with Jaffe's work, however, are instructive and should be read by anyone who flirts with the idea of writing a novel.

Also of interest to Sanford aficionado and casual reader alike are Sanford's observations of Hollywood during and at Depression's end, his thoughts on the dissolution of the Soviet Union, and his vacillating opinions on fellow novelist Nathanael "Pep" West, whom Sanford credits with his beginning a writing career.

All in all, these letters fascinate. They're often didactic. They're instructive. They're funny. They bristle and sizzle. They reveal a man supremely confident in his ability to write gorgeous prose but who could not seem to get published without a struggle. They reveal a writer passionate about language and social change. They reveal a man who dearly loved his family and his wife, a man who could be counted on to defend them against any aspersion.

These letters may not always indicate a warm and cuddly human being, but John Sanford is an outstanding and neglected American literary treasure. His politics and asperity certainly worked against him; given the quality of his writing, however, his relative anonymity is certainly unjustified. In the 20th Century no one—neither Maltz nor Dos Passos nor LeSueur nor Eastman nor Fast nor any other proletarian or socialist writer one may name—combined such high art with unyielding polemics. John Sanford stared directly into America's hypocritical face for decades and never relented nor varied his anti-capitalist, anti-war message. "Art is a weapon," he writes, and in a career spanning seven decades he used his art to club America's readers into fulfilling the promise in the last line of our "Pledge of Allegiance," "with liberty and justice for all." Unfortunately, we rarely seemed to have listened, or he could not get his writing more widely disseminated to where we all could hear him. Thankfully, he never stopped "screaming at the deaf."

Dan Giancola

THE LETTERS

1. To Ruth Shapiro

(John Sanford's sister, born in 1908. She went on to become an educator, moved to California, married Vernon Leader in 1942, and died September 28, 2001. The manuscript referred to here is The Water Wheel. *This letter was sent from Menton, France, during Sanford's second trip overseas. Mel Friedman is Ruth and John's first cousin. This letter features Sanford's early experiments in prose, inspired by his reading of James Joyce, which includes a lack of or odd use of capitalization and apostrophes, and idiosyncratic spelling.)*

February 8th, 1931

Dear piece of cheese

eye assure you eye was very sorry to hear about your i. eye hope that beye this teyem your i is feyen, but dont have too much confide in doc goldsteyen. He is many long sleyeces of knackwurst, and maybe even wurst than that. wheye, eye know more about is [sic] than he does. he is a fathead. he is a very big fathead.

well, it seems were talkin about eyes so i might as well tell you that mine dont bother me at all at all, even though I work many hours each day on the mmmmmssss. and read books by the volume. not bad. and no glasses at all. i cant understand it, unless going to bed early has something to do with it and also getting up before sundown. try it yourself. its supposed to be good for whats aylwin, as theodore whats dunton.

a verminous, bebearded, debraggled, seedy, villumous, looking creature got off the paris train the day before yesterday and impersonated a cousin of mine. it was too thin. i knew he was an imposter as soon as i onced him over north by northeast. can you beat it. he said he was melvin friedman. even so. of course i walked in his face and laughed away. he folleyed me down la rue and poured out intimate details about my life, about his own, too, which only a real friedman could be espectured to know, so i began to credents in his story. he turned out to be melvin friedman, a man we all know very well. It seems they wouldn't let him off le bateau to coin a dingdonger at le havre because he didn't look anything like the fotograf in his pass the port. they claimed he had stoling it from the wright guy, you know the wright guy, don't you. he looked as though the as-CAN-ia had been standing on the tips of her funnels for sixty years but when i asked him if he had had a ruff trip he said HELL, nO, that he was one of the best sailors since Leif the Great, mr MaGellan, cristophosphorous colombinimo, amerigo Vespucci, vasco de gama, capn ahab, dr kabatchnik, called cabot in the land of beans and codpieces, lord Nelson, caleed HalfNelson sometimes, THE CHAP at Vanilla Bay who said you may fire when THE Griddle is ready and even ALAIN GERBAULT. but none of his brags felled my opinion that he puked out yards and yards of guts and whats in them. he must have shot up every biscuit and cookie but the turbines and number four hatch. he needed four or seventeen shaves and had gotten bollixed up every metre of the way from le havre. his fast fright from there to paresis landed him in the oily of churches, rats, pimps and dolltearsheets at the wrong time. he booked on to menton and went across the street to a coffee to get cup of cafe. the train went. he did not go. i do not know why. he doesn't know either. it seems that through some misunderstanding with the railroad officials, the engineer forgot to wait for him, or forgot to go across the street to tell him that the departure was already an hour overdue, and wouldnt he please hurry up and finish that coffee. he wasnt a bit put out. he found out that if he waited long enough, there was another train going to menton. there was, but not the one he finally took. that brought up short and sharp at marseille at two in the morning and stayed there. no matter what he did, the train stayed there. so he went to a hotel, where he forgot to register. as a consequence, they wouldnt let him go up to a room and go to sleep, a procedure of course vastly different from anything in americas, so he sat on his ass in the lobby until the menton train pulled out, a matter of only five hours or so. before quitting paris, the man had sent a telegram that he only wanted o. to meet him. when he staggered off the train here he must have been damn sorry he didn't have enough foresight to demand an ambulance. he nearly needed a plank as it was. of course, his injunction was obeyed. i was walking down the street a few hours later and lammed into him in front of a cafe with o. swabbing down the cinders with a champagne cocktail. he looked like something you ate that didn't agree with you. this is not for publication.

any year now I expect to see something of him. he seems to be occupied with something or other. i havent been able to find out where he spends all his time. i think the adjective would be horizontal, but that's an awfully unfair thing to say about a man who is down. if you understand what I mean.

Proof of the pudding is in the cathartic you have to take later. Yesterday I got a letter from you dated January 22. swaller your words gal swaller them.

i am enclosing a clippin or two you may enjoy looking at. first read the stuff in the london times. even though many complementary laws are left out of the article deliberately, to throw the worst possible light on the enactment, nevertheless the whatever is in the article is the truth. then read the bilgewater in the daily mail and see if you can find out the truth. then, im also enclosing a pronunciamento of calvin r bitchpup. he speaks on america. as ezra pound says, he is a yellowbellied peewit, or notes to those effects. also charles shrapnels new flick has made quite a flicker. also the sporting page of the times, containing art notes, strawinsky, etc. not half bad, except the talk about the art crap.

that's

all

for now. . . . . . .but. . . . oh yes

so natan gave a party the other night. it sure must have been a swell affair. not even tea, eh. what were you supposed to do, bring your own lunch, or send down to a catererere-rer. just like him, but in his circle that goes for just forgetfulness. oh nat, why hes so intense and so vital, he just natchrally loses all sense of time and space. oh, don't mind that. you know he has a great big heart and would give you the back off his shirt anythime (that you can find him). oh yes you've got to overlook all that. he means well. hes so intense and so vital. garnet whaledriver sat before the ivories. his fingers strayed over the minor keys and suddenly dipped into hambletonians berceuse in r flat foir rubberhose and carpenters bench. mrs girlpish swined away.

oh hes so vital.

and that's

that.

2. To Jesse Greenstein

(Sanford and Greenstein met in Long Branch, New Jersey in 1927. Greenstein went on to become Professor and Chairman of the Astrophysics Department at Caltech and authored the pamphlet "An Astronomical Life.")

Mar 12. 31

Dear Jess

Veni Vedi but not the rest! Eliot returned the mss of the story this a.m. with a kindly and benevolent—which means usual—obituary burying the ex-bridge player with simple honors. Almost the sort of thing where the master says "Better stick to the law, my boy; you have every qualification for success *there!*"

But he made the mistake of winding up his note by saying hed be happy if I looked in on him again before I sailed. So I phoned him this a.m. and he gave me another appointment for tomorrow. Therein he doubtless will enlarge on the slender merits of mystery, overlook benignly the overwhelming defects and shake my hand warmly (or as warmly as T. S. E. can do anything). And send me off vainly happy. So that he can sell more books. What a life!

In restaurant last night, saw a guy who looked familiar. Sent waiter over to snoop around and see if the guy with smoked cheaters on was really Joyce. The bloody fool of a flunky walked straight up to him and put the question. Joyce owned up, but asked not to be "disturd". So I didn't, which makes 2 up for the other side. You know, you can't do much better than to be turned down by Joyce + Eliot. That's shooting pretty high. And Heigh Ho!

Sail from these chalky shores May 15 on SS Deutschland, reaching New York on May 22 if all goes well and the ship doesn't take it into its head (whose head?) to stink. Gave up plan to sail on Geo Washingtoilet for this reason: no money to stick it for another week. Furthermore, I just can't wait to see you. My soul yoins for you and my fist is just itching to crack you one on your ugly schnozzola.

But save me a good piece of roast beef and a hunk of schmaltz herring, will you?

Take care of yourself, kiddo, and look out for me one of these days.

Kiss [indecipherable] and tell him Uncle Christ is coming home.

Sincerely

3. To Ruth Shapiro

(This letter previously appeared in Volume 2 of Sanford's autobiography, The Waters of Darkness: Scenes from the Life of an American Jew, *pp. 87–88.)*

March 26th, 1931

For Ruth

At once its just what I expected and yet nothing like my expectations and its gay and lively and theres lots of nightlife and noise and joking and arminarmwalking and shouting and sitting around in front of cafes and parading up and down the streets doing nothing more important than enjoying life and crazylookingdreamsoldiers and singing and squealing and children run through your legs and with all innocence in their eyes look up and ask for five centimos and hurdy-gurdies playing thumping Spanish melodies and beggars and merchants with all their stock spread out on the pavements and students behaving madly as ever and always with talk of revolution and shouts of song and squeaky horns on rickety old taxicabs and outrageous nineteenthcentury marble monuments adorned with women as large as horses and horses as large as trolleycars and trolleycars as small as wheelbarrows and men in hussars uniforms and carpetslippers and women with lightbrown skin that looks dusty and murky but clear and soft and fine and eyes that are wet black buttons and hair that shines like strings of black beads and streets full of flowerstands and all are utterly nameless but the filthiest street is as scented as any forest and there are stands of banked birdcages filled [with] canaries that are so yellow they look like butter and parrots that fill your eye with blazes of colour in perfect design and parakeets and cockatoos and birds that are pink and birds that are green and black and red and birds I never saw or heard of and the trees above them filled with thousands of sparrows whose noise and chatter I can hear over the roar of traffic and American names and American signs and American clothes and American habits that can never cover nor does anyone want them to cover Spanish souls and lotteryposters and sellers of lotterytickets and posters for prizefights and bullfights and jack hylton is playing the mavra of Stravinsky here and Lillian Gish is here in an American picture and wide avenues that are incredibly wide lined with blooming trees and palms and shrubs and then huge benches of granite and loitering sauntering people with babycarriages and horsedrawn cabriolets with coachmen and footmen sitting proudly and rigidly up on the boxes and gesticulations and armwaving and loud talk and remarkable facial contortions and excitation and excitability and eagerness and continual quest and search and desire not to miss anything but no one knows what there is to miss and then overpowering lambasting smells punching out of doorwaydruggets and markets crammed and piled and loaded with meat and maggots and cheeses and leeks and bottles and bread and grain and crumblylooking fruit and wizened vegetables and harlots and knockdown bodypowder and men who slide up alongside

and exhibit a fakegold watch as though it were the greatest treasure in all spain and you

can have it for forty pesetas and he would fall down in a trance if you offered him ten and

peanutroasters and chestnutstands

and it is

BARCELONA

4. To Ruth Shapiro

(Sanford mentions this letter in Volume 2 of the autobiography, p. 88.)

April Second Thirtyone

Dear Severest Critic:

Your letter of March Twentieth to Paris was forwarded to Madrid and I received it yesterday. Even though you managed, as sometimes you do, to report nothing of the remotest interest to me, it was a welcome piece of mail. I hadn't had a word from America in the two weeks prior to its arrival. I think Im going to stop writing letters. Its an unproductive pursuit; nothing comes out of it. No one bothers to answer, so to hell with them. Hereafter Ill write them when I bloody well feel impelled to write. No more of this writing because I think the addressees will be tickled stiff to get letters with foreign postage stamps on them. As a matter of fact, to hell with the whole goddamned world. To hell and to hell and to hell. Tomorrow and tomorrow and tomorrow.

But youre excluded, of course. Why, my little hunk of Stilton, you didn't think I meant you, didja? Your humour is always delightful. Its good humour, too. You aren't "caridaboo", areya?

Don't gnaw your fingernails so about having written to the cousinly bribe. I dashed two letters to the Royal Monceau at Paris, one from Barcebaloney and one from here. I ought to be getting a reply any year now. Unless the bribal party comes to Spain, Ill see nothing of them. I think too highly of the Pardo to dust out of here on the run to see the fambly or any part thereof. Excepchu. Ive been here 5 days and to the Prado 5 times. And all Ive done there has been the Goyas and a short preliminary survey of the Velasquez. I haven't so much as entered the room where the El Grecos are, nor do I even know where the Murillos are kept. In the reading room of this hotel, theres a biography of El Greco. In the back of it, theres a sort of chart telling where (in 1908) the paintings are to be found. It was interesting to note that in Madrid alone, there are 86 of them. This includes only his paintings, publicly and privately kept. In Toledo, 90 kilometers away, there are 78.

Boston --------------1
Chicago-------------2
Philadelphia---------1
New York------------4
Pittsburgh ----------1
Paris -------------- 44
Greece --------------3 (all private)

Of course, there have been many shiftings in the past 23 years, but only among the privatelyowned works. The stuff that gets into a gallery stays there for keeps. The 3 that are, or were, in Greece was a curious note. Domenico Theotocopuli was a Greek, as you should know, and yet only 3 of his paintings are in the homeland. I wish the United States would do the same thing with John Singer Sargent, who, by the way, owned a fine El Greco, according to this book.

I got rather tired the other day hunting around for symphony music so I went to a discshop and gave them a cockandbullstory about having sent to America for my Victrola and that until it came I was just shopping around. The dopes fell for it and gave me the run of the place, thinking that I was about to place an order for a million pesetas worth of records. Strangely, I chose to hear only two numbers. The first, which moved me as before when I heard it in Carnegie, was the Bolero of Ravel. The maker of the record, even though in slightly altered spelling, was the Orquesta Sinfonica de Boston, bajo la direccion del maestro Serge Koussevitsky. The melody is more than the "cheap Musichall" theme that our young, but none the less eminent musiccritic has pronounced. I need mention no names. The music is not Bach because it isn't meant to be Bach, and for the same reason, it isn't Beethoven or Wagner or Strauss or Brahms. Although Ravels a Frenchmen, nonetheless hes gotten down into the nationality of Spanish music and succeeded finely where many a true Spaniard has failed. Its reminiscent of what Glinka has done, and Borodine and Balakirev. Youll have to understand without more explanation now. No time. The other composition was Leonora, Obertura Num. III. Need I tell the name of the composer? It was por la Orquesta Filarmonica de Viena [sic], bajo la direccion del maestro Franz Schalk. Only Schalk isn't a maestro. He smells to heaven and so does his orquesta. He went after the lyrics so hard that he forgot the music was still by Beethoven. The fact, too, that Beethoven had written so many oberturas to an opera he never wrote, or had to write after the overtures, was absolutely lost. My next thieving venture will be Tchaikovskys 4th Symphony, a piece Ive wanted to hear for so long Ive gotten disgusted waiting for it to come around. I propose to hear only what I wish to hear. After the Tchaikovsky, the 7th Symphony of the real maestro, the 2nd and then the 5th. Then, if I can find it, the Mozart Jupiter Symphony. Then a Brahms. Then as much Russian music as I can hear without creating the suspicion around these turbulent parts that Im a Nihilist.

Tonight, at seis y media, or sixthirty Americano, I go to hear the Orquesta Iberica de Madrid. This is psuedochamber music by an outfit of some 40 strings, most of them guitars and suchlike. The programa consists in pieces by Chapi, Albeniz, Tarrega, Breton, Anonymous, Bassa, Soler, three parts of a suite by Bach, Turina, Salazar, Halffter and de Falla.

On the 7th, the Orquesta Sinfonica de Madrid, bajo (pronounced Bacho) la direccion del maestro Arbos, is giving a concert which includes The Meistersinger overture, the Cesar Franck symphony and some things by Cherubini and Haendel [sic]. Am I going. Well, baaaaaabee.

After this evenings concert, dinner, and then to the Fronton Madrid (or Pardid, I dont know for sure), where pretty girls play raquets.

No more toros, though, even though the meet the day after tomorrow is one of the best that's to be held in town all year. Sort of a windup for the Holy Week. I enclose the programme. You can see for yourself. By all means, keep this intact for me. I want it. If I remember correctly, Hemingway, in one of his stories about bullfights, writes about Villalta, the toreador (pronounced Biyalta). I cant recall the name of the story, but Im certain of the name. The other big blade in Spain is this Gitanillo de Triana. At the bottom of the prospectus, the prices are listed. In Barcelona last week I had what they call a contrabarrera, which means exactly what it sounds like. Its a place way down toward the ring up against the barrier. It set me back 18 pesetas and damn near all Id eaten for three years. Sol means that your seat is in the sun. The Sombras are sought after and therefore more expensive. I note that the barreras here run as high as 35 pesetas. A peseta is 11 cents American, so the seat runs way up the line. Like a frontrow for a Follies opening.

Short summary of a bullfight: The show opens up with a rootin tootin parade coming out of one of the entrances. Through some strange oversight, the bulls are not permitted to show themselves and take a bow. This seems unfair when you consider that the bulls are to furnish a good part of the entertainment. But then, perhaps they were invited but were too stuck up. Isnt that punny? The Matadors, the picadors, the toreadors, the swingingdoors and the cuspidors, together with all kinds of hangerson, rubbers, towelswingers, swordcarriers and horses come charging out into the ring to take the deafening cheers of the crowd. From the fuss raised, one would think these men and animals, or just plain animals, were about to set out on a Crusade and get back the Holy Land from the infidels. If Lindbergh, Lincoln, Cervantes, Columbus, Cortez, Georges I, II, III, IV, and V, Rasputin, Buddha, Charley Ross, Maam Macpherson, Mrs. Schlobotky-Shitlovsky and Jesus Q Christ were to make an appearance in pajamas, the crowd wouldnt even wave handkerchiefs. But when it hears the word "Bullfighter", hell breaks loose. The horses are some sight. What was the name of that nag in Don Quixote?

Rosinante? Well, by gum, they are all Rosinantes here. They are scrawny and thin and emaciated and scarred and raggedy. Ready for the glue factory, each of them. The picador who rides him weighs invariably about 360 pounds, considering his armorplate that would stop a shell from a 16 inch rifle. If the Maine had been lined with picadors, thered have been no Spanish-American War. Each picador carries a long lance with a flexible handle and a short murderous fouredged blade. The banderillos smile and simper at their girlfriends. The matadors gaily flag their beautiful cloaks of purplyred satin, lining yellow. The toreadors come out with the weight of the world on their shoulders, as well as a hell of a lot of goldbraid that would make a Costa Rican majorgeneral die for envy. Just as "McAfees are never on sale", just as "Witherspoons, sir, never divorce", just as "Fools never learn"—so, too, "A toreador never smiles". For concentration, hes a composite Einstein, Confucius, Aristotle, Plota, and Moses—and a damn sight more important than all of them put together.

The ring is cleared. Only a few matadors are to be seen. A gate is opened and out stamps a big fat, excrementsplattered brown bull. He stares for a couple of seconds (he really cant see because hes been kept in the dark for the past few days) and then makes for a red spot he sees opposite him. He lowers his horns and gores it to death, but whats this? Nothing has happened. He goes for it again, catches his horns in it and tosses it to hell and gone. Nothing happens. He does this 30 or 40 times but never wises up that all he has to do is make for the man holding it and the shows over. A fool never learns. By this time, the bulls a bit overworked, but not before hes scared the hell out of a couple of matadors who run like streaks for their funkholes when they get the idea that the bulls making for the substance rather than the shadow. The way they leg it when they get out of position is the funniest part of the afternoon. They throw themselves over the barrier, they dodge into crevices, they scoot away like rabbits, the dirty little bastards. They aren't supposed to get hurt. That's what the bulls there for. Now that the bulls a little tired and a lot confused, the banderillos come parading out. These guys have a real hard job, without fooling about it. They hold these spears, about two feet long, one in each hand, call to the bull, stand still until hes about ten feet away, step nimbly to one side and hang the darts on the top of his back, right up near the horns. The chances are one out of three that the banderillo will stick, and one out of five that the sticker will get stuck himself. This little fun is twice done. Two pairs of banderillos are jabbed into the bull. He cant shake them off because theyre really long fishhook contraptions, but they hurt him like all getout and he gets madder and madder. After this out ride two brave picadors on nags like hobbyhorses. The horses, or the attacking sides of them at least, are heavily padded.

This does about as much good as trying to stop the 20th Century Limited with a rubberband. The picador rides over to about 40 feet from the bewildered bull and curses him and telling him lies about himself and running down his reputation and his family. Naturally the bull gets sore at this, even though he was willing to call it all off before, and he puts down his head and makes for his defamer. The picador tries to jab the bull on the back of the neck, the same spot as before, with his lance. Sometimes it works and the bull gets a huge hunk of meat torn out of himself for his trouble. Sometimes it doesn't. Sometimes the picador misses a holding spot, or sometimes the lance breaks, as I saw happen, and the bull takes the old nag up on its horns and throws him about ten miles high and when he comes down, he comes down on the horns of the bull again, and finally gets all his entrails torn the hell out of him, as I also saw happen twice. The only consolation in this case is that the picador takes a fall that's worse than that of Adam and Eve, that of Babylon, that of Rome, that of Troy. Sometimes, as I saw happen, the horse rears up and falls back on him, which was the only time I had a chance to laugh all afternoon, and applaud, too. The picador is usually knocked stiff and then the matadors have to leave their funkholes and try to wave off the bull with their cloaks. Sometimes they succeed. Sometimes they have to put in a call for a brandnew picador. After these picadors, if they live, finish blessing the bull in this gentle manner, the matadors tire him a little more by waving their cloaks at the bull. Then to the earsplitting yells of thirtythousand throats, the big cheese makes his appearance. He comes out armed with a red flannel flag, a twofoot sword, a prayer and a good pair of legs in case rag, sword and prayers fail him. He annoys hell out of the bull. He makes all kinds of trick stances, he dodges in ten different ways, he calls the bull all kinds of ugly names as it vainly goes by. He makes a paso por alto. The crowd goes mad. He makes another escape in another manner. The people outside who couldn't get in now go wild. He makes a third. People in the next province throw babies out of windows. Then comes the call for blood. The toreador now steps back, slowly waving his rag at the bull. The latter is now just a little leary and a damn lot weary. Hes been charging at that red thing for fifteen minutes and still its waving. Whats the big idea? The toreador draws his sword, makes a last invitation. For the last time, the bull is bullheaded enough to accept. He runs right square into this blade, the force of the charge ramming it home to the hilt in the top of his back. Hes been bleeding a lot before now. Now he becomes a Niagra and his knees give way and soon he sinks to his belly, all the while looking wonderingly up at all those confusing people, and I thought, a trifle pleadingly. No use. Hes dying.

And a man, no part of the big show, sneaks up behind him and plants the blade of a long dagger into his brain and that's the finish.

Out come gorgeously attired horses, three of them in tandem. The dead bull is hitched to this trio and dragged quickly out to the screams and whistles and cheers of the mob. Hats and cushions and money are thrown into the ring. The toreador, having accomplished as much as Shakespeare, takes a long low bow and goes to sleep with someone called Estrellita Extramadura or Rosita of Castille. But first he collects his ten thousand pesetas.

Continue with the Paris address.

Love and so forth.

5. To Ruth Shapiro

(The Putnam mentioned herein is Sam Putnam, founding editor of The New Review, *which published Sanford's submission, "Prose".)*

April 16th, 1931

Dear Snips,

I hurry to write and tell you of my return to Paris, which I reached at midnight last night. I made straight for France et Choiseul and in some way felt as though Id finally reached home after a long hot walk.

As I wrote you from San Sebastian, Spain, I made a stopover there to cure a cold. This I accomplished in jigtime with the kind assistance of countless Hot Rums (Grog Americain). At one in the afternoon yesterday I took [a] train for Paris. As the cars passed over the border, a narrow creek or inlet, with the French flag flying on the far side of the bridge and also from the stern of a fastlooking revenuecutter, and with the new red yellow and purple of the Spanish Republic on the near side, I felt a sudden rush of affection. I was sorry to leave Spain. I like it so much. I even went so far as to say to myself, but aloud: Spain! Adios! The latter word was piercing and keen and sad and I thought of the Spanish music that I love so.

Very happy you admire Proust. Although you should read further than Swanns Way, I don't mind telling you that you'll come across nothing in all Proust better than those two volumes.

I explained about the New Review several times before, but Ill do so again if its still not clear. Putnam found after the first publication, which he wrote me went like the proverbial wildfire with the pisherkees who are supposed to be in the know, that there was too stinkin much work to getting out six issues a year and too little time to devote to each issue. So he cut down the number to four a year and in every way increased the size and content of the review. Of course, he couldn't do better than employ me to write an entire issue, but Im not bent on selling myself for a pess of mottage. Or even a pot of message. Or a mot of pessage. AND THEREFORE, he postponed issue number two from March 1st to April 15. What Pete said, as usual, was all cocked up. None of these socalled literary reviews EVER is on time coming off the press. In fact, it's a bad sign only if they are ON time. It shows theyre eager for the bizz. The good review can keep the public garsping with impatience. Like Morada. McKenzie told me that he and McLeod, the American editor, got in some kind of misunderstanding about who was to supervise the publication of a certain issue. The result was that Number 4 Morada never appeared on either side of the wet, each guy thinking the other was producing it. It got under way again with Number 5 recently.

Id forgotten about Paysock. All I thought about was Easter eggs and bunnies. And if there were any matzer boards in Venice, as you asked, they must have made gondalas out of them. The guy in charge would then style himself "The Yiddishe Kiddishe Sonofabitch of a Kosher gondolier".

So you just stuck some Sharpe on your Dohme. Hope you feel better by naow. To read that the Seder at the Friedmans was dull was not to read news, as the man said who was told that a puppy had just urinated against a pump. But if the pump had urinated against the dog. . . . . !

I received a letter from Gladys and Ed posted at Nice. They say theyre returning to Paris on the 18th and ask me to look in on them. Ill do it, although not with any great eagerness after the way they treated Dad, just to keep peace in the family.

Whats the noise about a penname for me. I agree Julian Lawrence is oke, but how can I change now that Ive made a great reputation for myself with a Shapiro hung on the end. My public, remember, my public.

Give my love to those who deserve it. You are exempt from the requirement. You get it any old how. Da best, babe, da best.

How would this look at the end of an article, or on the flyleaf of a first edition:

Julian Lawrence

With his compliments

6. To Ruth Shapiro

(This letter was written in Warrensburgh, New York, where Sanford and Nathanael West were renting a cabin to write books. West wrote much of his second novel, Miss Lonelyhearts *there; Sanford continued working on his first book,* The Water Wheel, *the only one of his books published under his birth-name, Julian Shapiro.)*

July 28th, 1931

Dear Snip

Everything going along swell up here. Its turned out even better than advance expectations. We are all set and firmly installed. I commenced work yesterday, youll be glad to learn, on a short story, merely to see whether or not my hand was in, and it isn't far from in, I assure you. Not that its coming easy. Nothing in writing ever does, but when I need to say something in a certain way, I don't worry about finding a solution. Enough. Ive decided not to write about my writing. I dont want these letters dragged out years from now with I told you sos smacking me right and left. If I cant do it, why I cant do it. And if I can youll know soon enough.

Tell me the news in town.

Forward all mail as soon as it comes in.

Don't go to too many concerts, and when you do, sit in the dollar seats. Ill make up the difference to you, but how I don't really know.

What are you reading.

Enjoy your nice little self. Thatll do nicely. Try to make me forget you are a nasty little slob. Especially, whats the latest re Melvele. I understand Nat didn't go to Europe.

Be good to Pop.

I heard a woodthrush this morning. I want you to hear it too sometime. Ill tell you when, or come up anytime you want to. Try to get Dad to come up, but have him wire me several days in advance when and where to meet him. The fishings grand and the swimming and sun even better. And he wont starve because we learned a trick or two about cooking. Love all around, you, Dad and Aunt Jo.

Regards to Phoebe.

Affectionately

7. To Ruth Shapiro

August 13 (1931)

Dear Ruth

Received your letter. Funny theres little news on either end. Except perhaps the fact that, contrary to what you think—or hint at—, I am doing work. And of both kinds, with the hands and with the head. We get up around 8 (Im using this filler because Ive nothing to say), cook and eat bkfast and then wash dishes and pots. A little fooling around with the rod and gun, like the Rover boys, until ten or so and then the typewriter until one or after. Lunch, the same routine with pots and dishwrassling, and then back to the opus from about three to seven, when dinnertime looms up like—opin your own figger. After that, conversation around table until we get used to the fact that the dishes wont wash themselves. And then whatthehell remains but bed, but I generally read Fowlers Modern Eng. Usage, The Oxf. Eng. Dict. And now Irwins sent me Don Quicksoat. Rilkes here, Peps, but haven't read it yet. Glad you like him. When I read book, Ill talk to you about it.

Sam Levy drove up with George Isreals yest. Stopping near Pottersville. Will come over again soon. No other visitors. WCWilliams was supposed to come up to see Pep. Knows him from Moss and Kamin, but didn't after all, though may stop in on way to Montreal. Sent manuscript of The White Cassock to Bernie Bandler, who asked for it in letter not long ago. Havent heard, but its only three days since I sent it. Apropos, Bee Turell wrote that Jesse is going around West End, or is telling her at any rate, that I flung money ins face. True, but incomplete. You know story. Pep and I getting along real well. Quarrels and all that but nothing serious. Minding our own business and doing work. No interference. Good stuff. Food mostly out of cans but good. Favourite dish, Boston beans and brahn brot. That's about all. Except of course my love to Dad and Aunt Jo. And you. Regards Phoebe. You could make package and send me some underthings left over when went away, pajamys, etc. Not too much, only stuff you think I absolutely need. Hdkfs not to be sent, nor underwear nor sockos. In fact, cant think of anything except paj. Late magazones, like sympozeum or criterial or hahnd and hone, transitory etc. Like that very merch. Do it. And love again.

8. To Angel Flores

(Angel Flores was editor and publisher of Dragon Press, located in Ithaca, N.Y., where Flores was a Professor of Languages at Cornell University. The Dragon Press published only a few books—Sanford's The Water Wheel *and William Carlos Williams'* The Knife of the Times *among them—before the Depression took the Dragon Press under. The "Green" mentioned in this letter refers to one of the book's distributors, Duffield and Green. "Melvin" is Sanford's first cousin, Melvin Friedman, who designed* The Water Wheel *and worked for the printers Haddon Craftsmen. "Abernathy" refers to Milton Abernathy, editor of* Contempo.*)*

Jan 8 [1933]

Dear Angel

Read your telegram an hour ago. Tickled silly that you've decided to increase the edition to 1500. Many thanks for that, and for the authority on the dustjacket. Melvin will be struck pink when he gets the order. My only hope is that the book gets disposed of. I'm trying my damndest to sell all I can for you. Have tackled each member of my family personally. Expect to nail them all. As for friends, maybe you were right when you said I'd be finding out how many I had when I began asking them for two and a half bucks. However, of some of them I still have high hopes.

As soon as Haddon strips a proof of the jacket, I'll mail you a copy. I want you to see what everyone thinks is a first-rate job. I don't ordinarily go bugs on anything, but this, I think, justifies it. The job is not only striking, a first requisite, I understand, but free from the garish, in addition to catching a glimmer of the meaning of the book. But wait—you'll see for yourself.

Mrs. Flores wrote that you were a little put out because I seemed to have nothing but 'The Water Wheel' on my mind when I wrote to Ithaca. But believe it or not, I've been thinking nothing but the book, and working on nothing else for the past six months. The editor of Lion and Crown asked me for a story; so did Whit Burnett of 'Story', but I was forced to tell them that I had no time. Also I was supposed to send Sam Putnam something for his New Review Number 6, but I let it slide completely.

In case you do not already know it, 'Contact' is flooey. The 3rd number wound it up. Williams wrote to me to that effect about 4 weeks ago.

James T. Farrell turns out to be a right guy. He reviews for the 'Sun' and the 'New Republic'. He told me the other day that he will do his utmost to get a review of 'The Water Wheel' in the paper, and at least a note in the magazine. In addition, he is arranging to have the book reviewed by the Nouvelle Revue Francaise. More than that a friend cannot do, I guess.

Abernathy was here with his wife over Xmas. He wants to know exactly when the book will appear, so that he can run a second ad for us, which he promised to do. I'll write him soon and give him the date; the ad will be in the issue nearest publication.

About the dustjacket once more: Green suggested what copy the jacket should contain. I drew it up and will show it to him tomorrow before turning it over to Haddon. The back cover will repeat the three blurbs of Williams, Komroff and Putnam. The back *flap* will run the same (practically the same) 75 words about the author, and possibly a mug (suggested by Green). The front flap will have a condensed version of what appeared on Page 2 of the circular.

I'm still playing handball regularly. The only effect I notice is a greater hardness and a better-played game. On thinking it over, I recommend it to you again.

DeJong also turned up the same night Abernathy was here; he came in with our pal Jose Garcia Vila. DeJong said he received his stories, but is glad you have retained the poetry.

That's about all for now.

Best all around.

Sincerely,

9. To Angel Flores

Feb. 28th , 1933

Dear Angel,

Got your letter yesterday and was all busted up to hear that D. & G., after their big private ballyhoo, are flivvering with the sales. Also sorry you think Haddon Craftsmen are padding the bills. Will see Mel for lunch today and put up a hot argument for reductions all along the line.

As far as your hint that I'm expected to pay the difference between 10 3/4 [cents] and 21 1/4 [cents] is concerned, I want to say you must be a little cracked. When did I indicate that I was paying for part of the publication of the W.W.? Firstly, your alleged minimum price is cockeyed. Haddon never for a moment considered less than 14 [cents], or something like that. As for the difference, I can't recall any promises to pay. All I know is that I said I'd get you the cheapest presentable volume. You know yourself that the stuff Haddon showed for 14 [cents] stank out loud. We couldn't have used it and gotten by at all. However, there's no use knifing each other so soon. Let's straighten this out when you come to N.Y. for Easter. O.K.?

RE foreign rights, again I think you're wrong. Can't recall any phrases in the contract specifying a universal disposal of the W.W. to Dragon Press. However, this, too, will be ironed out when I see you. As far as Spain and France are concerned, you proceed as if *Dragon* owns the book; do whatever you wish and make all arrangements you think necessary. As for England (for want at present of a better understanding), I'll proceed as though *I* have the rights. Later, we'll make a settlement of the issue. The reason for this is that you have the Spic and the Frog connections, while I have a lead among the beefeaters. I'll ship one of my personal copies to the Roastbeef lead and see if I can't get some action. As for you, my good man, try your very very very very very very very best to get a publication in France and Spain. I'm more interested in those countries than in England and the U.S. rolled into one.

The last account I rendered to Dragon showed a balance of $1.96 in my favor. Against that, I held on to a sub from Arthur Larschan (1708 Undercliff Avenue, N.Y.C.). That left a balance to you of 54 [cents]. Don't forget to send a copy to Larschan, of course, since he's paid for it.

Lately, I received another sub from

Mr. and Mrs Murray Kahn
Hotel Park Crescent
87th St. & Riverside Dr.
New York, N.Y.

I enclose the cash for that sub, the book to be sent them right away, and also the cash for a sale of a personal copy to a friend who saw the book in my house. That makes five bucks enclosed.

I just got a choice list of 40 names from Milton Abernethy. After

I send these out, your 54 [cent] balance will be wiped out, and there will again be a tiny bit due me.

Try for Spain
Try for France
Try for Spain
Try for France
Try hard, you big bum
Try very hard. You'll not regret it. You'll emblazon the name of Dragon and the name of Flores in all the heavens that surround the civilized world. Children will gaze on high and cry for it. At night, they'll sing themselves to sleep to the tune of Flores Dragon Flores Dragon Flores Dragon. Some may murmur the name of Shapstein and get very sick, but in the Arts we do not stop for the weak, the halt, and the lame.

Ah France
Ah Spain
Ah Dragon
Ah Flores
Ah Tempora
Ah Flores

When you come to N.Y., call me right away.

Take good care of Iris and pray for a boy. Girls are only in the way; they cry like sixty and pee like Niagara. Pray for a boy, my friend, pray for a boy.

A bientot,

Suggest you send out the paid-for subs right away. It'll give just that much extra talk about the W.W. before the Ides of March.

Send me a copy of the W.W. to replace the one sold, and also a second one to replace the one I'm sending to England in this mail.

10. To Angel Flores

April 30, 1933

Dear Angel :

Enclosing two checks, one from Robert M. Pincus, and the other from my bank. Both represent sales of the Wheel. And both books were delivered from my private stock, so kindly send me a couple of Wheels right away as I'm getting low.

Green took me to lunch at the Harvard Club two weeks ago, and tried to talk me into signing a contract with him for the second book, but when I put my proposition to him, that of supporting me with advances until the book was completed, he folded up and talked no more of contracts, nor have I heard from him since in any capacity, either about the new book or the old.

In my opinion, he's mismanaged that Wheel so that he ought to be ashamed to look an author in the face, or even dare to talk to him about publishing his second book. Ive never in my life seen a book allowed to go so completely dead after only 5 weeks of publication. The sonofabitch cant even get the Tribune or the Post or the Sun to run a note on the godamned book. Im bitterly disappointed about the whole thing as I expect to be about anything in all my life. I don't say the Wheel is the great American ball of fire, but it's a dirty shame that it was allowed to die the way it did when worse books are setting the public on its ears. Im going down to see Green today and tell him what I think of the whole bloody thing.

You were pretty vague about the translating of the book when I saw you here in town. I want to know exactly what youve done, and exactly whats being done. I want to know also who youve asked to do the translating and their addresses, if that isnt such a great secret. Ive gotten to the point now where I can see that nothing further is going to be done for the Wheel in America, and Im anxious therefore to see what I can do for it on other continents. As I see it, this matter of translation is of the utmost importance to me, and if youre really my friend youll do everything in your power to see to it that the Wheel gets translated as soon as possible. Id like to hear from you in this connection right away.

Tell me also whether anyone else has ordered the Wheel direct from Ithaca, that is, any of my friends.

Give my best to Iris and kiss your baby for me.

Bien sincerement,

It looks to me as if Covici-Friede will get the call on the second book. They've been after me hot and heavy and are not averse to putting up the coin. Will know this week.

11. James Farrell

(Farrell was a novelist best known for Young Lonigan, *published in 1932.)*

March 1, 1934

Dear Jim,

I was glad to hear from Parks that your book is going into a second printing, and I'll be progressively happier when it goes into a third and fourth. You've worked hard and sincerely, and you haven't "sold out" to the public. You deserve all the good that I'm sure is on the way to you.

William Trag gave you a corking write-up in last week's Nation. I'd have bought a copy for you, but where would I get the 15 cents?

I'm enclosing your review of "One Way Ticket," as you requested.

No news yet from Knopf. In this case, "no news is not good news," for Knopf is particularly hard to please, and I've no great hope of his falling for my brand of writing. In any event, I'll keep you advised.

I had a note from Alex Buchman, the Cleveland chap who published some of Dahlberg once upon a time. He's in China now and, evidently, hardup.

Fanya Foss must have heard about the fracas at Dahlberg's that night, for when she greeted me at the lecture I mentioned she said, "I hear you're a fascist." Dahlberg—who doubtless smeared the story—ought to get a little common sense slugged into him. Why does he persist in his opinion that if a man isn't an active Communist, he's automatically a fascist agent? Will he never grow up? And if he does grow up, will he ever learn to mind his own God damned business? I don't like to be undermined by stories like the one he seems to have related to Fanya, and I'll know what to do if another such is sent on its lying way. You can tell Dahlberg for me that I think he's a complete fool, and that he's got his gall attacking fascism when he isn't even a member of the Communist party himself. He told me that the reason for this was that he had too much to do, and couldn't put himself at the disposal of the party leaders. What an attitude for a Communist!

Best to you and Dorothy.

Sincerely,

12. To James Farrell

April 5th, 1934

Dear Jim,

As you say, it's no good raving about the choices of the Guggenheim Committee; they've been neither more nor less stupid and heartbreaking this year than they ever were. But this is my point : with certain evident exceptions, no current writer in America is worth a prize of two thousand dollars, or, indeed, any part of that sum. The Committee isn't wholly to be blamed for tossing the money to hacks : excluding the advanceguard, there was no one else valuable enough to kick out of the country. There never will be until there's a purpose behind all the words that find their way into print each year; and there can be no purpose while the sole apparent aim of writers is to secure a publisher and a market at any cost, to attract attention, to attract even derision, to make just one miserable little squeak before oblivion catches up with them.

Dahlberg deserved a scholarship in preference to Halper, but intrinsically he was no more entitled to one than I was. He's shown very little; far less, surely, than Caldwell. His first book was a confusion of unimportant and dull episodes in the life of an unrealized character, a character remaining unrealized even though projected into the second book. Not a tenth of 'Bottom Dogs' was worth printing in any literary era, even in one like our own. It revealed nothing but a desire on the part of the author to rebel, to be honest and penetrating, but no amount of desire accomplishes the end of desire in the absence of talent. As for 'From Flushing to Calvary,' for me it was a slight advance over Dahlberg's first exhibition of clumsiness, but not enough to convince me that he was the Great White Hope. He is not, of course, and no praise of his sincerity will make him so. Janet Lewis is superior to Kay Boyle. If she had had written the second half of 'The Invasion' as carefully as she wrote the first, she'd have been entitled to the prize without more. I know nothing of

Josephine Herbst, but if the tales I hear are even partly true, then she, too, has been cheated. As far as I'm concerned, there are no other young women writing in America today.

Giving the poetry prize to Isidore Schneider was a towering joke. I'm willing to bet there are twentyfive poets in this country who are his superior, and among them are Tate, MacLeish, Ransome, Bishop, Winters, Stevens, Williams, Rakoski, Blackmur, Aiken, Cowley, Baker, and even Mister Horace Gregory. The last, however, has always been a pretty doubtful musicmaster in my opinion, and is not entitled to shed many tears over his failure. If he feels low, let him read his contracts.

I haven't read the particular story of Thomas Wolfe you referred to, but I did read another some time ago, called, I think, 'Death the Proud Brother,' and if prizes were being awarded to the most inept, I'd have no hesitation in calling Mister Wolfe to the platform. Somewhere he must have heard that he was a veritable man of power, and now he stalks through his own too numerous pages like a palpitating conqueror who's smelled the blood of his victim—the reader. His power, such as it is, pours from him without restraint; he leaks power; he drips power—but when you put it all together, it's simply a callow display of muscle. I've been trying to force my way through the thickets of 'Look Homeward, Angel,' but I find that I'm stopped dead in my tracks. After reading seventyfive pages, I threw the book behind a collection of old rubbers and torn umbrellas, cursing the undisciplined, unmotivated, untutored, unkempt bastard to high heaven. He has nothing to say.

Henry Bamford (Mike, to you) Parkes gave me his manuscript, 'The Puritan Tradition.' I'd have liked to read it all the way through, but I'd promised him speedy action and had to turn it right over to Knopf. I gave it to Kronenberger, who assured me of a most careful reading. I gave the book the highest praise I could memorize, for I wanted to help. I think Parkes is the goods in his particular field.

Lately I've been reading all I can lay my hands on relating to the Agrarian South, Sectionalism, etc. I'm very deeply interested in these fallacies; I want to understand why fine talents have been led astray by a trashy and reactionary substitute for the inevitable—Communism. As it's being applied, Agrarianism would seem to be no more than another name for Fascism; as such, it must ultimately fail. But I can't help wishing that writers like Ransome and Tate would steer clear of the group on the porch sitting around somewhere near Lynchburg waiting for Beauregard to return from Bull Run. Let me hear from you on this.

Best love to you and Dot.

Sincerely,

13. To Ruth Shapiro

(Albert Boni, of the publishing house Boni & Liveright, wanted to change the title of Sanford's second novel, published in 1935, and did).

August 2, 1935

Dear Ruth,

I think you and Hortie and all the good folk of Cincinnati are right in claiming that 'The Trampled Vineyard' is infinitely superior to 'The Old Man's Place', but there's very little I can do to convince Boni that we know more than he does. In a sense, he's better fitted to say which title is the one more likely to click; he's published at least three thousand books in his time, and if by now he doesn't know what the public catches its dress on, then he'll never know. He may make a mistake in particular cases, of course, and I can only hope this isn't one of them.

When I got your note and Hortie's enclosure, I really did get worried. I called Boni and even read him the passages I thought would influence him. He still thinks 'The Old Man's Place' is from every angle the proper title to use, and remember this, that I submitted some forty others to him during the past two weeks, some of which I think are better than either of those under discussion. Here's one that he put his foot down hard on: 'A Little For A Rainy Day'. Here are some more: 'Never Sick A Day'; 'A Nice Refined Woman'; 'A Romantic Correspondence'; 'A Social Call'.

I did get Boni to consent to this: by next Monday I'm to have a list of the reactions of 100 strangers, and if the overwhelming majority are in favor of 'The Trampled Vineyard', Boni will do some reconsidering.

About the name of the author: it's to be John B. Sanford, the same one I used for myself in 'The Water Wheel'. There's no point in it, I admit, for nobody will ever associate the author of the new book with the character in the old. I'm doing it simply because a change of name was demanded by the publisher. What little identification there is, I want to have as a purely personal matter. It doesn't make any real difference whether the name is John B., or John L., or Julian L., as long as we have the Sanford finishing it off. As far as J.L.S. Nevins was concerned, Dad was the one who balked at it. I think he's pretty sick and tired of those six letters, particularly since you've done it to death among the three-ninetyfives, and when I mentioned it to him he made a face and refused to talk about it.

The book jacket, my idea, will be ready on Monday. I haven't seen the artist's sketch, but I'm told he knows his business, and furthermore that he's following my suggestion. This was to have the rim of a hollow in the foreground. Deep in the hollow is a rundown farm, behind it a backdrop of trees, and over it all a cauliflower of ominous clouds. Standing with their backs to the observer and facing the farm below, are three figures. These dominate the entire foreground, and because of the perspective, the entire scene. The single touch of fact about the picture is a whisky bottle that one of the men is holding behind his back in view of the observer. Now, if this god damned artist follows orders, we'll have something. The scene calls for retching colors, tomato red, rawspinach green, sulphur yellow, etc.

Dad, according to reports I've had has been pretty well lately.

I'll know for myself later in the day, for it's Friday, and I'm off to the wars, I mean shores. Or should I have said, I'm off to the whores?

I bumped into Abby Vogel Pollack last night in a restaurant. In addition to her unfortunate gland trouble, she's once more pregnant. If she weighs a pound, she tips the beam at 275, and I give you my word of honor that I'm not exaggerating. I tell the truth when I say that I didn't recognize her until I saw Ben with her.

Nonie's address is:

South Lake Drive, Elberon, New Jersey. You'd better stick the name Kitay alongside, just to make sure. I've spent a lot of time with her, and she's just as charming as ever. She's a pretty fine sort, very much like our Hortie.

Give my love to everyone. Take care of yourself. Write, if you get time. Even if you don't, write to Dad and the folks. You ought to get your fat little ass kicked hard for sending him only one letter every ten days, and I don't give a good God damn how busy you've been. There's absolutely no excuse, and if you think I'm stating only my own opinion, then you've got a flock of other guesses coming to you.

That's all.

Affectionately

14. To Ruth Shapiro

(On the strength of his second book, The Old Man's Place, *Sanford landed a job writing screenplays for Paramount Pictures. "Hats" mentioned herein is Ruth and John's older first cousin, Hattie Friedman. "New Orleans," a potential movie Sanford was assigned to write with his partner, the novelist and poet Joseph Moncure March, who later introduced Sanford to his future wife, Marguerite Roberts, was never made. The novel Sanford says he's revising at the end of this letter is* Seventy Times Seven. *"The O.M.P. refers to* The Old Man's Place *and marks the lifetime habit of Sanford referring to his book titles by their*

initials. J.M. is the actress Jean Muir, whom Sanford dated.)

18 October 1936

Dear Chick:

The folks are in. I met them yesterday morning, got them through customs, and drove them up to L.A. in my flivver. In a half hour, we found an apartment, and they moved right in. The place is directly across the street from the Shapiros hotel (Shapiro the jeweler). It's in a good section of town, a stone's throw from the Hotel Ambassador. Full details in a letter to Hats in this same mail. The folks look great, you can tell Dad, and had a splendid trip. The reunion was swell. You'd think we hadn't seen each other in years.

Glad your throat is relieved. Keep up that spraying business. You say it doesn't hurt except when you forget to spray it. Well, for God's sake, stop knocking your head against the wall. It seems there was a guy in a nuthouse, and he was hammering his conk against the concrete, and somebody came along and said to this guy. . . . .

I'd like to set you straight on that option-renewal business. When I make mention of the fact that it may not be renewed in March, I'm not trying to tell you that I'm not trying. On the contrary, I'd like to stick it here for a couple of years, and I'm doing all in my power to get them to like me around the lot and to turn in the best possible work, but all effort is in vain if your work doesn't add up to box-office returns. You can be the loveliest guy in Christ's world, and people can think you're just too sweet for description, and you can have sweated blood over that screen play for five months, and you can have the most intelligent producer and a director who adds 50% to the script—but if the film doesn't make dough you're out on your fat ass, and there's nothing you can do about it.

If you think I'm out to let this chance slip through my fingers you're crazy in the head, that's all. I've had five years without a dime in my pocket, and, to put it mildly, I don't like that kind of situation in the least. If 'New Orleans' should happen to click—and it seems to have a good chance of doing so—I can write my own ticket out here for years to come. That's the way it is. You can cash in on one success till the cows come home. You can take your own good time, take a vacation in the desert, pull all kinds of tempermental stunts—and the verdict is that's your way, the way of a 'GENIUS', and the whole place marks time till you hand in your next script, which may be a year from the time you had your success—and it's all O.K. with the front office if they can make money on your work. If they can't, you're on your way home, with no appeal whatever.

March (you can tell Dad his father is Moncure March, a well-known New York lawyer, also that he's a nephew of Peyton C. March, also that I had his other uncle as a prof at LaFayette) has had his ups and downs out here—he wrote Hell's Angels and Journeys End—and at the moment he's on the rise again. It's lucky for me that this is so. He's absolutely grim about writing a good script, and he'd keep going all night long if I let him. Add to this that there's nothing he doesn't know about the technical side of screenplay-making, and you get a fair idea that I'm in with somebody who's just as determined as I am. He was so jittery when that first batch went to Revnes that we almost bit each other's ears off, and he went to the extreme of calling his agents and telling them to have another job lined up for him on a 24-hour call (he's on a weekly contract at Paramount), so that he could quit here if Revnes began pulling any of his wellknown tricks. I was out when Revnes came sailing in so delighted, and Joe called me all over town to pass on the news, even though we parted thinking of hatchets at ten paces. That's the way things get you out here. You ride high in the morning, and by midafternoon you're fighting like Hell to come up high enough to touch bottom. We're way into the play, and it's going like a house afire. To prove I'm making progress with March, possibly one of the most taciturn guys that ever lived, he actually asked me to his house to dinner last week. I was having dinner with J.M., however, and I had to refuse. He's told me a good deal about his wife, whom he thinks the world of (she's the former wife of a louse by the name of Theodore Von Eltz), and I'm anxious to meet her.

Stay away from 'Valient is the World for Carrie'. By all means see 'The Gay Desperado.'

Your not getting a bang out of Henry any more only confirms an idea I've had about women for years—that they're screwy from the word go.

I'm working swell on the revision of the novel. I've gotten organized, and I'm giving it a good hour and more a day. If I have any luck I'll be done with it by February 1st, maybe sooner. I plan to make it the hardest book ever written—I know you won't like that, but I'd like to say that by 'hard' I don't mean brutal, as 'The O.M.P.' was. I promise you you'll like it.

Love all around.

Affectionately

15. To Ruth Shapiro

(The Tones mentioned herein are Franchot Tone and his wife, Joan Crawford. "Haddon" refers to the book manufacturers Haddon Craftsmen, for whom cousin Mel worked. Joe Mankiewicz refers to the MGM producer and screenwriter. Raft is the actor George Raft. Harold Salemson published Tambour, the first periodical to publish Sanford.)

Nov. 22, 1936

Dear Monk :

The admission that you've been depressed lately has troubled me ever since I received your letter last Friday, and it'll continue to trouble me till I learn the exact cause of those low spirits. Of course, it doesn't take a wizard to make a shrewd guess : I know you're making fine progress physically; you must be fretting about the indecisive actions of your boy friend. If that's the case, and it probably is, I'm a little offended that you haven't taken me into your confidence earlier than this. We've always been such close friends in these matters that I've gotten to expect that I'll be let in on them as soon as they develop. I can fully understand why, at the present time, you wouldn't want to annoy Dad with any such stories, but I cannot at all understand why you hold anything back from me. I've got plenty of worries on my own head, but there always is and always will be room for any that you may care to dispose of.

Assuming that my guess is well founded, I must say that you're forgetting a good deal that you learned over the past four or five years. The biggest lesson, the one I had sworn you got down pat, is that you never get anywhere with a guy by showing him that he's important, even if he really is. A man may indicate his feeling to a woman, for her vanity is usually satisfied by knowing that she has an admirer, but when it's the other way 'round, the man is apt to become a little careless, to take a little too much for granted, to let his attention wander around whatever public place the two of them happen to be in—and that's bad. The woman always has a much harder time resuming the casual mask than the man does. He somehow can turn it on and off at will, but once the woman has too completely shown her hand there can be no retreat. Therefore she's wise if she doesn't show it at all until she's reasonably sure of what she's doing. I don't know what's between you and Joe, but I'm sure that if you spend your spare time thinking about tactics, legitimate tactics, you'll fare much better with him than if you put in that time at swelling the sales of the Kleenex Corporation of America.

In any case, be good enough to write and tell me all.

My darling cousin Melvele sent me ten copies of 'The Water Wheel'. They got here yesterday (Saturday) afternoon, and I nearly fell down when I opened the package. The books were unbound ! All that came was the sewn signatures. I don't know whose fault that was, but the fact remains (where've I heard that one ?) that I'm in possession of ten pounds of worthless paper—and after paying Haddon twobits apiece for the books ! I was particularly annoyed because I was heading for the Tones again last night for dinner, and I wanted to make good on my promise to her. I had to go empty-handed again, and I felt like a liar all evening.

Most people who know me at all well are told very quickly what my real name is. I don't see anything to be gained in trying to hide it indefinitely, especially when I start off by having people know me in all quarters. If I were in Australia, it'd be a different matter (I'm not so [sure] about that even), but here it's a futile gag to try to pull, and I'm not keen on hiding my religion anyway. On Friday night I went to a Chamber of Commerce meeting with Jean, who was pinchhitting as a speaker for Fred Keating, and in the lobby later I bumped into Sylvia Kleban. A chap came along who knew her, a mick if one ever lived, and Sylvia said : "Mister Sanford, Mister Sullivan." I shook hands with him, saying : "The real name is Shapiro." He nearly floored me by saying : "That's all right. Mine's Solomon."

At the same meeting, I meet Harold Salemson and his sister Paula, and three or four others, some of whom I've known since Paris days—and nights.

The dinner at the Tones last night was again small, but I'm sure you'll agree that it was select when I tell you that in addition to Joan and Franchot, there were Gary Cooper and his wife Sandra (Rocky, to you) Shaw. The others were George Murphy (the actor) and his wife, Lynn Riggs, myself, and Joe Mankewicz of MGM. Lynn was feeling particularly high, for his 'The Plainsman', with Cooper playing Wild Bill Hicock, had been previewed in Glendale the night before, and all the papers raved their brains out about it. Again I was at Joan's left, and talked to her throughout the whole dinner. I have to suppose that they like me, or else they wouldn't have me to their house three times in ten days. It's always hard for me to realize that that's the reason I'm with people—because they like me. I'm usually wondering what's on their minds. And it'd seem that Joan actually liked 'The Old Man's Place'. She's already bought 18 copies, and doesn't even own one herself. Many times during the meal she reverted to the book, and I tell you truthfully that I was embarrassed, for I rate the book away down the list. But what's my opinion worth, after all ? She told me that of all the books she's read in the past five years, she likes Hilton's 'Lost Horizons" and "The Old Man's Place' the best; she gave away 40 of the former, so that when she likes she likes. She got the Coopers interested, and also Barbara Stanwyck; I'm sending more copies along in a day or two. What can I do ?

I'm sorry to hear that Joe's mother hasn't been well. Give her my best wishes through him next time he calls. If I recall rightly, he owes me a letter.

The script will be finished Monday night, and Revnes will have it in his hands the following night. We have only a couple of tag scenes to write, and we expect to sail through them on Monday without much trouble. In any case, even if we strike a snag or two, the most we can be delayed is a day or so. Raft came crawling back to Para twothree days ago, and Variety carried notice that he goes right into 'Souls at Sea' with Cooper, and after that 'Sapphire', our opus. I'm not at all sorry. We have the kind of role for him that he can do to perfection.

If my option is picked up—how'd you like me to stake you to a trip to Paris next summer ? I've got a lot saved up right now, and by that time I won't mind cutting you in for five hundred. Let me know whether the offer is accepted.

Remember, now—take care of yourself, and no more Kleenex.

Write soon.

Call Mel and find out what happened. See if he can get me some bound books at once.

Affectionately,

16. To Ruth Shapiro

(The reference herein to "Schulberg" refers to B.P. Schulberg, who ran Paramount until 1931 and became an independent producer in 1936.)

November 29th, 1936

Dear Ruthie:

In writing as I do now, I'm giving you what I think is my best advice on the subject of your relationship with Joe. You're not bound to follow it, of course, but I think you'd eventually be a good deal happier if you did.

You say that Joe is too smart to fall for any of your tactics, but I say that no man is too smart to fall for tactics if he really cares about the girl. For a married man, I think he has considerable gall to come out baldly and state that he has no intention of remarrying for years to come, and if I were in your shoes I'd most certainly take up the challenge with a readiness that'd quite knock the breath out of his body.

You've reached the age where most people sit back and take stock of their opportunities, and if you fail to do so now or pretty soon, you may find that you'll later regret being a softie and taking the short view of things. I agree that what I have to suggest reads a good lot easier than it'll work, but none the less I feel bound to say you ought to send Joe packing through the door of Number 12B, with the cool statement that if he isn't serious [as] you are, that you can no longer afford to waste your time on giving him a couple of dates a week just so that he can be seen in your company and just so that he can have a place to park his hat and rid himself of a handful of traveling salesman's jokes, that you misunderstood his intentions, but that now they're perfectly clear you're no longer interested.

These are heroic measures. They either cure or kill, but at least you'll have the satisfaction of knowing that you shot the works fast and got the sickness over with one way or another. Look at it from this angle : if these measures don't work, it'll only mean that you've learned in a hurry and at one fell swoop what it'd otherwise have taken you painful months to discover; if they do work, you'll have saved yourself an equally lengthy time of anxiety. To my way of looking at things, the quicker one learns how the wind blows, the better off one is.

There are other ways of telling a guy that it's a case of tochas offen tisch, and perhaps the brief outline I gave above is the crudest of all, but there are others galore. One of the best, in all probability, is the vacation dodge. With me out here in California, it'd be the most natural thing in the world for you to start planning a long, a very long trip to the Coast. You might even be away from New York for three or four months, you know, and you might be laying plans to leave starting with the receipt of this plot. And with my 'connections', mighn't it be possible that you're ticketed with a job as, say, secretary to my producer, with the intention of remaining here permanently? This is a suggestion, and you may take it for what it's worth.

But you've got to do something, that's perfectly clear, and I've always been one for having the cards laid out face up on the table. If you flop, well, then, you've flopped, and maybe you'll feel very blue for a short while, but you've gone through the worst of these affaires du Coeur (God help me with my rusty French !), and you know as well as I do that none of them can ever even touch the poignancy of the first.

When you're up against timber like Stanley, etc., you run the show as if you owned it. When you crash into the merest suggestion of experience, you come to grief with the most astonishing rapidity. I suppose you'll never be able to do better, but that's nothing to worry about. The big thing, it seems to me, is the backing out once you've gotten into things deeper than you find comfortable. Regardless of how unique you think Joe is, you'll have to admit that there are many counts on which he takes a bad second to at least a dozen others that each of us could name. He may have a very winning manner, a nice smile, lots of consideration and thoughtfulness, an extensive wardrobe, and plenty of money, but with that description of him nobody would be able to pick him out of any crowd, small or large. You're very pretty, and you're intelligent, and you're young, and you have a good family, and you have a brother who'll do anything he can to help you out and who looks as if he might have a wad of dough himself if things go along as they have been for the few months (excuse the touch of Babbitry; this is a practical letter), so why fret your heart out for just one little guy who comes along into scene five years after the big Affair?

I can't quite persuade myself that you regard Joe as ONE BIG OPPORTUNITY. He no doubt looms large because he has no competition, but without meaning to do him an injustice, I think he'd begin shrinking if there were someone else on the horizon. Remember how you felt about Henry early this year? Try to remember. It's all pretty hazy by now, I'll wager. Well, substitute the name Joe for Henry, cut the period of mourning in quarters, and you'll have a pretty exact picture of what you'd be in for if you cut Joe adrift.

On the other hand, he might not be so damned anxious to be cut loose, and if that's the case he'll have to go away back and sit down and be very quiet, lest you drop him a second time and for good.

I think it's worth a stab. If the trick fails to work, and in order to have the slimmest chance of its working, you have to believe that you don't care one way or another—I say, if it fails to work, you can always fall back on me and come out to California, and to Hell with New York and grief. You're entitled to a damned good time after what you've been through (or let yourself in for) during the last several years, and I'll give it to you whenever you like.

I'm open to further discussion re the above at your pleasure.

Don't give up the ship. You'll be back on your feet in another couple of months, and then to Hell with everything.

*

Tamara came in by plane yesterday. I happened to see her name in the trade papers in the morning, and I arranged with my agents (they're hers too) to drive out to the airport to meet her. I thought Erwin was coming too, but she came alone. He's to follow in another two weeks if her tests for Schulberg are satisfactory. I don't know what he's got lined up for her, but I'll find out next time I see her. Schulberg's lot is right across the street from Para, so we'll probably get together for lunch daily, Schulberg's outfit having no commissary of its own.

I'm having lunch with my agents on Monday. I spoke with them over the phone on Saturday (today's Sunday, in case you want to know), and they told me that the renewal of the option is practically in the bag. That'll mean a jump to $400 a week, in which case I'll jump Dad to $100, thus splitting the extry $50 with the gent. Don't tell the guy yet, though; I want to surprise him. I'll call it a birthday present, even if it comes on March 1.

The news about Gladys draws a note from me at once. Bravo.

The note in the papies about Para's doing a N.O. story of the present day is hooey. Ours is laid in 1832.

The Mufson chap is not a phoney. I know him from the Y.M.C.A., and last time I saw him, around the beginning of August, he said he was having some writing trouble, and I offered to straighten him out if could. I had once before, about three years ago.

Almost forgot. Taking Tamara into the Knickerbocker yesterday, I ran smack into Sylvia Blankfort and her husband. They said they'd been trying to get a hold of me for a long time, invited me out to their house. I'll go, but later in the week. I tell you, the whole world is out here. Everywhere I go, I run into people I know from the East.

Bing—just got a phone call from Tamara. Arranged to take her to Aunt Sarah's for lunch today. I was going alone, but managed to drag her in. Chicken zooooop, roast chicken, obble sauce, tchai (prekuzkoi, if you like), und efsha a schtickel schtrudel (or should I say stru*delle*).

Longest letter since I last had a sweetie. Signing off.

Love to you and the Governor.

Affectionately,

17. To Ruth Shapiro

(Leland Hayward was the New York agent who placed Sanford at Paramount pictures.)

September 12, 1937

Dear Ruth:

You asked me three or four times in your latest letter not to take what you were saying in the wrong light—and I'm going to astonish you by granting your request.

I'm not hiding anything from you or Dad, and therefore I can't give you a 'confidential report.' You know at your end all there is to be known at this time. About Mankiewicz, I've told you nothing but the absolute fact. "The Bride Wore Red," the Crawford picture that was shooting over the last three months, is still in the cutting room, and that's where Mankiewicz is to be found whenever he's not holding story conferences on his new Crawford opus, 'Mannequin.' I've been in constant touch with his office, and so has Leland and his entire staff, and it would be a very simple thing for Mankiewicz to tell us that he doesn't want any part of me, now or ever—but he hasn't done that. He's under no obligation to us, and if he'd definitely made up his mind that I wasn't the guy for him, there'd be nothing to prevent his being outspoken about it. Instead, he's asked us to be patient, and since you can't get a job at the point of a gun, I think the least (as well as the most) that we can do is comply.

But we're making other efforts too, and one of my own was

to uncover something at Schulberg's through Theodore Reeves. It seems that for months this chap's been singing my praises to George Auerbach, who is head of Schulberg's plant, and last week we had a three-corned interview, the upshot of which was that I submitted a copy of 'The Woods Colt' and a copy of 'The Old Man's Place' to Auerbach for his approval. I have an appointment with him tomorrow to discuss the stuff, and I have his personal assurance that if he likes it he'll either plant me at Schulberg's or land me a spot elsewhere. All this, not being compulsory, sounds very encouraging, but since you want facts and not hopes, I'll have to ask you to wait until facts develop.

My third 'iron' is the submission of 'The Old Man's Place' to Warner Bros. by Leland Hayward. He's been in New York since the Labor Day weekend, but he returns in the morning, and we ought to have some word early this week.

My fourth 'iron' is the new book, of which you seem to think the success is problematical. You think, further, that even if it's very big, I'll not be able to cash in on it until next Fall at the earliest. Well, if all that's so, it's just too bad. What would you have me do about it?

There was every temptation to get so God damned mad at your letter that I'd made up my mind never to write to you again, but I thought that I'd accomplish more with you by holding in my temper. You simply must understand that I'm doing what I can, and that no amount of goosing and no amount of bad business in New York can make me go either at a faster pace or in a different direction. I've done pretty well despite your opposition in the past, and it's a great mystery to me how you have refrained from acquiring just the smallest amount of respect for that success, especially in the face of your own complete failure. It's a mystery too how you've come this far without acquiring some little understanding of how to deal with various people. Some may need a kick in the pants once in a while (that's your type), but others whirl and bite when they're nagged (and that's mine)—and you've never grasped that fact about me for even the briefest time.

Another thing that I might have resented very deeply if I didn't believe you were just being stupid was the crack about listening to my 'yes' friends. You have only one such friend in mind, and since you know a great deal less than nothing about her, I'll thank you to limit your animosity to thinking about it.

Now, I think I've been very tolerant about all this, and in return I have a right to expect a reward. It's simply this:

Since my arrival in California I have received 35 letters from you and 17 from the Governor (I just counted them for the fun of it). Dad's have been so wonderful in every way that I wouldn't part with them for a thousand dollars a page, but yours, with no single exception, have been the most distressing communications that any man has ever gotten from his sister under conditions ten times worse than what ours are, in every way, and without exception even in a single instance, they have served precisely the opposite purpose from which they were intended; they depressed me instead of—whatever you were trying to do. It isn't that I need or want your encouragement. In fact, it's just the reverse; I can get along beautifully without it. But hasn't it ever struck you that it'd be ever so much more pleasant to feel that we were on good terms rather than on bad? Hasn't it ever occurred to you that I'm under no obligations to you whatsoever, and that if you're taking without giving in return you ought at the very least not to squawk if you don't exactly get what you want? Hasn't it ever occurred to you that I have fully as many rights as you have, and that I've proved well qualified to handle my own affairs without interference from one who cannot handle hers? Hasn't it ever occurred to you that you've been bombarding me for favors with no color of right, legal, moral, or otherwise? In short, hasn't it ever occurred to you that I'm your brother and not your servant?

We come now to the reward I was talking about : Henceforth you're not to write to me at all unless you can do without

1) malice
2) complaining *
3) whining
4) nagging *
5) threats
6) irritation
7) demanding *
8) belittling *
9) griping
10) every other objectionable quality

*very serious

If you find that you must incorporate one or more of these annoying characteristics, throw the letter away and wait another day. If you should make just one more mistake along these lines, you'll pay for it very deeply, I promise you. The next letter from you will be the pleasantest one you're capable of writing, and woe unto you if there's a single reference to anything along your usual lines. If you think I'm only joking, try me out. That's all—just try me out!

Hoping that this doesn't bring on a fainting spell, and attack of the heaves, nausea, a cold in the chest, biliousness, vomiting, or, what's worse, a statement beginning "The fact remains', I have the doubtful distinction of subscribing myself,

Your brother,

18. To Ruth Shapiro

(Lunt and Fontaine were a husband and wife theatrical acting team associated with Noel Coward. This letter contains the first mention of Maggie—Marguerite Azora Smith, whom Sanford would marry in 1938. Max Gordon was Albert Lewis's Broadway producing partner.)

Sept. 23rd, 1937

Dear Ruth :

The facts, briefly, are these : I report on Monday at 10 A.M. to begin my assignment at Metro for the fair-to-middling salary of $500 per week. It's a one-picture deal for the present, with no time limit stipulated; if the script sequences turn out to be satisfactory, the deal may stretch out indefinitely; if they stink, I'll probably get the sack in a couple of months. But the set-up is too good for any such sour conclusion, to my way of thinking. I'll have to be very very bad to get the air, much worse than I think it's possible for me to be at anything in the writing business.

Without doubt, I owe the break to Joan Crawford entirely. She introduced me to Joe Mankiewicz at her house one Saturday night last year, she gave him my book to read, she arranged my first interview with him in April, she had me out to the MGM lot time after time when she knew I'd run into him on her set, and lastly, she must have put in a good word now and then when I wasn't around. It's true he'd not have taken me on if he weren't convinced I could deliver, but there are many in Hollywood who could deliver with a set-up like this, but I happen to have gotten the call because of my friendship with Joan. If I could think up a gift that she hasn't already got nine of, I'd buy it for her; as it is, a dozen American Beauties will have to convey my gratitude.

The property is Keith Winter's 'The Shining Hour', and if you get it you'll see that it's a story of landed folk from the north of

England; when it appears on the screen, however, the locale will be Kansas or some place else in the Bible Belt. Mankiewicz has some fine ideas for adapting the piece, and he's already outlined the direction it should take if Crawford's to play the lead, as he fondly hopes at the moment. It was originally scheduled for Garbo, but it's way off her line. Some notions I still retain from 'The Stranger's Return' will stand me in good stead; in fact, I think one of the first things I'll ask for is a re-running of that film.

Maggie just fell into the biggest opening of her career. Albert Lewis, for whom she used to be secretary some years ago and who's now producing at RKO, called her up and asked her if she happened to have an original for Colbert. She didn't but she said she had, and in three days presented him with an original that she cooked up out of thin air. He went so wild about it that he's going to have her write a play around it and produce it with Max Gordon on Broadway. They're even talking Lunt and Fontanne for it !

'The Old Man's Place' is under consideration at Warners, and we should have some word about their attitude in a week or so. I'm keeping after the Hayward office day by day.

The new book is within a week of completion, but that'll probably stretch out to three weeks now that I'm back on salary. An hour a day for that length of time, and it'll be on its way to New York. It's about 70,000 words long now, and it'll be about 75,000 by the time I show it to Knight. I like it so much that I've offered to buy it back if they won't give it the promised advertising campaign.

Sorry I missed the Governor when I called tonight. Give him my love and tell him to take care of himself.

I got the new job just in time to make you a birthday present. It'll be along in next week's mail.

Best love to you both, and tell all the folks the good news.

Affectionately,

19. To Ruth Shapiro

October 21st, 1937

Dear Ruth :

Your letter in the bag. I was glad to hear from you, particularly in your new and most becoming vein of sister-in-fact as well as sister-in-law. It's a treat to know that you've let up on your carping, and I want to assure you I realize the change.

The book did not go off to Knight as planned last week. It was finished and ready for its journey, but Crawford niggled around and finally asked me to let her read it before I sent it away. She's had it three days now, but I know she didn't read it till today; she had a day off from the lot, and I believe she devoted a good part of it to knocking off my seventy thousand words. I'm seeing her tomorrow, and then I'll get the verdict from her. And it may not even get mailed this weekend; Metro got wind of the fact that I had a book ready and asked to read it before it went to press. I haven't decided what to do yet; I may let them have it, and again I may hold off till it's in galley.

I've promised Mankiewicz the first sequence by the early part of the week, and naturally I'm trying my best to get it in the best possible shape. Maggie will look it over during the weekend, and Monday I'll hand it over to a stenographer. By the way, I'm working on Sequence 1 all alone; Hertz is roughing up Sequence 2 in the meanwhile; we hit on that way of handling the job, first talking over the potential content of each sequence, of course, because we felt that we'd get a better flow to the dialogue.

I see Crawford every day on her set, and at least three times a week she calls me over to her dressingroom for lunch. We're very pally, and I'm convinced she likes me as much as her actions in my behalf would indicate. She had Maggie and me out to the house last Sunday night for dinner and a picture. The party was small, as usual, consisting of the Tones, Jerry Asher, George Murphy and his wife, and us two. I'd seen the film, so I took Franchot into the library and gave him a terrific licking at two-handed pinochle (which I hadn't played for ten years). The session cost him a cool fifty cents.

Maggie's deal is all set. I drew up the preliminary agreements last night, got them signed by the producer this evening, and secured $250 as an advance, another $250 being due on delivery of the first act, which'll be on Saturday. Everything will be handled through the Author's League, so I guess all Maggie has to do is write a good play. From what I've seen of it so far, I think that's what it'll be.

Yes, Hertz is the playwright you've heard about.

Too bad about 'The Bride Wore Red'. It was meant to be a pretty good film, but it went awry in the writing, and nowhere else. Crawford and Arzner tried hard, but there never was a film in the script. I read it, and it was just too dull to contemplate. It was a foul affair from the fade-in to the fade-out, and it was perpetrated by one Bradbury Foote and one Tess Slesinger. Crawford seems to like my dialogue. Every time I get on the set, she asks me to listen to the lines and make suggestions. There's very little but tempo to criticize in 'Mannequin'. It's no profound writing job, but the dialogue is alive, and it seems to play. The new lead, Alan Curtis, is kind of slow on the uptake; if Borzage cures that in the final takes, the picture should be Crawford's best of the year.

Love to you and the Governor. I'm enclosing my weekly check herein. Be good enough to deliver it into the hands of Boss Shapiro.

Affectionately,

20. To Ruth Shapiro

*(*The Shining Hour *was never produced.)*

October 30th, 1937

Dear Ruth :

I forgot to tell you a few weeks ago that I was working alone on 'The Shining Hour.' I turned in the first sequence yesterday, and Mankiewicz must have liked it, because I'm going ahead solo; he said that if the finished script needed anything, we could always recall Hertz for a valve and carbon job at that time. Mankiewicz finally acquainted Crawford with the story yesterday, and when I saw her on the set she told me she was crazy about the set-up.

Her picture, 'Mannequin', is finished, and after retakes, which'll probably carry her over to November 15th, she goes on a two-month vacation according to contract. When I spoke to Joe the other day, he told me that if he gets the script he wants on 'The Shining Hour', that'll be the next Crawford instead of 'Shopworn Angel', with which I gather they're having plenty of trouble.

Yes, that Sunday evening a couple of weeks ago was Maggie's first visit to the Tones, but when you ask me if she was impressed I really don't know how to answer you except by saying that she's not the type that's impressed by anything but out-and-out talent. Glitter and fame and opulence, after tasting them for the better part of ten years, leave her cold. I know she admires Crawford for what she's accomplished with herself, but she kept her head admirably in the face of an armful of star sapphires.

I was over there again for dinner last Wednesday night; it was the night Crawford was finishing her film, and knowing that she was going to be late at the lot, she asked me over to keep Franchot company. I stayed till about eleven, taking another fifty cents away from him at pinochle.

As you've no doubt heard by this time, the book is in New York. I had a wire from Burt Hoffman yesterday telling me that the manuscript had arrived safely, and that he'd write after reading it. . . . On re-reading the above I realize that the only way you could have heard about the book was through Mel, and thinking about Mel reminds me of the fact that I haven't had a rumble out of him since last June or July. Why this is so is a mystery, and if you know of anything that has prevented his writing, I should like to hear what it is. Can he be angry at something I've done or not done, or just exactly what ?

I'm writing a letter to Uncle Arthur immediately. I was, of course, very sorry to hear of his illness, and I earnestly hope that he pulls through with no ill effects. I see where this may make the Governor feel that he has to go down to 11 West 42nd St. and start in moving desks around and chewing his nails off to the elbow. Let me tell you, if I hear of anything so nonsensical I'm going to get good and mad. There's absolutely no need in the world for him to fret about those stink-pot clients now, and you're the one to boss him around about it. See that you do.

Sorry to appear pikerish about the negatives. I was only lazy, though, and didn't want to go down to the corner drugstore with them.

A letter from Uncle Dave reveals the fact that he's in Havana, unless he got sick of it between the time he posted the note and I received it—which wouldn't stun me in the least.

The Al Lewis in the clipping you sent is Maggie's Al Lewis, all right. Her first act went over with a bang with him, and she got her second two-fifty as per the contract. I think there's a very funny play in sight here, and there will be unless I miss my guess by a wide margin.

Hortie just dropped me a line, complaining about your silence. Speak !

Love to all, and write again soon.

Affectionately,

21. To Ruth Shapiro

(The book referred to here is Seventy Times Seven, *published by Alfred A. Knopf in 1939.)*

November 12th, 1937

Dear Babe :

Sorry about that old caracul coat. How are you ever going to get it out of hock ?

Crawford, Tone, and Mankiewicz liked the book very much, but I'm a slight more interested in what my publisher thought. I heard from him today for the first time since he received the book. I'd been prepared for some little enthusiasm, but according to the way he writes, he's discovered another Dostoevsky ! His letter is eleven pages long, and there are five or six hyperboles to the page. He has several valid suggestions to make regarding phraseology, elaboration, and the like, but on the whole he's so tickled that he seemed to have written me the letter while dancing. He repeats his promise to give the book the works as far as advertising is concerned—which means full pages everywhere that a book-reader might look.

Quotes from the letter : . . . I sincerely believe that you have written a grand book. . . . Your style, naturally, is good—to my mind just about as good as I have ever read. And from your past experiences with me, you know that I am a crank on styles. . . . the variations of presentation held me only as James Joyce (oof !) has held me in the past. Not that I am drawing any comparison between your style and James Joyce's. It is my candid opinion that you can write rings around him (oof ! oof !). . . . You have written a really great book. . . . I read the manuscript twice. . . . and I did it only for one reason; I couldn't help myself. You can forget about Boni and all the other boys that have had a hand in exploiting your writing in the past. I mean to make you satisfied with our terms so that contract or no contract you would never think of going to another publisher in this country. . . . .

And more of he same.

Got a letter from Mel today, enclosing five snaps of him and his baby—really a lovely looking little critter.

I've been thinking of a trip east around the holidays, but in this damned racket you never know from one minute to the next exactly where you are. All I can say is that I'm going to try to make the break. But if I'm still on 'The Shining Hour', and it's unfinished when I want to get out of here, all I can do is stick to the job. So don't make any plans.

I've no plans for 'The Old Man's Place'. Warners turned it back to me at least two months ago, and it's lying flat on its back in my garage. I got all rights back from Hayward, and the book is mine and Boni's to dispose of, but without time to plug it I'd rather let it lie for the time being.

Selma's relative was her uncle, Dave Nierenberg.

I was rushed during the few days he was here, and I had to meet him on the fly at the Knickerbocker bar, and then but for half an hour.

Maggie and I took a brief jaunt up to Frisco over the weekend, our first outing since we all had that fling last June. Jack's and Pierre's are still serving that grand food. Pierre himself remembered you as the lade weeth ver poor appetite. He autographed a few menus for you, and I'll send them on when I get hold of a long envelope.

How are Aunt Sarah and Uncle Arthur getting on ? And how's everyone else in the family?

Love to you and the Governor.

As Ever,

22. To Philip D. Shapiro

("Knight" was the original publisher Sanford found for Seventy Times Seven.*)*

November 24th, 1937

Dear Governor :

I haven't heard from you for three or four weeks. What's the matter ---the old imaginary writer's cramp ?

I had a confab with Mankiewicz the day before yesterday, and I've been commissioned to go ahead with 'The Shining Hour' on my own. Hertz was taken off it four weeks ago, but he was being held in reserve in case I failed to make a go of the script. I understand from Hertz that he's been put on another assignment. Mankiewicz went to New York yesterday for three weeks, so I guess I can count myself on the payrool at least until he gets back.

By this time you know that I scored a bullseye with the new book—at least as far as my publisher is concerned. I'm hurrying with the revisions he suggested and also those that occur to me as I go along, hoping to have the job finished by December 15th as Knight asked. Assuming that I meet the deadline, the book will be in galleys by January 15th for three solid months of plugging before publication, the date for which has tentatively been set at April 22. You've always been tough to please, but I feel reasonably safe in saying you'll be pleased with this book.

I'm very sorry that there's been so much illness in the family. I hope that you're being sensible and taking things easy. Next time you see Aunt Sarah and Uncle Arthur, please give them my love.

About getting away for the holidays—if I get bounced when Mankiewicz comes back, I'll most certainly take a two-week flyer to New York. And then, even if I'm not bounced, maybe I'll be able to sneak in some kind of trip. I'm really most anxious to see you and the kid and the rest of the family again, and if it's humanly possible to break away I'll do it.

Enclosed is a snapshot of the author working on his new book last summer.

Affectionately,

23. To Ruth Shapiro

1.14.38

Dear Ruth :

Your letter and Dad's give slightly different versions of the state of affairs prevailing at 170 West 73rd St. Forgive me if I regard his as the more accurate of the two.

It's a bit late for me to say this now, after your evening with Joe on January 2nd, but to keep the record straight I have to observe that you did not, from your own account, handle the matter very ably. I think you'd have had much more self-satisfaction if you'd give Joe the bum's rush instead of waiting for him to take the hint. In those fifteen minutes of silence you might have recouped much of the pride you've lost over the last couple of years. The ways things are now you're only waiting for him to call you back, whereas what we were after was a pass which would make his calling back impossible. We agreed on surgery, and you used laxatives.

But after all, the time is ripe for a breaking off of this affair by one means or another, and whether he got thrown out or just walked out is really immaterial; the big thing is that you don't see him. I'm not as callous as you may think. Indeed, I'm very feeling—but my feeling is all for you, not for the situation. I honestly don't care how the job was maneuvered. I don't care about how you're steeling yourself to the consequences. Suppose you are lonely a few evenings or even a few months. At least you'll know you're free to take up whatever happens to come along, and you'll be much more than wise if you use these next few months to build yourself up physically so as to be able to take advantage of any opportunity that comes your way. You may feel that all opportunities are shunning you, but that's only because you're looking at things from the outside in. A room looks dark, even in the daytime, if you look from the street. But just go within and look outward, and there's brightness. I've been through a few ordeals myself, and in the not too distant past, and therefore I know that what I say is the truth.

In many ways, in most ways, you have much to be grateful for, and I know that you have the quality of gratitude, as well as many others, but you've just sewn yourself up in some kind of impeding garment, with the result that your best self is stultified. No one has clamped down on you, as you seem to think; no one is against you—in fact, surprisingly enough, there's nobody that wouldn't help you to the limit of his powers. . . . . provided only that you come to the realization that you're important enough to yourself to want to help yourself. No one wants to waste effort on a losing cause; no one has much respect for a person that won't respect himself.

It's up to you, Ruth. I told you years ago that you'd have to find a different slant if you didn't want to come a cropper. You listened, but you went your own way, with the result that you went on your face three times in a row. People lose sympathy with a person that makes the same mistake so often; they feel that you'll never learn.

I feel that you will learn, that you have learned much. All that remains is a perfection of method, and that's the hardest of all. But I feel confident that you're in for a better time if you make up your mind to it. It's in your own hands.

I caught a cold on the train, and I was laid up for four days on arriving in Hollywood. My house was kind of dampish, so Maggie made me go out to hers and park there till I felt better. I'm O.K. now, and I've been working furiously at the final revision of SEVENTY TIMES SEVEN. It's half way done now, and I expect to have no difficulty in meeting the February 1st deadline. Quinn Martin, Story editor for Paramount, has been after the book from this end, and Richard Halliday, the same on the N.Y. end. I've promised both a copy of the very first galleys.

There's a lull at the moment in film production, a reflection of the general "recession" throughout the country, and few studios are signing anybody on except big names. But frankly I'm not at all anxious to get placed till the book's on the fire.

Love to you and Dad, and take care of yourselves.

Affectionately,

24. To Ruth Shapiro

("Maggie's play" mentioned herein refers to Farewell Performance, *which was never produced.)*

1.30.38

Dear Ruth :

Well, the book's finished and in the mails ! I put the last few touches on it yesterday and sent it to Knight, hoping that it comes somewhere near what I think it is. I improved it immeasurably by the revision that I gave it since coming back to California; I went through the entire manuscript, cut out all the dead wood, added a few explanatory passages, and in general gave it a thorough overhauling. I'm confident I did a very wise thing in refusing to let it go to press while I was in New York. I'll have galley-proof back to me in two weeks, and then I'll be able to tell more about the presentability of the book. But even now I know it's far and away the best writing I've ever done.

Knight sent me a sketch of the jacket last week, and it was simply stunning. It's by Hawkins, the chap who did the jacket for OF MICE AND MEN. He has a peculiar technique; it embodies a rather airy blur for all the backgrounds, making whatever is important in the foregrounds stand out very boldly. And why shouldn't it be airy? He uses an air-brush to get his effects. Anyhow, I know definitely that you'll like it miles better than the jackets on my other books.

About conditions in Hollywood : The moving picture companies are dead or dying, with only 25 films in the process of being shot as against 45 at the same time last year. No company is taking on help at the moment, but the quiet period is expected to end at any moment, for every outfit has a certain number of pictures sold to exhibitors, and sooner or later they must be made. The big trouble out here is the utter sheepishness of all the executives; nobody wants to make the first move for fear of walking into an axe. But when some hardy soul throws caution to the winds (er), things'll start humming again.

As far as I'm concerned, I'm really not looking for a job. I'm tired of writing, and I'll keep on being tired of it for a good several weeks. I want to take it easy for a while (I've been writing steadily for three or four years) and in the meantime dream up some scheme of selling THE OLD MAN'S PLACE to the movies. Warners owns OF MICE AND MEN, and as soon as they get around to putting it into production, every other studio will be screaming its head off for a similar propitty. You and Dad just sit tight and quit worrying either yourselves or me about being under salary.

Paramount has first call on SEVENTY TIMES SEVEN. I got a letter from Sam Goldwyn yesterday asking for a copy of the book. In addition, Metro wants it, and so does 20th-Fox.

I'm waiting to hear what Stivelman had to say about your condition. If you haven't gone to see him, do so at once. And if you've jobbed me on that touch, you'll never get another cent from me as long as you live. Go to see Stivelman TODAY !

I heard about Sidney and Adler long ago. All I can say is Adler would have a lot easier time of it if he just handed his bank account over to her and called it quits. She'll take him for his eye-teeth.

I saw SNOW WHITE myself the other night and had a grand time. The only thing I didn't like was the scenario. It was truly a dull and pointless story. But what was remarkable was that I completely forgot, after the first few minutes, that I was looking at an animated cartoon. The figures, especially the animals, were real.

The books arrived in perfect condition. They stacked all around my joint because I haven't yet had time to go out and shop around for some secondhand cases.

By way of contradiction, I'd like to say that this grandson of Sitting Bull knows a lot less about George Armstrong Custer, greatest fake-hero of American history, than I do, and for a perfectly solid reason : old Sitting Bull was even further from the battlefield on June 25, 1876, than I was. As soon as he heard that a battle was coming off, he grabbed a horse and lit out for the mountains to do a little 'praying,' and every authority without exception says he was so far away when the fight took place that he couldn't even hear the firing. The attack was led by Gall, Two Moon, and Crazy Horse, one or other of whom, with about fifteen hundred men, cut Custer off from the main body of his command and killed them to the last man. Many of these 250 killed were not scalped, and if Custer got away with that indignity it was not because he was the great Custer, but because the Indians simply did not know they were fighting him that day. None of them had ever seen him, and if they had they wouldn't have recognized him, for that far-famed 'long yellow hair' of Custer's had been clipped very short for the Sioux campaign—and he did not wear a 'fringed buckskin jacket'; he dressed like the others, in calvary blue.

Thanks for the story, though. It's just another fairy tale, a little less dull than SNOW WHITE, but a fairy tale all the same. I still have a brief piece about Custer in SEVENTY TIMES SEVEN, but it's satiric and very bitter. Those historical passages of mine, by the way, were most unclear in the version you read; you'll be glad to know that a long explanatory passage now precedes it.

Maggie's play was accepted by Lewis, and he forwarded Dramatists' Guild contracts for her signature. He had several suggestions for changes in Act III, however, and therefore I'm going to try to wangle another $500 out of him for her. He says that the Lunts are definitely interested and begs her not to reveal the contents of the play to anyone at all. If I inadvertently let slip to you any of the plot, for Maggie's sake keep it strictly to yourself.

It was rotten of me not to have called Lydia while I was in town. I take it that excuses you made for me were the usual ones—family, book, etc.—and when I drop her a line, I'll repeat them. They happen to be strictly true anyway.

You can't complain about this letter being short. Let's see you do as well. Give my love to Dad, and the same to yourself. You wrote nothing about Joe, so I take it he hasn't called. How are you taking it, though ? Sensibly, or in your best 1930-1938 manner ?

Best to all the family.

Affectionately,

25. To Ruth Shapiro

(The "original story" Sanford refers to here is "The People Against Johnny Doe." It was never produced.)

March 21st, 1938

Dear Monk :

Your letter just arrived, and I'm replying to it at once because I happen to have ten minutes to spare, this being a much longer breathing-spell than I usually have these days.

I'm devoting all my time to the original story. It started out as a stab at a grand or two, something to catch some producer's eye and make him cough up a piece of unimportant dough; at first, I was simply going to sketch out the idea in true original form, a job that'd require about fifteen pages at the most. But once I'd begun work, I realized that there were possibilities in the story and that by giving it added time I might easily rake in a sizable hunk of change by some extra labor. I've been on the job for two weeks now, and I hope to complete it within three or four days; it's at least two-thirds done right now. Maggie tells me that Al Lewis is dickering for his old job at Radio for a four-month stretch and that there's a definite chance of his being interested enough in the story to take it with him and produce it. At any rate she's going to push it with him. We'll see shortly.

As for the novel, I'm allowing Mel to handle it his way. Of course, it was a shame that Knight had to pull its ears in when it did, but look how much better off I am that the book wasn't being bound and distributed when they had to stop work. It's too late now to make any spring list—that much is definite. It's at Viking now, and if they like it, they'll put it out for the fall; if they don't, it's on to the next in line. Mel wrote last week to say that he regarded it as too bad that I was pressing him for time, for he thought it to my best interests to wait out some good publisher rather than shop around and finally wind up with Knight; he says that Knight, although they may make a comeback in the fall, have irreparably injured their standing by missing out on a season's list, and that even if they open fire again this fall, it'll take them a solid year to re-establish their reputation. He asked me for permission to withdraw from Knight altogether, and I granted it.

As far as Crawford is concerned, I'm afraid I'll have to be the judge of what's permissible and what's not. When we parted at San Berdoo, it was understood that she was to get in touch with me within the week. Here it is ten weeks now, and still no call. Not, of course, that I'm afraid to leave the phone for fear of missing her call. It's just that her omission to call means that she doesn't want to call. Her circle of friends is small enough for her to remember me once in a while, and if she wished to do something about it, depend on it she would. In some circumstances, pride is more important than friendship out here, for if one lacked pride he'd damage certain tenuous relationships by opening himself to the criticism that he's only sucking around. That's not my attitude, certainly, but I'm unwilling to risk having anyone accuse me of it. So if I get a call, I'll be as friendly as all get-out, and if I don't. . . .

The war, that is, the coming war, is the one single subject that I'm interested in too. I avoid casual conversations and gossip like twin plagues; the only possible center of interest is Europe, with occasional sorties into China by way of supplementing European guesses. My reading has switched abruptly (this a matter of a year's standing now) from fiction to interpretations of power politics. I'm reading CAPITAL for the first time, in addition to Engels, Lenin, Dimitroff, Palme Dutt, Strachey, and all the sympathetic periodicals such as New Masses, Nation, Inprecorr, and occasionally New Republic, the last of which has a positively repulsive isolationist bent.

Write again, and soon. Love to you and the Governor.

Affectionately,

26. To Ruth Shapiro

March 29th, 1938

Dear Ruth :

Stationery ! Isn't that envelope part of the box I "bought" for you in Brentano's about five years ago ? Remember ?

The Shining Hour. Yes, I knew Hertz was back on the assignment. I've seen him two or three times this year at meetings of the Screen Writers' Guild, and on each of those occasions he wept bitterly into his beer about his fate. As for a screen credit, a writer's entitled to that only if he's contributed substantially (25%) to the picture as shot. It makes no difference whether he's written four complete versions of the material; if the finished film doesn't embody at least 25% of the ideas he created, he gets no credit. From what he tells me (Hertz, I mean) he's discarded all the stuff we did together and all the stuff I did alone.

The original story goes apace, and I expect to complete it this week. I'd have had it done at the moment, except for my giving over a couple of days to typing Maggie's second act for submission to Lewis; she's landed a job at 20th-Fox, and is pressed for time. Sam Marx at Columbia has promised to read the original himself, without turning it over to a reader, so I look for quick and expert action immediately.

Still can't see it your way re Crawford, and that's that.

Despite your prejudices, or rather your fears, about reading Lenin, perhaps the best book on the direction to be taken by power-politics is his 100-page pamphlet called 'Imperialism.' It can be had in the Workers' Bookshop for, I think, 30 [cents]. It may look formidable, and it may seem difficult to read at the start, but once you get the hang of a very gaunt and specialized prose, I think you'll have little difficulty with it. It is incomplete, of course, since it was written in 1916, but there's no possible escape from its implications, and those you can draw for yourself. As follow-ups, which will undoubtedly clear up any misinterpretations, I recommend two books by the English-Indian, R. Palme Dutt : "Fascism and the Social Revolution" and "History of World Politics, 1914–1936". In addition, you always have Strachey's book right in your library.

Reading the New Masses weekly can't hurt you a bit, but reading the New Republic will. You ask whether I'm for or against isolationism. Against, by all means. If you look over the recent columns of the New Republic and nothing else, you may get the notion that by taking an isolationist stand we can avoid war no matter what happens in Europe. That's about as false an idea as one could possibly entertain. Simply because we're isolated geographically doesn't mean that we're isolated economically—the reverse, in fact—and as our financial interests lie, so will our politics. There's no doubt in the world that the anti-new-dealers in America, the Republican Party, and the big interests are definitely fascist. Any understanding of the meaning of fascism inevitably leads you to that conclusion. It's definitely at the moment to the interests of finance-capital that we do not intervene in Europe. By keeping our noses 'clean', we strengthen the advance of European fascism, the only continental opposition there is to the Communist movement. If you read the works I've suggested, especially Palme Dutt, you'll see that this was the precise reason behind the great capitalist support given to Nazism and Fascism at the start in the early days of the movement, 1921-1923. The only way to break down that power is to ally ourselves with the real democratic movements in the world as at present exemplified by the French Peoples' Front, which combines liberals of every persuasion and color, from bull-red to old rose. For proof that this united front is the only successful way, consult your daily reports from China. With the alliance of Chiang-Kai-Shek and the Red Armies under Mao-Tse-Tung, the Japs for the first time tasted the might of the Chinese Nation. At the moment, they're tasting it to their complete sorrow, as the whole along-the-line Japanese retreat reveals. For the obverse of the medal, see Spain. There, with no intervening or very little, the Loyalists are being crushed. Take your pick. Which do you want?

No word from Mel for two weeks !

Take care of yourself and see to it that the Governor does too. And write soon.

Affectionately,

27. To Ruth Shapiro

(The reference to "George" is to one of Sanford's oldest friends, George Brounoff. With whom Sanford attended kindergarten and may have dated his sister, Olga, the O.B. of The Water Wheel, *and the woman to whom Nathanael West referred when criticizing Sanford in Warrensburg, N.Y. for the transparency of his early drafts.)*

April 12th, 1938

Dear Ruth :

Your letter was very revealing. That part about George showed such a passionate desire on your part to protect me from the possible touches of my friends that I hardly know how to thank you, sister dear. Read it back; your chest will surely swell with pride :

> . . . Unless I miss my guess, I have a pretty good idea as to the contents of (George's) letter. He asked you for a loan, didn't he ? . . . . and I was glad I told him you haven't been working for several months . . . *I do feel sorry for him as he has a tremendous expense and no money but after all—Ye Gods, you can't be expected to support all your friends and relatives . . . But maybe I'm wrong—maybe he never even asked you for aid . . . I hope I am.*

How does that look in print compassionate one ? And to take a great load from your mind, do you know what I'm going to do? Just this : I'm not going to tell you what he said in his letter. How's that? Neat?

It would be fitting if I also withheld a report on the original story, but fearing that you'd turn blue in the face, I hasten to inform you that the story was handed to Sam Marx of Columbia and to Howard Green of 20th-Fox yesterday. Ain't that great ? Now you can start figuring how much money I'm going to be offered. You can get out your adding machine and try to dope out how much I have in the bank (for my friends and relatives : see above) if both Columbia and 20th-Fox started bidding. Look—suppose Columbia started off with an offer of a flat $5,000. I could go around to Fox and pass the word along, and maybe they'd counter with an offer of $7,500. I'd take that back to Columbia, and maybe they'd raise the ante to $10,000, take it or leave it. I'd say I was leaving it, and speeding to Fox, I'd get them to tilt the pot to $15,000. By this time, all Hollywood would be onto the fact that J.B. Sanford had an original that was hotter than Hell. I'd be about to close with Fox when Metro stepped into the picture and knocked up the price to $25,000. That's put both Fox and Columbia out of the running, but not Paramount. Throwing its hat into the ring, Paramount would startle the industry with the unheard of bid of $35,000. Sore as a boiled owl, Louie Mayer would tighten his belt, clamp down harder on his ten-dollar cigar, and holler $50,000. Now Madeleine Carroll over at Selznick's would have gotten a gander at the story, decide it was tailored to her measure, and induced Dave Selznick to go after it hot and heavy. With my pen poised over the Metro contract, in rushes Leland Hayward waving 75 crisp one-thousand dollar bills. I don't sign with Metro, not because of the Selznick offer, but because now there's a national syndicate (composed of Republic, Universal, Monogram, Condor, Larry Darmour, and Hal Roach) that's entering the picture. They offer 100,000—but do I take it ? Not on your life ! The reason is Warner Bros. has just snapped the rubberband off its bankroll and staggered tradition with a bid of $150,000. As far as I'm concerned, that's the offer I've been waiting for, and I'm on the verge of closing with Warner Bros when I get a phone call from you, pleading with me to hold out for another boost. I urge upon you the fact that I've just about bled Hollywood white, but you insist that if they go to $150,000 they'll go to $200,000, and with all those friends and relatives of ours depending for their bread and shelter on little J.B. Sanford, it's my duty to get as much as the traffic will bear. I'm a little uneasy about it, but I give in because you've an unbroken record of being right about such things. So I wait around for somebody to top Warners offer. It's no go, and fearing that I'll lose the Warners tie-up, I go in and lay the story down. They now say they only want to pay $95,000, so I tell them the Hell—I can get at least $100,000 from the syndicate. I hurry around to the syndicate, but somehow or other they're not prepared now to go over $65,000. That doesn't sit so good, with Selznick, through Leland Hayward, offering $75,000, so I turn it down and speed around to Hayward—but he's a little dubious by this time, and it's $40,000 or nothing. I laugh and say it's nothing, and why shouldn't I, with Louie Mayer bidding $50,000. But whatta ya think ? Louie aint in such a lather any more; he says I can have $25,000, with a quick yes or no. I shrug and say no—what with Paramount splitting a gut to pay $35,000. But something must have happened because now Paramount only wants to shell out $20,000. Of course I don't take that with Louie Mayer's $25,000 fresh in my ears. I go back to Culver City, but Louie sends out word by his secretary that top price is $10,000. Hell, it's only three miles to 20th-Fox, and they always wanted to put up $15,000, so I tell Mayer to go jump in the lake, and it's off to Fox for the $15,000. I don't know what's the matter, but Fox says I get $7,500 or bupkes. Who wants bupkes, though, with Columbia bulging to pay $10,000 ? Columbia, however, is offering only $6,000, so I shoot back to Fox to get their original $7500. In the meantime, this figure has shrunk to $2,500, leaving me with the alternative of accepting Columbia's original $5,000. Well, $5,000 is better than nothing, so I go back to Columbia to get it. The offer is now $7.25. Shucks, I say, that's no money compared to Fox's $2,500, and back I fly to Fox, only to find that I can't get in without an appointment. Needing gas for my car now, I figure I might as well take that $7.25 from Columbia, but when I finally manage to bribe my way onto the lot (by promising the gate-man $7) I find out that Sam Marx has resigned his job and gone back to pants-pressing. . .

So that's why I'm writing to ask you if it wouldn't be possible to get a loan of $7. You know I wouldn't ask you for it if I really didn't need it—but that God damn gate-man is bothering the life out of me. . . .

Much love,

28. To Naomi Greenstein

August 2nd, 1939

Dear Nonie:

Got home from a 6500-mile tour of the west yesterday and found your letter of July 21 waiting for us. Started out for nowhere on July 3, and if you punks had kept in touch with us, as you promised, in all probability we'd have headed your way. Your long silence, then, cost you the company of two of the most interesting people I've ever known.

Christ, where were we not? At one time or other we were in each state west of the Rockies—California, Oregon, Washington, Idaho, Montana (the Custer battlefield, naturally), Wyoming, Utah, Nevada, Colorado, Arizona, New Mexico . . . . and we came home glowing with the knowledge that we live in the most wonderful country in the world. It has so much, its possibilities are so great, its history is so shabby, its people nevertheless are so fine. If the trip did nothing else, it solidified at least my plans for the fourth book. From a mere memory of America, I had dreamed a novel that would tell its story, and I have now facts, realities, with which to document that dream, not all, not nearly enough, but something to spring from. I'm very eager to start writing again; I know I have something splendid in mind; it all depends on whether I can surround it with words.

I haven't read West's book because I simply can't tolerate the man. It's the God's honest truth that he's the only human being on the face of the earth that I really detest. I've been publicly punched in the jaw by people for whom I have more respect. There's nothing in the world that he stands for on the same footing that I do, and it would be impossible for me to read anything of his, however good, with an open mind; I know the living body of the 'writer' too well to lose myself in his prose—and it never was that good.

I remember an anecdote (from the life of Baudelaire, I believe) that Pep dug out of a biography ten or twelve years ago and related to me with great relish. It had to do with Baudelaire's being accosted by a crippled beggar and asked for alms. Shouting that he was not poor enough to give alms, Baudelaire kicked the beggar in the face and walked on.

Whether the great citizen was Baudelaire or Nietsche or Rodin makes no difference; the point is that Pep has always approved that kick in the face—more, he has always done the same booting for his own account. No single whole he has ever written is free from some of the most unaccountable brutality between covers—not the brutality of life, which sometimes in the mass steps on and squashes a small fragment of itself, but the brutality of deliberate and conscious selection, the brutality that stinks of the lamp, the brutality of the occasional vindictive bully—who is yellow. Pep writes of cripples, and he does not weep for them: he kicks them in the face, like the hero of his piddling anecdote. He takes the clubfooted schoolteacher who painfully climbs five flights of stairs to get to her fifty-five-cent seat at Carnegie Hall, opens the ceiling to dump tons of excrement on her, and then boots her down the stair-well. He is not poor enough to give alms. He takes the exceptional case, the dwarfed body, the moronic mind, the cheap soul, and he treats them as if he were one of their own kind, dwarfed, moronic, cheap. No man that I've ever known has less pity for the insulted and injured, less nobility in the face of a life that constantly tends toward making man seem ridiculous. It is a bad thing that life makes some spines look like a corkscrew; it is a contemptible thing that one of the lucky ones jeers at the result; and in Pep's literature there's always some hunchback who has to pay double, once to life and once to Mister West.

You make a mistake when you say that Pep does not understand "these poor people who come to Hollywood to die". He understands them well. He is what you would call an intelligent man. It is precisely this intelligence that makes his obsession so criminal. His selection of "these poor people" hasn't got the excuse of ignorance; it's deliberate, as deliberate as Hitler's selection of the inconsequential Jew as a suitable German goat. Mister West chooses his dwarfs with care. They're hand-picked to yield him the maximum amount of revenge on a fate that failed to include in him those elements which go to make up a Hardy, a Melville, a Dostoevsky. In a low moment he once bemoaned the fact that he was only a third-rate Huxley, and now on reflection, I can't think that Huxley would be flattered.

Nothing would make me read The Day Of The Locust (which is Pep?), but I'd very much like to hear Jesse's views about the book. Ask him to write soon.

Maggie is grand. She loves you two and speaks of you often and with deep affection, as I do. We took 41 rolls of film on the trip, and if two of the shots turn out all right we'll send you prints—not that all 328 were of ourselves.

Red Masquerader has pneumonia while we were away, and now Maggie's sleeping in his stall to make sure he doesn't get it in his other lung. My God, is she crazy about that horse? But I like it! Minnie will lick the envelope of this letter by way of remembrance. And as a matter of fact, so will I.

With love, as ever,

29. To Philip D. Shapiro

("Sit Down and Fight" was another Sanford original screenplay, also never produced.)

August 18th, 1938

Dear Governor :

Ruth dropped me a note from the West End last week. She also dropped me a hint, letting out that for some time you've been chewing out your fingernails about my not having had a job since the start of the year. That won't do, my good man, that won't do at all. As I said before, I hate to write letters about things that look promising and then flop, and this business is loaded to the gunwales with them. I want you to know, though, even if I make no mention of it, that not a day goes by but I'm trying to squeeze into some opening. I see agents, writers, producers, directors, story editors, everybody from top to bottom and side to side, and if I haven't been successful yet, it's been due to my unwillingness to accept a salary cut. I could have been working at Universal right now if I'd been foolish enough to drop part of my salary, for I had a straight take-it-or-leave-it offer from Sackheim two weeks ago. I left it. You work hard out here to build your salary up to what it is, and once you agree to let it sag, it takes you ages to re-establish yourself; often you never do, for they get the notion that you've slipped. The trick is to make them want you at your own price, and that's what I'm working on. I was hot when I came out here in 1936; I'm cold now. The thing to do is to make myself hot again. How do you go about that ? Not having a book coming out in the near future, the only thing you can do (lacking credits) is write original stories. If they click, you click along with them.

SIT DOWN AND FIGHT has gotten nowhere, and the field has been pretty well covered. I can't coast on that any longer, so I'm writing another, and to my way of looking at it, it has a much better chance of going places. The idea is absolutely original. In all my reading and movie-going, I've never seen anything that came even close to it—and that's something that should sell without more. I'm not contenting myself with the originality of the idea alone, though; I'm doing a full dialogue treatment of it in the hope of being able to peddle myself along with the story. It's moving along fast and should be on the market within days. I'm going to use quite different merchandising tactics this time. I won't say what they are, but in all cases I'll know on the spot whether I've made a sale or not. Speaking very frankly, if I pick my spot correctly, I should sell it first crack. As soon as I've registered the story, I'll send you a copy.

So rest easy, will you ? Worry is bad for your health and peace of mind. I've got the talent and that talent will ultimately crash me through.

Let me hear from you soon. My love to you and the kid.

Affectionately,

30. To Philip D. Shapiro

September 11, 1939

Dear Governor:

Maggie and I were very glad to hear from you, the more so because your letter had news of the Arbitblatas flight from France; it's good to know they're safe and well. How they got away, though, is a little puzzling from your account. You say that Nick stole away in the dead of night and, getting to Southampton, found Sylvia and the child on board. How was that? Didn't he know where they were? Did they leave before him? Or did they take a powder, as they say in the G-men pictures? Let's have some details.

There's no doubt that the picture industry is going to be affected by the war, but it's hard to say exactly how at this moment. The first instinct was to grab the war as a reason for lopping off overhead, for cutting and slashing in all directions, but within a few days it became apparent even to these brilliant minds that run the business that the United States wasn't the only country in the world, that England, France, and Germany also existed, and therefore that so far from having to shut down over here, we actually might have to expand to take up the slack created by the crippling of film production on the other side. A great stink has always been made here about foreign markets. Producers have constantly dinned it into our ears that 40% of film revenue came across the water, but you need only a different level of approach to realize that the reason for this fictitious claim was to keep movies free from propaganda. Producers were afraid to tap the American market for democratic ideas; they didn't want to gamble their foreign market for "entertainment" against the increasing American demand for "truth". Slowly they've come around to the notion that any censorship we may submit to must come from ourselves, and one at a time films have been sent down the ways as trial balloons. Jobs like "Blockade", "Confessions of a Nazi Spy", "The Road Back", and two or three others have paved the way for better pictures as a whole, and foreign markets have little by little been abandoned, sometimes deliberately, sometimes by the action of foreign governments. So all the noise about those markets dwindles to this: they made up perhaps 10% of our revenue.

It's true that contracts which call for a cancelation in the event that war interferes with distribution have been suspended right and left. Maggie's, I'm glad to say, has no such clause, and therefore it'll stick at least till next March 15th, when her option comes up.

My original is finished, but I'm not handing it to my agent till I see how he fares with what he has. I've authorized him to dicker for "The Old Man's Place", "Seventy Times Seven", and the old original, and if he can't sell those or place me on the strength of them, I'll save the new job for a fresh agent. I'm giving my present one till the end of this week to come through.

That's about all for this time. Please find time to write again soon. Maggie joins me in sending love to you and Eleanor.

Affectionately,

31. To Ruth Shapiro

(The book Sanford refers to in this letter is The People From Heaven, *and he's prescient: it was published by Harcourt Brace, not Knopf.)*

April 13th, 1940

Dear Ruth :

Your long letter came this morning; I'm answering it from the studio, for I drove Maggie here and stayed to take her home after a conference. I gather you haven't received the letter I sent the day Dad left for New York, or else you'd have had something to say about it.

As for your criticisms of "Johnny Doe", I didn't get one of my famous "mads" at all. You're entitled to your opinions, and although I'm supposed to be entitled in return to knock you down for them, I won't be such a bully.

In order to write a good, or at least different, detective-story, it is not necessary to be acquainted with the latest Hammett or Van Dine. The reverse, in fact. The more you know of other methods in such a special field, the greater the temptation, unconscious or otherwise, to recreate them. I'm no detective-story writer, but happening across what seemed to me to be a mystery-idea, I decided to handle it in the manner that it suggested—the result being what you've read. It may not be so successful as those you've read by professionals in the field, but certainly it has some original angles to it, and after all that's what I was after; to have reproduced the work of others would have gotten me nowhere. I've gotten nowhere as it is, but hardly for the reasons you name.

If Johnny Doe had actually committed the crime, as you suggest, the story could not have been sold. I'd played with that notion, but always, when I reflected that the work was commercial, I ruled it out. Surely you'll not maintain that the studios rejected the story because the hero proves his innocence.

As for the "static" quality you find, you defeat your own criticism when you allow that action may be mental as well as physical. There's almost no "movement", as such, in the original, but you can't let yourself be fooled by the fact that you can't detect a lot of arm-waving and hurly-burly. What goes on in the minds of the characters seems fairly exciting, much more so than any spectacular action could have been. The situation alone is dramatic, and if the dialogue supports that drama, keeps it boiling, than the alleged lack of action is no defeat.

You don't care much for the dialogue, and I think you're very wrong. It's staccato, it burns along like a fast fuse, it hits the heart of the idea almost always, and it serves to characterize. Much more than that you can't look for in an original for the screen under the present set-up. It's tough, certainly, and it touches the Hays line in several places, but no studio would think of rejecting a work in toto simply because it offends here and there. The basic idea must be censorable for such a ruling out, and you can't say that of "Johnny Doe" even though the Mayor of New York gets the bump-off. And that didn't stop them either. They know as well as us that the locale can be changed just by a snap of the fingers, and the story will lose precisely nothing by it.

The best scenes in the piece you seem to be disgusted with—I mean those in the last third involving Yale. And here too I believe you're wrong, because here, if anywhere, are most of the originalities of the story. I know of no such handling of a denouement in all the many mystery stories I've read or seen, and if you think the excitement isn't intense up to Yale's apartment (even though they're talking football and other off-shooting subjects), you simply can't translate the words of the story into the pictures they'd make on the screen. That's the greatest defect among producers in Hollywood, so I can't blame you for suffering from it : the man here who can visualize words-as-movement is the man who makes the pictures that get talked about. A screen-play isn't literature; it's the foundation for another art-form, and all criticism of it must be in that other field. A screen-play is sort of a marionette in repose; it comes to life, and therefore is either good or bad, only when the strings are pulled, by which I mean only when the breath of life is breathed into it by living actors in a plausible setting photographed in motion and sound.

But all this is neither here nor there. The story hasn't sold (it got an amazing send-off here at Metro, but died in conference), and I'd be hard put to it to say why. Some say it's too psychological, others that it isn't psychological enough.

The last I heard from Dad (yesterday a.m.) he was somewhere in eastern Arizona, but he'd written the note on Wednesday, so he must be well east of there by now. He said when he left that he might put in a day at Greeley, Colo., to see Maggie's sister, but I understand Eleanor's nose (hers, not Dad's) has been bleeding from the altitude, so they may have pushed right on to get down the long central slope as quickly as possible.

I don't recall all your questions, but I know you asked about the book. All I can say is that I'm at it hours every day, and though it comes slowly, what comes is good—to my mind, naturally. It'd be impossible to say whether Knopf will put it out when finished; I've a contract with him for three more after 70x7, but he may reject what he doesn't want to take a gamble with. My feelings won't be hurt if that's what happens with Number 4. Don't worry; it'll appear, even if I have to publish it myself.

You'll be delighted to hear that Nonie Greenstein is going to have a baby, probably some time in the fall. I heard from Jesse the day before yesterday, and he broke down and made the admission.

Maggie'll be back any minute now, so I'd better wind this up.

I'd like to repeat my request that you extend yourself to be kind to Dad. Try that way for once, and I'm sure you'll never regret it. I'm convinced that your intentions have all along been good, but you have a way of letting small incidents blind you to the main issue; Dad's health and happiness. So overlook fancied slights, refrain from competition for Dad's "Hand", and smile once in a while. It's good medicine.

Oh, yes—you wanted to know about Gladys. I didn't answer her letter because I resented her interference in matters that didn't concern her. If she could pull that fur-coat stunt on you, it seemed reasonably clear that your welfare (which was what she seemed to be writing about) could not have been very dear to her. And further, at the time I heard from her, I knew it was a fact, from your own letter written to Dad at the middle of February, that *she had not yet had you to her house!*

Maggie just blew in, hungry and hot. Don't worry about her credit on "Escape". She'll get it, all right.

As Ever,

32. To Ruth Shapiro

(Sanford refers here to Pandro Berman, an MGM producer. The film Soapy Smith *was written by John and Maggie both and released as* Honky-Tonk, *giving Sanford his only screenwriter's film credit)*

11.30.40

Dear Ruth:

I started a letter to you a moment ago in longhand, and it got so bad after a paragraph or two that I chucked it away. On the level, my penmanship gets worse by the year; I can't read it myself now after a lapse of a day or so; it's like a strange language.

Pete was here last night with Mildy for dinner (they're divorced, you know), and both of them asked for you.

Berman took me to the football game today (USC vs UCLA), so I don't have to say I'm still at MGM. And Maggie's out to the movies with his assistant (Jane Loring), so you know she's still in good. After the game, Berman drove me to his home in Beverly, and we talked script most of the way. It seems there's a great chance to land Gable for SOAPY SMITH, and he wants to be sure to have something ready for him when he comes back from vacation on February 1. We've got plenty of time and ought to get in under the wire.

Naturally you're right about a person knowing all there is to know about the medium he's working in. I was putting in a bit of a side when I said I hated pictures. I don't, really; I only hate what's being done with them. A good picture has often found Maggie and me driving twenty miles for the privilege of being in the audience. They're rare, good films, but when there are GRAND ILLUSIONS, the Baker's Wife, Port of Shadows, and things like that around, we're there, you may bet. But Bittersweet? Pure and simple shite on a stick.

There's something I'd like to discuss with you, Ruth. It's Dad's proposed trip to California. As far as I know, there's nothing definite about it yet. But it's in the wind, and I'm not sure you sympathize with it. It's true you'll be left alone back there, but I know when you consider the good the climate and change will do for Dad, you'll see eye to eye with me on the advisability of his coming, even join with me in urging him to come. That would be the act of a daughter who had her father's interests at heart—of a piece with Harriet's wanting Aunt Sarah and Uncle Harris to spend all this time out here—an act you'd not have cause to regret. I'm certain. It seems to feel you've changed for the better during the past year. I may be wrong, but I don't think so. I note something of a different tone in your letters, and it can't all be my imagination. I think you've in some way learned that other people have rights, and if that's so you've certainly swallowed a whole bookful of knowledge;

it's a jumpoff to being real bright. So why not prove to me that I haven't guessed wrong? Why not insist, as I have, that Dad pick up sticks and shake the New York winter?

Pete and I were talking about Brounoff last night, wondering how he's making out, where he's living, etc. If you have any information, pass it along.

Ziegfeld Girl has every chance of being a smash. They've been shooting 25 days, and it ought to be done (as to shooting, that is) in another 20. We still see the rushes, and they still look entertainmentish. Garland is very winning, and for the first time Turner acts. And acts well, which is a surprise to me. Nothing of LaMarr has been shot yet, but she never could act and always was counted on only for decoration. Stewart really is something, and the find of the piece is a lad named Dan Dailey, who'll be a star in a year, or I know nothing at all. Horton's in there pitching with that gnome-like puss and those famous double- and triple-takes. Kelly, Winninger, Al Shean, Jackie Cooper, Philip Dorn, Tony Martin, all of them are reading lines like little gentlemen. Disappointment of the thing so far is Eve Arden (remember the slangy bit she had in Stage Door?), who is telling Ray June how to light for his camera and Maggie how to phrase a quip. They hate her on the set, and they're giving her the works. You know, they have ways of lighting and shooting that'll simply ruin anybody, and they're using them all on the tart. She comes out in rushes like an eighty-year-old witch, baggy under the eyes, gray, flat, and wrinkled. Wow. It's all right, though. She'll wind up hearing her lines come over scene, or with her back to the camera. They take a close-up of each player in a scene, with all the dialogue coming over-shot, so when anyone's too bad to look at, you see her back and hear her talking to—somebody else. I forgot Ian Hunter. He's *[here the letter is missing a section]*

Minnie is fat and putrid. She lies here at my feet, listening to every approaching motor-car. She's never happy when Mag's away—which is just the opposite of how I feel. I'm never happy when she's around.

Reddy Boy has his winter coat and a roached mane. He's a little puppy, and a pest. He dumped Maggie in the park a month ago. Got scared of a matchstick, I guess, or made believe.

The Smiths have a puppy to take Minnie's place—as if that were possible. A Dalmatian (coach-dog). One enormous black spot around his left eye. Cuter than all get-out.

We have three cats at the barn: an alley-cat, a real Persian, and a half-alley half-Persian, the last with five kittens. Also a bantam rooster and hen. Plenty animals.

Write.

Affectionately,

33. To Ruth Shapiro

(This letter's opening paragraph refers to the news about the death of Nathanael West and his wife in an auto accident at a crossroads outside of El Centro, CA, in December, 1940.)

January 2nd, 1941

Dear Ruth:

It's been hard to think of anything this week outside of Pep and the terrible accident that cost him and his wife their lives. For some reason or other, maybe because I so much regret not having been on better terms with him, I made no point of asking anyone for details. I gather from one person here and another there that Pep was on his way home from a weekend of bird-shooting in northern Mexico when the crash occurred, two or three miles east of El Centro. At all times he was a poor and absent-minded driver, so bad that I'm told people refused to let him have the wheel while they were in the car with him; on this occasion, I understand he failed to come to a halt at a Stop Sign, and with a car coming toward him at right angles, the result was what we know. Pep's wife died as she was being put into an ambulance, and Pep himself lasted only until they got him to the hospital. There were no services in California. Pep's body was shipped east, and along with it the ashes of his wife. I suppose that the burial will be alongside Pep's Dad. The whole thing is more regrettable than I can say.

It gives me a pang to think back on what I owe him, not because the debt is a burden, but because I buried it for so long under a mountain of stupid and childish animosities that probably had little to bear them out. To mention one thing only: if it weren't for Pep, I'd never have written a line.

In any event, we'd have been quiet on Christmas and New Year's. As it was, we didn't have the heart for much of anything. On Christmas Eve, we went out to Marion Parsonnet's house for a couple of hours to watch his family open their gifts, and on New Year's Eve we stayed home, just the two of us and Minnie. I hope your holidays were pleasanter, and I'd like to hear about them. Before I forget, let me thank you for our gifts. The nightgown for Maggie was in good taste, but it won't be worn till the frost goes out. As for the book of reproductions, I think it's very beautiful, and I propose to keep it. I always loved the Impressionists, although after a few years some of them have lost their power to hold me (Manet is one). One thing surprised me: there wasn't a single plate of Seurat's, and if he wasn't an Impressionist, there never was one. There were several Gauguin's in the book, but he's another that lost his grip.

Soapy Smith is in its last few pages. We've submitted 145 pages so far, and all of them have met with no little approval. The remaining batch (about 80 pages) we'll do over the weekend. According to Berman, there seems to be a strong chance of getting Gable—so much of a chance that he's casting the female lead now. He talks of Lana Turner. He talks also of directors. Leroy, Conway, Leonard, Fleming, etc. The point is that he rarely talks without turning up with something. Maybe it'll [result in] a credit. In any case, I could use it.

Thanks too for our anniversary greeting. We spent the evening at home.

The fire's dying down, and the living-room's getting cold. That's the signal for more firewood or a quick sneak to bed. I think I'll make it the latter this time—the wood's out in the garage.

Maggie joins me in sending you love and best wishes for the New Year.

Affectionately,

34. To Jesse and Naomi Greenstein

January 2nd, 1941

Dear Jesse and Nonie:

By this time, you'll have heard of the death of Pep West and his wife—a tragedy that simply knocked the props out from under me when I heard about it. I hadn't been on good terms with him for a couple of years, but ever since he died I've been trying to think of the basis for the quarrel without success. I deeply regret anything I may have said about him, for when all's said he was responsible for my starting to write, and that's something no lapse of time can obscure. In addition to that, which would be enough to cause me regrets, he was good to me and generous, and almost nothing that's connected with my past is vacant of him. To cap it all, he was a respectable writer who, according to many reports, was just beginning to grow. I'm really sorrier about the whole thing than I know how to say.

Everything else at the moment seems rather piddling, but I'd like you to know that I bought a copy of The Scientific American and read Russell's piece about Jesse. As Nonie says, it does him more than justice. I'm being wholly honest when I say that Jesse is a great man—and now, not potentially. Both Maggie and I glowed at Russell's use of the word "Masterly" in connection with him; nothing less than that would have been suitable. I'll write some more at another time. Till then, for God's sake drive carefully.

As ever, affectionately,

35. To Ruth Shapiro

June 8, 1941

Dear Ruth:

Rest easy: both your letters arrived safely. It's true that one of them was left unstuck, but if any civil employee wasted Government time reading it, he returned to his job no wiser, however sad.

Maggie and I were rueful when we read of the final dismissal of this preacher in man's clothes—not because we don't sympathize with your conduct, but because the conclusion of anything at all that started out so high and hopefully must have been a disappointment. There are other pebbles on the beach, and if it isn't Virginia Beach, it might be Deal. Don't let it throw you (yourself) back where it found you. You've made, to our minds, some great strides forward as far as your personal life, your life from the inside toward the outside, is concerned, and more than anything else we'd hate to see you backslide because something on the outside turned out to be rotten. That shouldn't affect your outlook; you were above reproach.

Honky Tonk has been shooting for a week now, and no one but Maggie is on the script, so it looks as if we were in for a joint credit all to ourselves. The cast is great: Clark Gable, Lana Turner, Frank Morgan, Marjorie Main, Albert Dekker, Chill Wills, and Claire Trevor. Maggie has seen the week's rushes, and she grudgingly admits (we both detest this Jack Conway) that the stuff is good.

The Warner offer came to me through Robert Rosson, one of

their top writers (The Sea Wolf, They Won't Forget, Marked Woman, etc.) He tells me he was talking to the studio manager, I think it was Hal Wallis, and he was told that Warners is going through one of its periodic clean-outs—younger blood, fresh talent, and that kind of thing—and Wallis brought my name up as likely timber, with an authorization to Rosson to sound me out at a raise over anything I was getting elsewhere. Rosson did, but I told him I was out till the Fall on account of the novel. By that time, not only will the book be practically finished, but also Honky Tonk will have hit the screen, and I'll gamble my chances on that.

You'll be very delighted to hear that according to a note in Retail Booksellers' Weekly, Knopf is reissuing 70x7 at the original price. That can only mean there's been a steady demand for it over the past several months, something I was entirely unaware of, for the book was remaindered more than a year and a half ago and completely sold out. This may have gotten the book to a wider audience, and enough talk generated to create a fresh demand. I have a hunch Knopf originally printed 7500 sheets and bound 5000, half of which sold to the trade on publication, and half on remainder. The reissue probably consists of a new binding on the remaining 2500 sheets. In any case, it can be classed as a second edition, so your brother is IN! I told my friend, the bookseller, that if he could get hold of a second edition for me, I'd pay him more for it than for the first. Ha! Ha!

The title of the new book is satirical: "The People From Heaven". It's an extract from a letter written by Columbus to a certain Luis de Santangel, shortly after the discovery of the Indies. In describing to Santangel how the Indians received them, he wrote: "And the others went running from house to house to house and to the neighboring villages, with loud cries of 'Come! Come to see the people from Heaven!'" I'm deep deep into the book now, and another two-three months should see an exceedingly careful first draft ready for shipment (or delivery in person, perhaps) to Knopf.

Dad is well. I haven't seen him for over a week, due to our having had to move. We haven't a housekeeper yet, and I have to make beds and cook breakfasts myself, so I'm tied down like a nagging wife. Maggie just comes home, cocks her feet on the table, and puffs contentedly on her pipe while I work my fingers to the bone. I tell you, women simply don't appreciate what us men go through here at home!

We both (we three, because there's Minnie) send love.

36. To Ruth Shapiro

June 29, 1941

Dear Ruth:

I haven't received the book on witch-craft yet, but I know you ordered it from what you wrote to Dad, so I suppose it'll be along pretty soon. You're probably wondering how I come to need books of the sort I've asked you to send, and if it were possible to give you a precis of the novel I'd do so, but it happens to be another of those jobs that's easy to write but hard to explain, so I guess you'll have to wait a while before the mystery is unraveled. All the stuff, though, ties in with a plan I loosely outlined to you when I was in New York—a plan to incorporate within the framework of a novel the important events and trends of all American history. To illustrate: the blank verse sections so far written (and almost all printed in The Clipper) include The Aztec, Eric the Red, Columbus, Capt. John Smith, The Pilgrims, The first cargo of negroes landed in America, The Jesuits, and (skipping a long period because the section wasn't written in order) Whitman and Melville. Of the John Smith piece, Genevieve Taggard writes that it's the only good poem on the Indian ever written in America. At the moment, I'm up to 1692—the witch-craft trials in Salem.

It's equally hard in a short space, to say what I think the Soviet army will do against the Nazis. I can, however, make a blanket statement. The road to Moscow will be what the road to Madrid should have been—the tomb of fascism. From all I've been able to read on the subject, the Soviet army is at least the equal of the German in every department, and the infinitely superior in regard to mechanization, airplanes, and tanks. If their communications and transport lag behind, it's as much to their advantage as otherwise because of the nature of the terrain they have to defend—and they will not fight a defensive war if it's possible to effect a breakthrough, at which time the German roads will be as much help to them as they are to the Nazis now. Tactics perfected by the Russians have been aped by the Nazis, and there's every reason to believe there are more tricks where those came from. Observers of both incidents on the far eastern front with Japan report that nothing like the Soviet artillery has been seen in modern times. They laid down a few range shots at Changkufeng Hill and then turned loose a couple of thousand guns to sweep the hill of everything that lived or moved in the most stunning heavy caliber blast ever opened up on man. This is attested not only by the immediate Japanese capitulation, but by reports in U. S. Army journals. As for the air force, I don't suppose any one but Stalin actually knows how many planes there are. That the number must be staggering even to Hitler is proved by his decision, in August 1939, to take on all the rest of Europe rather than face Russia alone—and we know for a fact that England had two or three thousand planes then, France perhaps five thousand, Czechoslovakia over a thousand, Poland six or eight hundred, and Belgium, Holland, Denmark, Norway, etc. at least two thousand among them. So that we may deduce, even without actual figures, that Russia even then outstripped that total. Since that time, two years now, it's fair to suppose they've kept adding to what they had. Their tank-park, according to Werner (and the two leading German military strategists), so far outstrips the German that the latter can never overhaul them. In addition to all this, there is the matter of morale (nine years under the iron heel), the diversion of German forces necessary to police captured countries, etc.

Germany will not beat Russia single-handed, and it will be touch-and-go whether they will do so even with the aid of Japan, Britain, and the United States. It would seem that the masses of the people finally have something to say, as witness Churchill's unwilling declaration of sympathy with Russia as a victim of aggression. Because of his previous record, it is not to be supposed that he loves Stalin like a brother, yet he was forced to declare against Hitler in this issue. It will be up to the people to continue to exert pressure against the world's great enemy, Fascism, no matter where it's found. Not against the German people, but those elements among them that have driven them in the direction they have taken.

You seem to be worried about the outcome either way. You feel, and truly, that if Germany wins, you can kiss freedom goodbye. You feel that if Russia wins, she will continue her campaign against capitalism. If you value capitalism more than freedom in America (for we'll have fascism here if Hitler wins, make no mistake), then you'll do that most incredible of flipflops—you'll support Hitler. Only thus can Russia come even close to defeat. Mankind must make a perilous choice, but either way the old life is over. Nothing is ever quite the same after a war. Both sides lose, both sides change. 1918 was different from a 1914 gone forever, for it found the Soviet Union in existence, 194- will find something else gone that we once knew, but we must not regard that with regret, otherwise we'll be standing in the way of progress which mankind somehow or other manages to make no matter what the cost.

Uncle Jack's back and ready to garage it for a while.

I was on the Honky Tonk set again yesterday and met Claire Trevor after all these years. It's still remarkable to me how the resemblance to Olga continues. She seems to be a good sort and very much in love with her part. I also met Marjorie Main (introduced myself) and gave her your salutations as well as mine. Told her we've always had a soft spot for her. Gable and I had a talk too (it's Johnny and Clark now), sat in his dressing-room, solved a few character points together regarding Candy Johnson. The picture will finish shooting in two weeks.

I no longer hear from Brounoff. He's probably wrapped himself in some bundle and shipped himself off to Britain. I figure I must have made him sore with something I said in the last exchange, but if he can sulk with me, I guess there isn't much good left in him. Pete read his last two letters and was so thoroughly disgusted that he decided to drop the idea of corresponding again.

Mrs Smith has a new dachshund puppy that I got from a friend. It's king-pin, after Minnie, of course.

Write. Maggie and I send love.

Affectionately,

37. To Marguerite Roberts

(Sanford is writing from Washington, DC, after having been hired to work as a screenwriter for director Frank Capra in the making of American propaganda films for the American Officers Training School during WW II.)

Wednesday night

February 25th, 1942

Sweetheart:

You must be some such thing: this is the second time I've written you today.

We had lunch with Capra at the Carlton, discussed plans for work, and made bids for assignments. Mine, as I'd hoped, is Russia, and I'm to start reducing it to script tomorrow after a showing of the Milestone film at the Department of Interior projection room.

We knew all about the Wilkerson blast—had it from Capra.

At Harvey's last night we saw J. Edgar (G-man) Hoover.

At the Occidental tonight we ate at the next table to Martin B. Dies. P.U.!

Between trains in Chicago, I was standing at the news-butcher's when a bloke in a mink-lined coat, striped pants, and a black Homburg rushed up and said, "Have you got any copies of 'Mission to Moscow'?" The butcher said, "Sorry, but we're just out." The bloke turned to wink at his sabled lady—and he was Joe Davies! Just like an author: checking up on his royalties.

So far I've been introduced to four Colonels, one Lt. Colonel, five Majors, a Captain (Bartlett), and a Navel Commander. I've not yet met Franklin D.

Capra promised to introduce me to Archie MacLeish.

I was a dope for not bringing my own typewriter. I'm always a dope when I don't listen to my wife.

Jerry changed accommodations from Chicago to Washington, and he left the Sheraton for the Carleton after getting here.

S/K/Lauren has been friendly ever since I mentioned you were my wife. Respectful, even.

My work will be hard—I'm not fooling myself about that. How you could help me! But I'm on my lonely own, and I'm either a screen-writer or not on the basis of what I can show unassisted. We'll see, baby.

Kiss my doggie Juno for me.

Don't worry about blondes flourishing brief-cases. I'm crazy about you, and I'm afraid I always will be. Please write me early and often. I love your letters, and your drawings kill me.

Sincerely, even respectfully,

Addition after seeing the Milestone film and after another conference with Capra, also the army officers who drew up the lectures.

My problem, it seems, will be to represent Russia as a present ally without dwelling on how at one time she was held up to the American public as an enemy—a man-sized job, if I ever heard of one. There naturally, with such a limitation, will be very little I can dwell on except the resistance that Russia has put up, with emphasis on what a united nation can do. In other words, the attempt will be to talk militarily without touching on the political—an almost impossible job. However, I'll do what I can, and it'll be the best I can.

Capra is an odd guy. They tell me he's a Christian Scientist, and from his manner, I can well believe it. He's a gentle sort, soft-spoken almost all the time, and ineffectually emphatic. He'll say something like: THIS MUST BE DONE, this must be done, the soft repetition only revealing an uncertainty of why he was so emphatic in the first place. He's utterly inarticulate, even the simplest expression of the simplest idea torturing him to the limit during the period he frames it in fumbling Hollywood and-so-and-sos. Yet what a director he is! I CAN'T UNDERSTAND IT. It may only be due to his feeling himself in deep water here.

Well, I'm in deep water too, and if ever I swam I'd better swim now.

I got your letter last evening, but there's been nothing from you since the supposed bombing of L.A. the other evening. Please write often in times like these, will you, honey? You haven't said what your chances of making the trip are. I do hope you'll be able to; I hate to think of seeing all this without you. Try your best to manage things. Juno could be left in the living room with a can of Pampas and a box of biscuits. She'd understand.

Very much love to the best wife in creation. You're cute 'n sweet 'n pretty 'smart.

38. To Marguerite Roberts

March 9th, 1942

Dearest Pouch:

We had our conference yesterday—of all places, at the broadcasting station in the buildings of the Department of the Interior. The session lasted from ten in the morning till six in the evening, the program being a series of readings by each writer in the order that his lecture turned up in the course, and after each reading a general discussion and criticism. I wish I could report that the Sanford family enjoyed a complete triumph, but that would be the equivalent of saying that all of a sudden Hollywood writers changed their spots. I can say, from my own point of view (completely unbiased, of course) that my paper was far and away and many miles far and away superior to the best that my slender opposition could muster. It read like a burning flash, as pieces of my poetry sometimes do, and whether I got my measure of approval at the end or not, I had the others sitting in absolute and unmoving silence from start to finish, and at the end only Phil Epstein had decency enough to say the paper, in addition to being filmed, ought to be published. The others, Jerry included, would only express bare satisfaction. Capra, however, seemed to like it immensely, his aide saying that he was so bowled over by the style and excitement of the piece that he'd have to read it for himself before giving an opinion. The result of the general criticism shows, however, how slight the disapproval could have been, for I've got the green light to coast in to finish with practically nothing to be changed of what's gone before, twenty-two minutes, reading-time.

As for the others, Jerry was first off the mark, and his showing was astoundingly dull. His paper dealt with the general origins of militarism in the 1932-42 world, and where it should have been breathless it was plodding, and where it should have been eloquent it was pedestrian. One hour of criticism followed it, and it will practically be rewritten. Sam Laurin came next, and his paper, dealing with the Battle of England, was simply pathetic—I mean nothing less. Astonishingly, though, he got the biggest hand. He made capital of "blood, sweat, and tears", and "to so few for so much by so many"—you know, that Churchill drivel. It was [a] bald, halting, uneloquent, high-school composition.

The Epsteins had the Balkan campaign and the Mediterranean theatre, and their paper, like Jerry's, will have to be redone. It was a sad parroting of the written lecture, and if the letter was dull, theirs was even duller. I couldn't believe my ears when it was read. They stuck to the printed word, and they're stuck. I'd warned them they would be, but they refused to use any initiative. I know they can do better. By the way, they happen to be a couple of likable guys, much more so and much more human than my good frand [sic].

I followed the Epsteins, and then came Parramore, who isn't very far along with the thing; what he had to say was barely ordinary. He is not a writer and is way over his head on this assignment. It's proof all over again that a writer today must be more than a man with a pencil; he must be in touch with the world on the most realistic footing.

Spiegelgass was last and among the worst, for all his March of Time technique and his bombast. It was poorly imitative of the most blown-up American ranting. It was self-conscious, and while it had meat, it had no real and believing heart. It was mouthing from start to finish, and full of material for the trainees to fatten on and say "Oh, yeah"—like America's the land of opportunity, here you say what you like, vote for whom you will, give orders to your electee, etc. Oh, Yeah!

Over all, I'd say Capra has been roundly stuck with his selection of personnel. Jerry knows what should be said, but can't say it; I know what should be said and can say it. For the rest, they weren't worth their train-fare. I think Capra knows it too.

Please don't show this to anybody. Only you and I know that

we believe I'm a better writer than this collection of punks, and only you and I can talk about it without blushing for our vanity. Steinbeck, by the way, will sell half a million of The Moon Is Down, which, had it been written by anyone else, would get lost under Kathleen Norris. I think it's a simply terrible piece of trash.

I may be all sold on myself, but that doesn't now and never has blinded me to the fact that my wife, in her field, is as able as I am in mine, and that she is a simply adorable little sweet-smelling squirt, whom I love most abominably—together with dog.

How about coming east? How about coming east? How about it? Please come.

Yours—and proudly

39. To Marguerite Roberts

March 12, 1942

Pretty Pouch:

I had a note from Guy yesterday. It was what he called "a bread and butter, or rather a lamb and pie" letter. But what I wanted to quote from it was this: "I was amazed at the grasp Maggie had on world affairs; her strength must be added to ours." I know you'll be pleased, because there's nobody whose opinion you hold higher.

I hear indirectly that the evening after the big conference, Frank Capra was highly elated; he seemed to feel that he'd gotten a valuable series out of the gang. So it may be that my criticism was too harsh, that I was thinking, as always, in terms of the best. All the same, Len Spiegelgass said he was very much worried by the pomposity of his piece.

Rhea got in yesterday, and I saw her in the evening at a showing of some Canadian documentaries. She said Jerry had told her what a brilliant piece I'd done, and she congratulated me. So maybe punks are not always and in all departments punk. But what she said that really concerned me was that you were being worked very hard by the studio and were in rather low spirits.

First, I want to answer your question about whether you did the right thing re Ruggles. You certainly did. It's about time that you realized that you can't always protect incompetence, and when incompetence is hand-in-glove with ingratitude, as in Ruggles' case, the right thing to do is think of higher obligations and sink him without a trace if the necessity arises. To Hell with the bastard!

And to Hell with that Messenger bitch! If she knows anything about writing, Metro must be paying her to pretend she doesn't, for none of her opinions was worth taking the trouble to steal. If I'm not in error, she was awfully high on some of those foolish originals that Metro got sucked in by a year ago.

And now to cases. I'm going to insist that you come east and join me. You've taken it on the chin with this assignment, and the result is that Pan carefully uses you as a fall guy to save some sonofabitch's face. You've had enough, and you're simply not going to get involved in another assignment without a complete change of scenery. I say I insist, and I won't take any argument on the subject. There's no reason in the world why you can't be reading that god-awful tome on the train, in a hotel room, or anywhere else. You don't have to be at that desk, waiting for the next ton of brick to come shooting down on you. Phrig those lice. You take yourself by the hand either Sunday or Monday, and set sail. It's beautiful back here, buds are busting wide open, the air is like a swig of orange juice in the morning, and there are shows to be seen, and kisses to be exchanged. Come on, baby. Suppose it does cost us a few hundred pieces of green paper. What the hell. It's for you, and nothing in the world is too good for what can't possibly be less than the most wifely wife that ever wuz.

I love you, honey.

40. To Marguerite Roberts

(Because the American government would not allow Sanford to become a commissioned officer in any branch of the service, he was released from his screenwriting duties with Capra. He left Washington, D.C. and traveled to New York to see about the publication of The People From Heaven, *which, as this letter makes clear, was refused by Knopf, which had previously published* Seventy Times Seven.*)*

3. 28. 42

Baby:

It was good of you to call me last night to assure me you haven't lost confidence in your stinking husband on account of the Knopf turndown. Believe me when I say that I haven't lost confidence either. Publishers are a dime a dozen, and what Knopf can't see others can and will—and soon. Random House has the book now, but Mel has warned me not to hope for anything there because the book simply isn't their leather. He's arranging a pleasant reception for me at Viking, and after that, if necessary, at Scribners, Harcourt, and so on. We'll hit the big houses first and go right on down the line to setting it up ourselves on an old hand-press and selling it on street-corners or giving it away with apples. It'll see daylight—don't worry.

As I told you yesterday, I was to have lunch with Sid today and learn the intimate details of Frank's reaction. I just came home after a three-hour session, and I want to say that it would simply be impossible to tell you, in cold type, all the praise that was heaped on me not only by Frank, but also by Sid and his wife. When I see you in person, I'll let you wheedle it out of me, but honestly it's too much to expect that I relate the success point by point. Imagine the most extravagant praise and the wildest predictions of reward—and you'll get some faint idea of how I'm supposed to have gone over. The most important thing, of course, is that it seems to be an open-and-shut thing that Frank'll freeze onto me for the duration—at present under the arrangement you know about, later on under commission. I think it was smart of me to have inserted my nose into the roller of this machine and squeezed out pretty words: they always go so much further than the "and so and so" school of not-writing.

I'm glad you approve of my love-letters, and I'm glad you're snuffling like a dog (purring of course being ruled out). I'm glad, because the letters were what I intended them to be—little conversations between the best and most beautiful wife in the world and the worst and most foul-smelling husband. We'll get that farm yet, baby. It'll be after the war's won, but after much tweaking of ears, much pushing in of noses, many puppies and colts, we'll go gorgeously to seed—you cleaning Reddy's teeth and I tying trout-flies. A beautiful prospect—going to seed with you. It—er—always has been fun . . . . if you know what I—er—mean. Um um and sho nuff. I love you, foolish, and if you don't know it by now, you're worse than foolish—you're a dumb Kansas joik.

Pull Juno's left ear three times and her right twice—she's lop-sided, like you, the pretty little bitch.

Yonkel lovs egg-hed. Guess who?

41. To Frank Capra

(Hollywood director Frank Capra was tapped by the United States Government to head a division of the Signal Corps to make wartime propaganda films that would explain why our allies were working with us during the Second World War. Sanford was asked to write a screenplay for a film on Russia. Because of his alleged—and actual—political affiliations—he was dismissed from the project and was unable to serves his country in any other capacity during the war. Parts of this letter and the next letter to Capra in this collection (#50) appeared in Joseph McBride's biography of Capra, Frank Capra: The

Catastrophe of Success, *Simon & Schuster, 1992.)*

May 2nd, 1942

Dear Frank:

During the time I spent in Washington, I felt that you were trying to take my measure as a human being along with my size as a talent, and whether you were aware of it or not, the fact is that I was doing the same from where I sat in respect to you. I believe, therefore, that we know each other well enough for straight talk, as man to man, and that any pretense on my part as to ignorance of what has been happening would be an insult to you and a disgrace to me. In short, I know all about your having put me on the shelf because you suspect that I am a communist.

If this were a time for gags, I might suspect that I'd been made the butt of one of the very best: The United States Government asked me to devote six weeks of my life writing a pair of scripts establishing Russia as an indispensable ally, as a result of which effort I am said to have sold myself for thirty pieces of Moscow gold!

I think one would have to hunt for a week of Sundays for a prettier piece of clowning, but I feel no impulse to laugh, nor has anyone else who knows the situation been in danger of splitting a seam. This is not to say that the situation could not possibly cause any merriment. It could, Frank, but only in Berlin.

I shall not enter into the question of whether I am a communist, except to state plainly that I am not. What concerns me, and what should concern my country, is whether I shall be used in the war effort if I am *reputed* to be a communist.

In the language of my time, I've been given 'the finger', but what finger is it, Frank? What finger on what hand? What hand on what arm? What arm on what body? *What body is it, Frank?* . . . But don't get me wrong. I don't want to know its actual name—I detest it unknown, for it can belong to no one but a traitor, and a traitor, marked or unmarked, is always and only the one untouchable in the human race.

No, Frank, I don't want to know the owner of the finger. I want *you* to know him! I want you to know the nature and intention of the voice that you have listened to.

I don't propose to tell you how this war can be won. You know that as well as I do—better, perhaps, for you've beaten me to the punch and put on the only clothes (aside from overalls) that the day recognizes as respectable. I do propose, however, to tell you a rattling good way that this war can be *lost*.

It can be lost if we are divided against ourselves. It can be lost if Gentile is played off against Jew, black against white, rich against poor, labor against capital, hammer-and-sickle against stars-and-stripes. It would be foolish to deny that in each of those brackets there are conflicts of interest; it would be insane to suppose, however, that any such conflict was more important than the survival of the United States in the arena of history. It will not so survive if the Benedict Arnolds among us are any longer permitted to split us from within. As a nation, we are a great towering rock, but if a seed of grass can divide an actual rock, what can a seed of sedition do to a symbolic one?

I am Jewish-American—I am *not* an American Jew. As a Jewish-American, I am an American first, last, and all the time—the word 'Jewish' being merely a descriptive adjective, like 'tall', 'fat', or 'happy'. As a Jewish-American, I support the Constitution of the United States with a religious devotion the like of which I do not remember having lavished on Jehovah. As a Jewish-American, I own a love for these forty-eight states that takes second place to none. As a Jewish-American, I have had as fine a life as any man living or dead, and so far from accepting this as my due, I ask only for the privilege of paying for it with my salt sweat, with my limited talent, with all my fortune—and, if the chips are down, with that very life itself.

But here's the dazzling beauty of democracy, Frank—that if

I were a Christian, I'd be a Christian-American, and I'd still say the same things in precisely the same language; if I were a Negro, I'd be a Negro-American; if I were an Ogalalla Sioux, I'd be an Indian-American. I'd be *American*, Frank, and the adjectives would be there for the sole purpose of identification, and no matter how I was identified I'd put the broad interests of America before the special interests of my color and my faith.

To silence one anti-fascist voice today (whether it be the voice of a communist, a reputed communist, or no communist at all) is to spike one gun at a time when all guns—good, poor, and obsolete—should be shooting till their barrels get too hot to be held.

In the second script that I wrote for you—and, I might add, for the United States—I used certain words to urge the recognition of Russia as a full partner in our struggle to tractor fascism into the ground like the fertilizer it is. Those words are equally applicable to *my* being accepted as a partner in that same struggle, and I quote them:

> "I wouldn't ask that party at the other end whether he was a democrat or a republican. I wouldn't ask him whether he drank, smoked, or used bad language. I wouldn't pry into his business, and I wouldn't criticize his taste in women, clothes, or horsefeed. I wouldn't ask him what church he favored any more than I'd ask him how often he took a bath. That's all part of his private life, and nobody's private life is going to win a war. It's what he does in public that counts."

It's what a man or a country does in public that counts, Frank, and I think I may safely say that Russia has done something in public that no nation on earth has duplicated to this day. A fellow named MacArthur has called it the greatest feat in all military history, and if it's good enough for him, then by God, it ought to be good enough for the fascist sneak whose invisible finger was pointed in my direction. The communists in Russia are dying in droves not only for themselves, but for us and all the other civilized nations lined up against Germany—and if we can accept their sacrifice, if we can gain time to prepare at the cost of their blood and their broken bone, surely we must be out of our minds to spit in the faces of the communists in America, real or by reputation, actual or by getting 'the finger'.

I am not too good to be drafted, and therefore I do not try to persuade you that we can't win this war unless I fly a desk in Washington. I can peel potatoes, clean out latrines, or aim a Springfield at a fascist heart—and when the United States taps me on the shoulder, I propose to go without hollering that I'm better than the guy next-door. What I do plead for in this letter, though, is special consideration for those who *are* indispensable to your effort in Washington—whether they're Christian-Americans, like the John Does and the Richard Roes; or Negro-Americans, like the George Washington Browns and the Abraham Lincoln Thompsons; or Indian-Americans, like the Joe Longhairs and the Tom Moosehunters; or Jewish-Americans, like the Jake Levys and the Izzy Cohens. I argue for them, not for myself.

Sincerely yours,

42. To Jesse Greenstein

Oct. 8, 1942

Jess:

I don't know what in blazes you wrote in your last letter, and I'm not going to dig it up to find out. I've got some news, though, and we can worry it for a while: THE PEOPLE FROM HEAVEN is finished! I feel like I got fucked just four years ago to deliver, only now, a two-ton infant. I'm showing the bastard around to some of my friends here to get their reactions (mostly political, for there ain't a one can tell a metaphor from a razorback hawg), and within two-three days it'll be on its way to Doubleday-Doran, who wrote to ask for it some few months ago.

It's a good book, you beshitted astrologer, and if you liked SEVENTY TIMES SEVEN, it'll make you foam from your telescopic eyes. I've finally trained my ack-acks on humanity, and b'Jesus, I like what I find.

I've been filing away papers preparatory to storing them for the duration (I'll doubtless be drafted in thirty days), and in a neat white envelope yesterday I came upon Nonie's announcement of the birth of Gorgeous Georges two years ago September 30. May I be among the first to congratulate you ten days late? May the babe turn out to be butter on your bread!

Maggie just ticked off another b.o. smasheroo (Hollywood for turkey) in "Somewhere I'll Find You," a Gable-Toiner kiss-fest and titty-orgy. Hot? It should've been advertised: THE KIND OF PICTURE THAT MAKES EVEN YOUR WIFE LOOK ATTRACTIVE! SEE IT! LIVE WITH IT! COME AGAIN! BRING YOUR FAMILY! YOUR LUNCH! YOUR DOG! YOUR EXTRA TIRES! IF NOT SATISFIED, YOUR MONEY WILL BR MURDEROUSLY REFUNDED AND YOU WILL BE-FUND-DED.

Maggie thinx it stinx.

HOW's by you, Nonie, and the pisser?

Write often.

My sister got married here three-four months ago to a very nice guy. Name: Leader.

Mag and I send piles and hemorrhoids of love.

43. To Marguerite Roberts

March 7th, 1943

Dearest and best wife:

Little by little we're organizing the big push against Morley. Yesterday I had lunch with Woodburn and a close friend of his, an agent named Volkening, who, I gather, is something of an admirer: he'd have to be, for he went right to work to sell me a bill of goods on how much he'd like to represent me. I stalled that off, saying I was interested in one thing only (outside of you): getting Harcourt to take the book. Whoever pulled that off was my agent, no matter what his name was. We see more of each other come Monday and Tuesday. On Monday Cedric calls Morley for a lunch appointment, and during eats he comes around to Sanford. Woodburn picks that up later on in the day at the office. Woodburn and I see each other again this morning (Sunday), and I show him the wire I just got from Neely Swanson, which reads: TALKED WITH YOUR WIFE TODAY WHO SUGGESTED I WIRE YOU TO SEE IF YOU WOULD LET ME READ MANUSCRIPT YOUR NEW BOOK AS PICTURE POSSIBILITY. EDDIE CARTER IN OUR OFFICE SAYS HE DOESN'T THINK YOU WANT TO WORK IN STUDIOS BUT COULD I CONVINCE YOU IF I SOLD ON OF YOUR STORIES OR BROUGHT YOU ASSIGNMENT YOU LIKED? REGARDS. H.N. SWANSON. I will answer this favorably as soon as I finish writing to you. I also expect, at the early part of the week, to hear something from Angus Cameron of Little Brown. Can't say I think he'll want the book for his own outfit, as it seems too much to hope for that two houses will be scratching their beards at the same time, but I do look for hopeful suggestions, if not for another prong to the Morley pincer. Also this morning I go to Eddie Chodorov's for breakfast (it'll be my second), and although I've decided against letting him have the book at this juncture, I'm going to press for just what he thinks he can do at Random or along Bway. The Traube thing I skipped till the middle of the week. Found, too, that Joe Fields'll be home for a March 12 opening of MEN IN SHADOW, which is only Wednesday coming. And when I see Woodburn today, I'm going to ask for lunch with him tomorrow, including Mel and Terrence Holliday.

The big thing we're going to pull off, and maybe for Tuesday or Wednesday, is a lunch with Morley himself. Maybe I'll be the only one there. I find, and it's strange, that I've got a sort of personal drive that sits these guys back in their chairs, and they listen to me like mad. Maybe it's a combination of anger at the failure of the book so far, solid belief in its being good, and determination to see it taken fast—whatever it is, I think it's a better weapon than all the statecraft and chicanery we can muster, and with the rest of the gang or without them, I feel it'll go further.

I'm writing today to Ralph Ellison for an apptmt with him and Dick Wright, and on Monday I'm going to call Genevieve Taggard.

Saw Brounoff at his house on Friday evening, and b'Josh, who should turn up there but Jesse and Nonie! She'll be in town for another couple of weeks; he took the train back last night (Saturday), but I had them down to the hotel for dinner and a long talk before train-time. They love you.

Went up to Aunt Sarah's again yesterday afternoon, and just happening, just happening y'understand, to have your pictures with me, I showed'em to the Folks. Uncle Harris examined them carefully, looked up, and said, "She's beautiful!" I said, "Go on, she couldn't get into the Follies with a ticket," and b'Jucks, he laughed his sides off, just like it was a new joke. But on the level, he kept on insisting you were beautiful. Kind of embarrassing to me, since I'm so sure you're just a mug with a puss like a heifer coming fresh. He and Aunt Sarah were very particular in asking for news of the 'young' folks, and asked me to convey their very best wishes. He feels much better these last few days and is most cheerful and philosophic. Tell that to Dad. All others in the family are well except for a sniffle here and there.

My dear wife, I don't think I can make it clear in a letter exactly how wonderful a dame I think you are. Maybe the best way even to suggest this is to say that these last five or six days, since I left, are as unreal as any I ever spent or ever want to spend again. What's unreal mean? It's hard to say, except that I don't feel I'm doing anything I'm actually or emotionally a part of. This isn't my life, I don't live here, I have no friends here, I don't want to stay here, I sometimes can't understand how I ever managed to come away here: from head to foot I seem to feel I belong there—and there, of course, is you, a duck-bodied, squash-faced, jiggle-bottomed fright. Fright—that's what you are. What Daddy said about Mom: a fright. That's you, only streamlined. I miss you, baby, and most energetically. I love you.

Where are your letters?

44. To Marguerite Roberts

March 10th, 1943

Most delicious wife:

Things have been going along 'according to plan', and I am 'retreating to previously arranged lines'.

First flash from Eddie Chodorov (Jerry has the measles) is that he is very much excited about the novel. Excited or not, I am sure he will do all he can to organize a Random juggernaut. I'm having dinner with him and his wife tonight, and then we're going to see 'Men In Shadow" (first show for me), after which, or during which, I'll get his full opinion and hear his plans, if any. He has told me how thick he is with Moss Hart and Geo. Kaufman, and I've no doubt that the least he'll do is get either or both to put the script directly into Cerf's hands.

Yesterday I had an appointment with Genevieve Taggard, and a couple of hours talk with her was most encouraging. It seems that through her I'll be able to organize a Harper juggernaut. I know that she'll do everything humanly possible; it was easy to see that Sanora's letter had worked whatever wonders were necessary over and above Taggard's original admiration for that Clipper poem, and when I told her that poem was part of the novel (which I left with her), she was simply delighted. I tried my best all day yesterday to get in touch with Richard Wright, but neither his publisher nor his agent would even think of giving out his address. Taggard, however, put it right in my lap. She personally will get him to read the book, if we decide to work it that way, and in addition, she will pass it to Henrietta Buckmaster, another and influential Harper writer. Found her a fine woman, also her husband. Both send love to Sanora, whom I'd like you to call, saying so.

No word yet from Cameron of Little, Brown.

Lunch tomorrow with Woodburn and another Harcourt editor. Still waiting to hear the result of the Belfrage lunch with Morley. Saw Terrence Holliday yesterday, and he repeated all the fine things he's always said about the book, but being more a bookseller than a regular editor, he was on the helpless side regarding suggestions as to how to proceed from here.

Aunt Ray, Gladys, and Leslie leave New York for Kansas City come Monday—for good. Haven't seen them yet, but of course will later in the week.

These are the prospects, then.

a. Getting Harcourt to change its mind;
b. Random through Bway friends;
c. Harper through Taggard et al;
d. Little Brown through Maltz
e. Henry Holt (still untouched) through Woodburn.

After these, I'll ask for a couple of quick ones by Dial, Vanguard maybe, and Soskin, and S & S. Then home, and disgrace. I hope to cover all this ground in two weeks.

Baby, I wish you were here, or better, I wish I was there. I hate this town with a lovely hatred, and if I don't see it again for another ten years, it will be a great pleasure to me. I don't live here anymore, and sometimes I find it hard to believe that I ever did. Damn it, I like it better with you, you fat little corn-fed stinker. I suppose I'm in love with you. Or is it the Turrible Tike?

(just this minute got a call from Woodburn that he's coming up to the hotel this p.m. with a couple of Harcourt editors. Drinks are on me)

What was I saying? That I love you? Oh, that!

But I do, honey, so don't bite your nails off to the elbows. Only goil I've kissed so far is Horty Herman. Wait—I kissed Midgie Chodorov. Wait—I kissed Noni Greenstein. Wait—I kissed Lenny Tobias.

They none of them kiss like you, though, nor even like the Purpendicular Pup. So . . .

Give my love and a nice pinch of the cheek to Mrs. Ingele. Call my folks, too, sweetie, and tell'em I'm busy running around lugging books.

You write very seldom, my fine rat-face. And where are the drawings I was led to look for?

With all my love,

Are you taking care of yourself, really, or are all these assurances just suspicion-allayers? You go to bed early, and you eat heartily, and you lay off worrying—or when I get back I'll fan your can tan.

45. To Marguerite Roberts

March 15, 1943

Darling Wife:

This will be a sad excuse for a letter: I'm ripping it off just before keeping an appointment with Simon & Schuster—and I've got about fifteen minutes time.

A little hard luck to report. The book, as promised, was handed over to Curtice Hitchcock by Mrs. Taylor, it was read over the week-end, and it was returned with regrets yesterday (Monday). Taylor won't be back to town till the end of the week, and I'll no doubt hear from him on his return, but Reynal, Hitchcock, which promised to be a nudge to Harcourt, is now nothing. Woodburn doesn't know about the rejection yet, and I won't tell him for a while: he's still pushing Morley on the basis of RH's interest.

I also got Kyle Crichton to sound out Cerf. Cerf had read the book, but not understanding a line of it, had passed it on to Saxe Commins. Commins, however, is really going to give it a roll. Mel, who knows him well, had a long talk with him yesterday, and he was assured that Commins will enter into a re-reading without prejudice on the score of the script he saw last year. I hope for nothing from this connection, however. If something comes of it, it'll be gravy.

I've made up my mind to try only the first-line publishers myself. If I get nowhere with them (and that soon), I'll give the book over to an agent, leaving him the second-runs, and come home. I'm discouraged, I'll admit, but not hopeless. Nothing new to report at Harcourt, except that Morley has already received the McKenny letter (I've got a copy, and a good letter it was) yesterday, and he will have lunch with Cedric tomorrow. From these two events, something concrete may develop. I feel certain these are the reasons for Woodburn's postponing a getting together of me and Morley. He's trying hard to get in every possible lick before throwing us at each other. No word from Cameron, and of course no effort has yet been made to contact Henry Holt: Woodburn will do that when Harcourt is definitely out of the running. Taggard is putting me next to Ellison and Wright. I'll push that tomorrow.

Winter and Stewart dragged me along to a gathering on Sunday at Jean Muir's house to hear Will Rogers Jr., and yesterday I got invited to Jean's house for dinner tomorrow evening. She's got a nice husband and a pretty baby, but I'm also going to sound her out on Morley connection. She asked for you and sends her best, as did her mother.

Another call from this Volkening fellow, the agent. Lunch with him Thursday.

My dear wife, I can't possibly tell you in a letter how much I love and adore you, and nothing in the world would give me greater pleasure than to kiss you on your sweet mouth this very minute. You're the best woman in all the world, and if all the other women were loved half so well, Reno would turn into another Virginia City. I miss you more all the time, and I never want to go away without you again. I'm simply crazy about you, and if I ever utter a savage word to you in future, please trot this out, tap it coolly, and spit in mah mouf. I'm a terrible dope: I look at your pretty pictures all the time, and I beam like a bloody booby.

Keep on snorting to Johnny Woodburn. Who knows?

All love to you. Even Juno has to get her share from what scraps you may happen to leave.

Beautifully yours,

46. To Marguerite Roberts

March 18, 1943

Mag:

If I hadn't heard from you today, I'd have wired to ask what de hal was de matter; fortunately, I got two notes in the morning mail. I write this and one to Mrs Ing before going down to lunch with this Volkening guy.

Last evening a few good things turned up. Had dinner with Jean Muir, told her about the book and the situation, and got an immediate response. Two of her closest friends are Henrietta Buckmaster (a woman to whom I had been commended from Hollywood, and who has written, I understand, one of the most stirring tracts on the Negro in years: 'Let My People Go'), and Walter White, president of the National Association for the Advancement of The Colored People (NAACP), and a novelist in his own right. It has been arranged, through Jean, for me to submit a script to Buckmaster as soon as one becomes available, and to do likewise with White. The idea is to get both these pro-Negroes to support the book to Morley, especially White. And should White happen to like the book, of course the way will lie open to Richard Wright. I could have done this through Taggard, but her response to the book left something to be desired, and I think erroneously.

I can't begin to tell you how effective Cedric's lunch with Morley was yesterday. The whole picture has changed. Morley actually said that if he got time to set himself, he undoubtably would take on the book. His reason for asking for patience, as I gather it, is to protect himself against criticism in case the book is neither a critical nor a financial success. As he put it to Cedric, he has more angles to consider than Woodburn, and he wants to feel (through support, I suppose) that the house itself will not share in the failure of any of its books. I can sympathize with this point of view, but naturally it's tough on the nervous system. On the whole, though, I'm astonished at the calm with which I'm sailing through this apparently endless waiting-period (and that's a sentence that'd never get into any of my books, you can be damn well sure).

There's no use in dwelling on these things. I find it best to report facts, rather than hopes. A big fat fact, my dear and pretty wife, is that I love you better every damn day in the week. You're the God-Almighty best! It sure tickles me that you miss me, you much-married but little-learning fool! Hoka hey!

You've got all my love; what is there left to send?

47. To Marguerite Roberts

(Here, Sanford refers to a new book—Johnson, Daniel—*which he will later self-publish, in 1951, as* A Man Without Shoes. *"Seppy," I believe, is a mention of "September Girl," one of the Sanfords' many race horses.)*

Saturday, Mar. 20, 1943

Dearest and by long odds best:

Regular love-you-nique No. 10:

Let's see, now: how far back do I have to go to reach the last developments I reported? I forget. Anyway. . . .

As I told you, the McKenny letter reached Morley on Monday, and he had lunch with Cedric on Wednesday, and the two together made a deep impression, so much so that Morley is quoted to me as having said that Harcourt will take the book, but it must be given time, etc. Of course, that's not what I came here for: I'm after a contract if I can get one. But Woodburn is much perked up by the new Morley attitude, and this long hoped-for Morley-Sanford talk should be coming off during the early part of the coming week, especially since I slipped Woodburn the info on Thursday that I'd booked my return for next Friday, the 26th. I told him I had to do that to protect myself in case the trains were jammed, but that I'd cancel the reservations if any important reason for doing so turned up during the week. He knew what I was driving at and said at once that the meeting would come off within a few days—which has got to mean Monday or Tuesday at the latest, or I'll be unable to cancel the reservations. This chat came off Thursday afternoon, after which we had dinner at the Algonquin with Midge Chodorov, and then, when John had gone, Midge and I dragged off to see 'The Eve of St. Mark' on tickets she wangled through the Gordon office. The show was worth exactly what we paid for it: 60 cents in taxes. It simply stank me to sleep. All it lacked was people.

Now, to go back to Thursday lunch, which I had with Henry Volkening at the Ritz (Dutch). He renewed his effort to get me under his wing, and this time I was more receptive, mainly because (and I laid it out on the table) I felt the Morley thing needed a goose, and V. might be just the guy to come up with it. I haven't signed with him yet, and he doesn't even ask for that. I said I'd sign with the headwaiter if he moved Morley this much toward a 'yes'. V., it seems, has been doing legwork all along, and he mentioned he touted me up to the great Maxwell Perkins, of Scribners, whose very close friend he is, with the result that Perkins right now is reading 70x7 to prepare the way for reading TPFH. That's one thing V. has done unsolicited, and another blew in with the mail this morning, a letter from Houghton-Mifflin in Boston for a look at the script on the advice of V., and showing no little interest. Of course, Woodburn has been informed, and these things will only move him to quicker action.

Regret to say Dial turned us down, as has Reynal & Hitchcock, but on being told of this, Woodburn just lit another cigarette and said he now liked the book even better.

Yesterday (Friday) was a blank.

Today, through La Muir, I took the script to Henrietta Buckmaster, who will read it over the weekend. She's touted as a great authority on the Negro, and I'm running a risk in letting her read it, but it's a risk that must sooner or later be taken, so it might as well be now.

Also today, I bought you two nice presunts and Mrs Ingele one. You've got a nice surprise coming when you see them, but I won't tell you in advance what they are. I'm bringing them in person.

So as things stand right now, I'm set to leave come Friday on the Broadway Ltd., which'll give me several hours in Chicago on Saturday before pulling out late in the afternoon on the Streamliner; this gets home (and I do mean you) on Monday morning. This is one time when I will *not* say, "Don't meet me." I suppose I've never been so eager to see anyone in my life, and it would be a coupling of the grossest deception and the finest histrionics if I indicated the contrary. So do meet me, if it's possible. I regret that I must add there just could be a hitch necessitating my remaining here longer than I think I'll have to, but it'll be a hitch of the pleasantest kind.

Do I feel I've accomplished anything by coming here? Well, yes and no, but more yes, I think. The negative side is that I just have not got lying in front of me a signed and red-sealed contract that I could touch and rattle if I wanted to; it's a long-shot that I'll get one in the next six days, and if I did I'd be astounded; so I must say 'no' if you'll only count positive things like legal documents. The affirmative side draws strength from the fact (and it is a fact) that it took the trip to show that Harcourt was not done with the book—quite the contrary, to be exact. If I learned no more than that, I might feel justified, but I think there's a lot of other stuff to set alongside of it. For one thing, I've met and associated often with Woodburn on the friendliest of terms, the result of which can only point toward a continuation of his effort to pull the book in. I can say definitely that as long as the book is not taken elsewhere, he will not give up, and even if it is taken, he will use it as a needle on Morley for years. Further, the Henry Volkening thing may burgeon into something at any moment, and in any case, I could not leave New York without placing the book with someone for a coverage of the rest of the field.

As it appears, V. is as good (or bad) as the rest: it's the book that sells, but there are many little things an agent can do. For instance, Perkins will read the script even though he knows his house has already turned it down. That's far from meaning he'll reverse the decision, but I could never have gotten him to re-read the book. What else on the affirmative side? Maybe as much as anything else, I've satisfied myself that I did all I could, and it will surely be easier, even if we fail here all along the line, to get back to 'Johnson, Daniel' with the trip under my belt. Otherwise, I'd have been torn by the thought that I'd not gone all-out for TPFH.

And that's about all.

I have missed you more than I could convey on all the rest of the stationary in the building, more, I think, than I'll be able to convey during the many years I hope to go on living in the same room with you. It's impossible for me to know the feeling of a guy in a fox-hole in some tropical swamp, but again and again I catch myself imagining that I'm thinking about you as a guy would if he were separated from his dame by war, water, and regulations. Jane says that Matt writes to her, saying, 'You are the most beautiful woman in the world', as in truth to him she is, and I, walking in the park or drinking coffee, say with Matt, 'You are the most beautiful woman in the world', as if I were lying on my belly half a mile from the Japs. And you are beautiful not only on the inside, where I always knew you were beautiful, but on the outside, where sometimes I used to think you had a most peculiar face. I only wish I wasn't such a damned stinker; I only wish I'd done something in my thirty-nine years that could fairly be called a qualification for my most unusual reward. By juckies, wife, I love you.

Don't you wish you knew what the presunts were. I went to the limit to get them: they're the very best ever. Wish you knew? Ha, baby, not a chance. You wait. Damn it, if I talk about them much more, I'll be telling: they're so pretty.

Kiss my dog for me. And how about Seppy? Still no word about her. And no letter from you in four days.

My best to all, including, of course, Mrs Inge.

Simply,

If you have not put in for your lay-off yet, please do so at once!

48. To Marguerite Roberts

3.30.43

Most adored wife:

This is being written on Tuesday, March 30th, and although the events of the past week have run together as in a vorka-pich, I'll try my best to cut them up for you and set them in line. But before I begin, I'd like to say that you're the finest woman in the world, and I love you very much. After digesting that and going 'Prrrr-prrrr', you may proceed.

On Monday, the 22nd, I called Jack Goodman of S & S and caught him smack in the middle of TPFH. On Tuesday, I saw Angus Cameron of Little-B and got a report to the effect that although he had a few reservations, he admired the book very much and would be glad to pass it on to his superiors in Boston. I couldn't let him do that immediately, for I had an appointment with Woodburn and Frank Morley within an hour, and I rather looked for favorable action; Cameron asked for and got next refusal after Harcourt and S & S.

From the Cameron pow-wow, I went straight to the Roosevelt Bar, where I met JW, FM, and Dorise Schneider. The one hour I spent there was easily the most painful I've had in thirteen years of dealing with editors. Morley (as I thought then) was even worse than I'd been led to suppose him, and no approach to him that ordinarily would've had a chance as between one human being and another even suggested itself to me as a long-shot hope: he was simply crushing in his unwieldy bulkiness. From the start, he dominated the talk as a hard rain of sorghum would dominate a woman dressed in organdie. He simply smothered all three of us in his slow-running world of taffy-like maunderings, and I personally came away feeling as if I'd been practicing swan-dives in a cess-pool. He dealt with the book in myth and metaphor almost exclusively: it was a 'diamond with a flaw in it', although he could not say where the flaw was; it was 'brandy'; it was a prize-fight—it was anything but one word written after another in order to impel the people to action. He played chess with it, he engulfed it in fable (I later called it bullshit from Bullfinch), he shambled, shuffled, hawked, drank beer, apologized, picked his ear, and finally backed himself into the position of pronouncing the book unpublishable. Yet I was sure he had not meant to do this on his way over to the Bar, but finding himself faced by three people all hostile to his manana-attitude, he simply took the easy way and washed himself off.

JW and I stayed to pick up the pieces after Morley had run off to catch his train, but there were no pieces to pick up: Harcourt seemed then to be definitely out, and the two of us were sunk like stones. We parted, and he said something about refusing to give up trying, but it was out of his hands, and we both knew it. I had a dinner that tasted like a warmed-up Stetson, and afterward, because I didn't care any more, I went to see Thornton Wilder's 'The Skin of Your Teeth'. My fondness for life must have been under-rated, for at the end of the second act, almost vomiting, I found myself hurrying up a dark street toward room 1719. I got here to find a call from Midgie Chodorov, saying that she was at her hotel with a pot of tea and waiting for news of the Harcourt triumph. I bought a shabby little box of Nabiscos and dragged myself to the Navarro, where, over tea and crumbs, I received condolences till Eddie came in from rehearsals, and to his own wife's don't-take-it-so-hards, he added his own.

On Wednesday morning, I called Henry Volkening, told him he was my agent, and then started reeling in my lines preparatory to pulling out Friday evening. The first call I made was to Jack Goodman, and the line wouldn't come in! He'd finished the book and was raving, and two other readers at S & S were likewise. I jumped down there to deliver a second copy of the script so that both Simon and Schuster could read the book over the week-end, and I was promised a definite Yes or No before noon on Monday, the 29th.

I cancelled off the Bway Ltd. And the Streamliner, of course, fell in with the agents, and sprang the news on Johnny Woodburn. He positively went frantic at the possibility of losing the book to S&S and in addition to preparing the document I enclose (which went to every adult member of the Harcourt force on Saturday morning), he made a date with Keith Jennison of Henry Holt for cocktails, to which he brought a copy of the book. This was strickly against our orders, but he did it anyway, managing to leave the table long enough for Jennison to get a gander at twenty-odd pages. The result of this was an immediate phone-call from Jennison, offering to publish the book on the strength of what he'd seen alone. I gave him the stalleroo, and the whole troop of us went into the week-end, knowing that Monday morning would see plenty action. That's when I called you.

Monday (yesterday) came, and with it all action. I was awakened by a call from my agents, saying that Woodburn was already in their office with an offer from Harcourt backed up (at last!) by Morley and Don Brace. I dove into my rags, flew to the agents' office, and got in touch with S&S, caring nothing about what they said so long as they didn't want the book. It was a tight minute: if S&S had said Yes, there was no way in which we could've withdrawn; to have done so at that stage would've been to ruin me forever with S&S, to say nothing of the agents. Fortunately, however, I was informed, with real regret, that after an all-morning battle among the entire S&S staff, Simon and Schuster included, the house was rejecting the book. I laughed out loud, which I suppose I shouldn't have done, for the S&S editor very quickly caught on that somebody else was in the picture. She pressed me then, and has continued to press me, for the name, but I fobbed her off with something about not having admitted that there was interest elsewhere. Hanging up, I turned to JW, and he was crying!

The contracts will be signed as soon as the lawyer can draw them up, and, as I told you yesterday, I will roll in to L.A. on April 5th—for one time in triumph. The trip came off magnificently, luckily, and honorably all around. Before I forget, I should say I called Angus Cameron to tell him the news, and was delighted to learn that he would have accepted the book if it had ever come back his way again. In addition, I'm still to meet Max Perkins, Scribners' boss, for it turns out he liked 70x7 very much. Also Carl Sandburg comes to town on Thursday, and I'm to meet him; JW expects to get a hot blurb for the jacket from him.

I know you will approve a few gifts I just bought and delivered. To Doris Schneider went a pair of very beautiful gloves from Mark Cross. To Ursula Brennan (JW's secretary, first at Harcourt to read TPFH, and responsible for the note 'SPECIAL!' that he found on it on his first day on the job) a little Danish silver pin from Georg Jensen. And to Johhny Woodburn an alligator cigarette-case from Cartier: initials on the outside, and engraved on the metal frame inside 'FROM MAGGIE AND JOHN SANFORD TO JOHN WOODBURN, ONE OF THE PEOPLE FROM HEAVEN' . . . . Nice?

Let's see, now—what else? The letter from Jesse I've told you about, and of course I'll bring it home with me for you to read: all in all, it's a rave which, if it were in a review on the front page of the Times, would sell five thousand copies. I've never seen him let himself go like that. I read it to Erwin and George, and both were so deeply impressed by it, knowing Jesse as they do, that for the first time since I've started writing, George asked for (and got) a copy of the script. Erwin did too, and tomorrow night I'll have their verdict. It will not necessarily be final, for I still will be able to appeal to the public, but it will be interesting. I've written Jesse to meet me in Chicago if he can: I'll have eight hours there. He has a number of points that he wants to discuss with me in their context, and of course I will listen to them eagerly, for I respect his opinion (even when it isn't favorable). One or two good suggestions came from Genevieve Taggard and Henrietta Buckmaster, and I believe they will be followed: they're along the lines of making America Smith less symbolic and more real, which can't hurt.

As far as the colt (what a beauty he must be!) is concerned, I chip in with the name 'America Smith'. Consider it carefully: it has lots of points, not the least of which is the Smith part.

And now—you. My God, if I were to start telling you the part you've played in the creation, the writing, and finally the placing of TPFH, I'd still be here at this machine when the Bway Ltd pulls out next Friday afternoon, and I wouldn't want that to happen, for there's nothing I want more than to tweak your lovely ears and kiss your sweet mouth just as soon as same can be arranged. You are simply gorgeous and good and adorable—with monograms! I love you more each time I draw a breath, and therefore for your sake (as well as mine) it would be awfully cozy to keep on drawing for another fifty years. I wish I'd married you on August 27th, 1936: then I'd have had 2 ½ more years of you. I was a dope, but give me a chance, and I'll make it up to you. Please, if you can find it in you, love me just a teenchy in return.

Of the 72 hours that I still have in NY, I'll probably spend 40 with JW. He has a lot of suggestions to make for revision, all along the lines of cleaning up the obscenity and curing the obleekness (yahhhhh!). You may be sure he'll have his way unless the body of the book is affected but there's no chance of that, for, if anything, he's more satisfied than I am. He's no pushover, though: I understand that he's one of the most acute editors in town. It would be impossible to over-state the part he's played any more than it would be to over-state yours: with all that you and I put into the book, we still would have come a cropper if it weren't for John; it wasn't the book that put us over; it was the broadside he prepared, and to my mind it's one of the cleverest things I've ever read.

Again: all love to my best wife, plus beautiful presunts. Also my best to Mrs Inge and Juni-bug, both of whom will get presents. And Jane too.

49. To Jesse and Naomi Greenstein

7.6.43

Dear N & J:

I meant to answer you right away, in conformity with our compact to maintain a regular correspondence, but what derailed me was a sudden request from Harcourt for permission to strike out some fifty words and phrases (feelthy) and insert others of their own choosing. I went into a steep climb, and the upshot of the dispute was that I got the manuscript back together with the list of revisions and a gun pointed at my head in the form of 'OR ELSE!' Maggie smoothed me and smoothed me, and I finally made a three-point landing. On examination the list seemed not nearly so formidable, and I parted with some fine favorites a lot less reluctantly than I'd ever have imagined: maybe what contributed to this was a determination to find others, while less offensive to the eye, at least as offensive to the mind, and on the whole I think I succeeded. At this writing, the book has been on the press a good two weeks, and I should be receiving galleys any day now. Don't think I'm not cute enough to make an alteration or two back to what I had in the first place, especially where I couldn't think of a good replacement!

The book jacket, drawn by McKnight Kauffer, is a beauty. Black and white typography against a background of split-pea-soup green. The book will be sold at 25 cents per plate (croutons extra). I hardly need to say that the Greensteins are on the complimentary list: you'll be getting a copy in a month or so. I'll sign it some time when I hit Williams Bay.

Maggie nears the end of her script on 'Dragon Seed,' far and away the best property she's ever gotten her beautiful fangs into. At the moment, they're casting, with expectations of starting the shooting on August 1st. Far and away too it's the biggest project she's ever been associated with, the appropriation being $3,200,000 to do the job in sepia, and another $500,000 for Technicolor. Every part, down to the last bit and extra, will be performed by a star: it's Metro's BIG of the year 1943. We plan a three-month layoff for Mrs. Sanford, starting the moment the last page of script is turned in: this may be two, four, six weeks—hardly longer. The lady talks wistfully of a trip to New York, but unless that can be combined with some war-effort purpose, it will not be made; we'll go trout-fishing and play with horses and dogs. Me, I'm trying to drum up an idea for a 100-page novelette that'll sell fifty million copies and win this war as much as 'Common Sense" won the Revolution. You're crazy if you don't think I'll do it.

Our wonderful housekeeper (Ingeborg Emil) has returned to the fold! Allah be praised! Once more we chew celery in front of our (cold now) fireplace, and once more Juno groans in her rabbit-hunting dreams on the couch, alive with fleas, crusty with dried mud, stinking ever so gently, but man's best friend nevertheless.

Plant a kiss on George's moosh for us, and exchange one between yourselves—as we do . . . . so!

Affectionately

50. To Frank Capra

April 16th, 1944

My Dear Colonel:

This is a hard letter to write, but there's only one way to get a hard thing done, and that's to pull your shirt off, spit in your hands, and pitch in. Without any feints or sashays, then, I'm pitching in.

The work I did under your supervision in the early part of 1942 was the start and finish of my service to the country during these thirty months since Pearl Harbor. I'd be a self-satisfied fool, therefore, if I thought I'd done anything to be proud of—and this despite the fact that at all times I have wanted to do more, and that at all times I have been told to run along home and suck my thumb. I think you well know the main cause of my getting kicked in the belly every time I've hopefully tendered my miserable little talent to the Government, but what you can hardly know at all is the state of my feelings after five flat turn-downs, and I'm going to tell you something about that because I have reason to believe you are a friend.

In December, 1941, I volunteered my services to the Navy, and the application was shelved; in March, 1942, you offered me a place in your unit, only to find that I was listed as unacceptable; in June, 1942, Major Wyler asked me to join his over-seas outfit, and I consented, but from that month to this I've heard no more from him; in September, 1942, you renewed your own offer, and I filed forms on the same day, only to find out on the next that I was still unacceptable; and in October, 1942, I applied for admission to Officers' Candidate School, and after passing all examinations and being certified for active service, my papers were returned when President Roosevelt issued his order against the induction of all persons over the age of thirty-eight.

Being a five-time loser, Frank, I think I'd be justified in going about my business and working up a sense of participation by donating blood through the Red Cross, buying War Bonds, and writing speeches for the Writers' Mobilization, all of which I've done—yet I say to you in all sincerity that none of the rebuffs I've had has changed by a hair's breadth my desire to take an active part in the war.

There were times when I tried to persuade myself that there were many ways of becoming active—times when it almost seemed that if I were barred from wearing the uniform of a soldier, it was proper to wear the uniform of a worker or a farmer—but, Frank, I've never quite been able to make that go down. If I'm anything at all, I'm a writer, and if I'm ever to pay back what I owe the country, my currency must be words.

I take a back-seat to nobody in my respect for what's being done with the riveting-hammer and the pitch-fork, but the simple fact is that those are not my weapons. I have a weapon, such as it is, and I've put fifteen years of my life into learning how to use it, and it's a damned and crying shame that I've been told again and again to oil it and put it away. I have your words to prove that my words are good, and I protest to you—the only man I know who will listen—that words, good words, cannot be put away. This is not that kind of war, Frank: we will overcome bodies with bullets, but the mind is impregnable to everything but words, and we shall have won nothing if we fail to win the mind.

I'm now forty years of age, and therefore not subject to any foreseeable draft, but I still want to offer my words—my best lick—and I write to ask if conditions have so far changed from what they were that you can use me where I ought to be used. In the event that they have not, I ask you, out of your good will, to inquire into my chances of serving with the Psychological Warfare Division of the Office of Strategic Services: I understand that combat-correspondents are being trained for important work in that branch, and it may be that I can qualify no matter how unacceptable I may be elsewhere.

In any case, I should like to hear from you, and in all cases, accept my deep gratitude for your many kindnesses.

Yours sincerely,

51. To Marguerite Roberts

9.18.'45

Dear Maggie Darling:

I'm fresh from ten minutes with John Woodburn, and you're entitled to be the first to know that the book was turned down cold! There's no use going into the whys and wherefores, except to say that if it's possible for a man to miss your point so completely that he seems blind, then Woodburn has pulled off just that trick. He simply doesn't know what the book is about, and he'll never know, and I've taken it away. Tomorrow, it goes to Reynal & Hitchcock.

There was nothing to be gained by letting Woodburn go into detail. He wanted to talk about punctuation, about form, but it would've been a waste of time. Any man who can only talk form after reading 'Johnson, Daniel' is a man who never did know anything else. I didn't say that to him, but I did say that it was incomprehensible how he could've been taken in by 'TPFH' and not fall over dead before 'JD'. I said the one was as two-dimensional as a sheet of paper, for all its form, simply because it was blank of people. He was incapable of seeing that. He said the book blew up when I abandoned the rigid outline of the classification-card. Since I believe that's where the book began to have balls and blood, I was incapable of seeing it his way.

I tell you these things to show you how far apart we were. It was never a matter of revision. I've always been ready to [?] on from an editor, at least from Woodburn. But I knew that I could revise till I fell over and never get him to the pitch of enthusiasm he reached for 'TPFH', so I gave up on him and shook hands goodbye.

I'm sorry to have to disappoint you again, but, what the hell, honey, you're married to a writer, and you've got to be ready for these things.

I won't stick around here too long. There'd be no point in that with an incomplete book. But I think I ought to get a couple of readings, now that I know I'm once more without a publisher. I'll be able to take anything from the others; I just couldn't from Woodburn.

My best love, as always, to the best woman and wife in the world.

Lovingly,

52. To Marguerite Roberts

Tuesday, Sept. 25. 45

Sweet Bug:

As I've told you, I had a conference with Frank Taylor last Friday, and that, coupled with the reception I got when he took me to the offices later, made me feel justified in wiring you that things looked bright for us at Reynal & Hitchcock. The way things were left, Taylor was to have called me on Wednesday (tomorrow) and told me the verdict. Well, he called today instead and invited me to his house for the evening, saying nothing about the book. Naturally, I brought up the subject, but all he would say was: "My mind's made up, and you can relax." It would be hard to take that two ways, so I've relaxed.

If things broke right, I could easily wind up my business in N.Y.C. this week and start for home. But there'd be very little point in doing that unless I had real assurances of an affectionate and sincere welcome—a thing it is not too simple to infer from your infrequent letters, mainly on the subject of Shorty and the pups. Now, if I had, say, a three-page letter from you stating the exact nature and degree of your emotion toward me, I might be able to reach home in ten days. Failing that, however—well, there are other girls. None with such a pretty belly, I'll have to admit, but after all, what's in a belly? I never thought I'd have to complain about your stinginess with stamps, but I'm doing it all the same.

I suspect I'm being treated to some kind of lesson, or else worked for the same kind of declaration I just sought from you. To start the balls rolling (excuse the expression), I love you!

A telegram will beat this in if good things happen tomorrow at R&H. Otherwise and in any case,

Lovingly,

53. To Marguerite Roberts

(Sanford returns to New York, this time with a completed draft of Johnson, Daniel. *Harry Ford, at this time an editor at Reynal & Hitchcock, went on to become a respected editor and book designer at Atheneum and, later, at Knopf. Shorty is one of John and Maggie's racehorses. Daniel is Sanford's nephew. Heskett was Sanford's groundskeeper.)*

July 8th, 1946

Dearest Bug:

A line to say I called Frank Taylor this morning to find out what progress he's made in a week's time. Both he and Harry Ford have been reading like "maaaad," he said, and they're both "wiiiild" about what they've seen. They don't want to do any talking till they've had two complete readings and then several hours of discussion with each other. I can't possibly get final word, there, for another ten days, during which I'll just have to suck my thumb. I'll be going up to Westport, I think, over the coming weekend; Taylor and his wife need guests. But it's as good a way of killing time as any (except horse-racing), and I'll go.

Saw Eddie Rose again last evening for a fish-supper and a hot walk. I believe we'll make another trip to Jamaica on Wednesday to catch the Demoiselle. Whitney's first flight goes, and I'd like to see her in action. I'll be watching the form for Hollywood entries, but I can't understand why Leavitt hasn't given Shorty any works. You don't let a horse stand still for two weeks and then start him cold. Or do you?

Everyone here is well, and we all hope you and the Folks are the same.

I haven't seen Danny yet. He's still at school in Philadelphia. But this morning I got a letter from him, and the first paragraph is so funny that I'm going to quote it. I quote:

> "Dear Pal: It may seem quite strange that I'm writing a letter to you when I shall see you within a week's time, but my purpose is to ask your very valuable advice about something over which I am now deeply concerned. Don't become unnecessarily alarmed, for I haven't violated any sweet, young Philadelphian because of my restless passion and promiscuity, although I seriously intend to make a hell of a stab at it tomorrow night, but I merely seek your literary criticism of Charles Dickens."

End quote!

It's a beggarly game.

Your second letter (with charts) came after breakfast, and I devoured it (the letter). I love to hear from you.

In fact, I love you. In fact, I'm wiiiild and maaaad about you. You're the sweetest and best and most beautiful. Oy, it's a beggarly game.

With much love,

Best to Margaret and Jim.

Re that Heskett bill, you can pay it. There *were* two discings. And you can irrigate any time you like, but don't call Heskett to disc again till two weeks afterward.

54. To Jesse Greenstein

(The book mentioned herein is Johnson, Daniel, *later self-published in 1951 as* A Man Without Shoes. *The manuscript was begun in 1944; Harcourt, publisher of* The People From Heaven, *was the first to refuse it. R & H mentioned herein refers to the publisher Reynal & Hitchcock, which would tease Sanford by accepting the book for publication and then backing out after the death of Hitchcock, the liberal voice of the firm. When Reynal returned from the war, he was staunchly anti-communist and refused to publish the novel.)*

Xmas Day, '46

Dear pal:

Your malice about the cutting of my book noted and contents analyzed. In my own defense, I have to say that if it's remarkable how much trash I can accumulate in a manuscript, it's less remarkable how little of it gets into print. By that, I don't mean that all my published stuff is great; a lot of it fails badly, but not because it's larded.

Nor do I think Robert Penn Warren fails for that reason, either. I just read "All the King's Men" too, and I've read both of his other novels, and he is a total and absolute failure, despite your friend George: he's a flop because of his ideas, and it didn't take Ham Basso's article in Life to make me know it. No man ever wrote a first-class novel with such ideas as Warren has—making Huey Long out to be a misunderstood hero. In three books about the South, Warren hasn't seen fit to write about the only thing in the South worth writing about: the Negro. And come to think of it, God help the Negro if he ever did write about him. It's a pity too, because if it's at all possible to separate ideas from talent, I'd say Warren is a very good writer from 'way back, a poetical guy, sentient and observing. But he's lost, or, worse, he's in full flight, and not even the Univ. of

Minnesota seems far enough away to let him write what should be written, and us guys that've never lived in the South, only passed through it holding our nose, have to do the job for him. He's a louse.

The revision is finished. I sent it off to R & H ten days ago. So far, silence. But I hope it's only Xmas traffic. If all goes well, that is, if no further big changes are necessary, the book'll be out late this spring or early fall. The sixty thousand words I've cut are in the main the ones that gave you the impression the book's full of sideswipes. That usually happens. Stuff gets in you think is okay, and it takes time for it to fade. Most often it fades when you glare at it in your last look before shipping it off. The chips are down then, and you're under no illusions. I suppose some crap will have escaped me, but I'd be willing to go to press as is without fear of provoking violence from you. Well, wait and see.

I'm glad Peter reminds you of me. Something ought to, although I'd just as soon it wasn't his pissy little ass.

Your remarks about the Soviet delegation I pass over in contempt. Politically, you too often are pissy-assed, and your skinny little bony bottom drips Dew Pearson.

Maggie is on vacation—first time in years that idleness has overtaken both of us at once—and we propose to spend four or five weeks along the rail at Santa Anita laughing at you. Of course, we could do that anywhere, but somehow or other the tail-end of anything evokes memories.

Jesse (Herr Doktor!), we do love you, though, and we love your annually inflatable wife, and we love the produce of your love, so write to us again and soon.

Affectionately,

If you get here in Feb., buzz us, of course.

55. To Frank Taylor

(Taylor at this time worked as an editor for Reynal & Hitchcock. Here, Sanford responds to a list of twelve single-spaced general considerations and page by page suggested revisions.)

February 9, 1947

Dear Frank:

Your letter and list came yesterday. The manuscript is probably still on the way, and without it, it's tough to figure your references, especially where you make them by page-number only. But so far as I can dope out, your objections to A MAN WITHOUT SHOES fall into two categories: literary and political. The literary ones are many and various, but since I never heard of a novel's standing or falling on whether diavoles are used in kindergarten, I think we can pass them for the real objections, the political, which come to two in all: the thing you so feloniously assault with the title "Evocation of History", and the development of Danny from right to left.

These two elements of A MAN WITHOUT SHOES are the actual sticking-points between us, not diavoles, and it would be well, now that matters have come to a head, for me to say so and for you to admit it. My position, certainly, has always been clear to you. That I intended to "evoke history" has been in evidence since the earliest version of the novel and from its earliest pages, and in later versions the weight of that evidence has never changed except to grow greater. Without the "evocation," no such work as I ever intended to write would remain, and I see no possibility of cutting it out, or even down, and having left a novel that I'd care to sign my name to.

I hope I make myself clear about this. I hope you will understand that you could offer me no argument that would induce me to shift my purpose in writing the book, nor impose any penalty—meaning rejection—that would force me to write a book to no purpose. The lint, the trash that collects in any man's book, the so-called "preposterous" phrasings, the labored metaphors, the ill-used diavoles—all that is exactly nothing, and you know it as well as I do, because even through the overlay of it, you one time saw what you called (forgive the reminder) "perhaps the great American novel." There was doubt in your mind, as your putting it indicates, but I never imagined you'd try to remove the doubt by removing the "American."

It can't be done, Frank. At any rate, it can't be done with me. The kind of writer who'll cut the heart out of his book for a contract is the kind you can whistle in off the street—there's an Arthur Koestler on every corner—and you only have to know how to whistle to get your man. Me, I'd sooner fall down dead in a ditch than use the only talent I have to lie for a living. I don't think you consciously ask me to lie. I think you've merely deceived yourself, or been deceived, into believing that the American stuff is a matter of diavoles, and that the book would still be a book without it. It would not. It would only be the kind of movie I've time and again been offered two thousand dollars a week to cobble up and knock off.

Nor would the book be a book without Danny's right-to-left progression. The right is the America "evoked" in the American passages, and the left is far from reached when Danny becomes involved in the Sacco-Vanzetti case. Many a man was heart-and-soul for the Italians—many a Koestler, perhaps—who today is heart-and-soul opposed to what they died for. The Trotskyist position (would anyone mind very much if I said Trotskyite?) is dangled before every liberal that comes down the pike, especially before the sucker-Dans, and some fall for it, and some do not, and my problem was to dangle it before Danny. I did so in what I felt and still feel to be a natural way, let the J.T. Farrells fall where they may. It's true that Vivian is no anti-Soviet giant. Indeed, who is? I claim only that she operates on a level that's plausible and, from my own experience, fairly common, and it being my intention to treat of a common guy for a common reader (not for Paul Valery), I reject the word "cheap" as a criticism of my approach.

It comes down, in the end, to whether one is sympathetic to an attack on Trotskyism, or, to be more inclusive, to whether one is satisfied with Danny's growing away from the America of Georgia and Huey Long and the NAM and Vandenberg, and toward the only reality the masses have had offered them in a century. America made an offer once, but the last American in a position to honor it was shot in the back of the head. The offer comes no longer from America, with its drivel about "free enterprise" (Standard Oil), "free elections" (the South), "free press" (Hearst), and "free God Almighty" (Father Coughlin and T.S. Eliot). Nor does it come from the Trotskyites—either the nymphomaniac Vivians or the intellectual Koestlers. It comes from the Soviet Union.

This is a far cry from diavoles, Frank, but it couldn't have been diavoles that made you say, "If you don't accept these suggestions, I frankly don't know where to go from here." It could only have been the whole essence of A MAN WITHOUT SHOES. Well, it's your right, I suppose, to pull out at the last minute and refuse to print the book I wrote unless I mutilate it into the book you want to print, but I have a right too, the right to refuse, and I do refuse, and I'll keep on refusing even if the book is rejected by every publisher in America.

I owe it to the people I spent four years of my life writing A MAN WITHOUT SHOES for, I owe it to myself, and I owe it to you, to say that I earnestly hope you won't carry out your threat to call it quits on what you still admit is "a very good book." To that end, I again offer to make a trip back east to keep the relationship alive. Unless you back down by mail (which, from your tone, seems to me most unlikely), the relationship is on its last legs. Sending for me would show great good faith on your part, but, more important to the issue, it would show that you have an open mind to the politics of the book. Mine is closed, and that's why it rests with you to say whether I may have one more whirl at convincing you, or whether it's curtains as of now.

But either way, Frank, keep one thing before you. You personally have been a right-guy, and I like you, and I know that you've honestly, though mistakenly, tried to improve the book, and I don't raise my voice to you, and you would not be hateful if you stuck to your guns, which are made of wood, and I would always like to be friends with you.

Sincerely,

56. To Dan Lyons

June 25th, 1948

Dear Sir:

The writer of the official chart for Race # 51974 used the following language to describe the performance of a 19-1 shot in the first race at Hollywood Park on June 24th, 1948: "WIN BAG quit after showing speed for half a mile and fell dead after the finish."

It was my bad luck to be at the track on the day in question and to see Win Bag die right before my eyes, and I think all who saw what I did, even those who had wagered on the horse, never let the word "quit" enter their minds. They had watched a cheap old gelding pack 119 pounds for the three-quarters of a mile at the greatest rate of speed he was capable of, and if they regretted that he faded in the stretch, they were horrified—bet or no bet—when he dropped to the ground while he was being unsaddled. Their two bucks or their c-notes were pretty much forgotten, if their faces were any criterion, and I think they realized very keenly that it doesn't take a Man O' War or a Citation to show gameness. A four-thousand-dollar horse can try just as hard as a stakes-horse—in fact, he can try hard enough to break a blood-vessel—and, to put it mildly, it was pretty cold-hearted of your chart-writer to usher Win Bag out with an epitaph centering around the word "quit." It's high time, it seems to me, to drop "quit" from the language applicable to horse-racing, because I know of no sport where the word can be so inaccurate that a participant can be said to die from not trying.

The border-line between quitting and tiring is thin enough to justify the substitution of the latter word. In any case, the best sports I've found around a racetrack are usually the horses, whether platers or champs, and if they could speak when man had run their hearts out for them, I have an idea they'd say something gentler than: "Joe Doakes quit after showing speed for a half mile and fell dead after the finish." I think they'd mumble a piece about dying game, and let it go at that.

Yours very truly,

57. To Bucklin Moon

(Moon was an editor at Doubleday, where A Man Without Shoes *had been submitted by Sanford's agent, Henry Volkening of Russell & Volkening.)*

January 21st, 1949

Dear Buck:

I'm going to be as frank with you as you were with me, and the risks you ran with my friendship I'm going to run with yours, but because you emerged with that friendship and regard intact, it's a fair assumption that you'll serve me as you've been served.

"A Man Without Shoes" was submitted to you not only as an editor, but also and equally as a writer. In the latter function, you reveal a deep sympathy with the aims of the book and a first-hand knowledge of the enormous effort that its writing involved. As well as any man going, therefore, I think you understand that books of this kind are not simply cobbled up; they're made with pieces of your own bone, and they hold some part of your blood, and they drain your brain of the best it has stored from your total experience on earth. That sympathy and knowledge should not have been put aside when you came to function as an editor, yet I think they must've been, or you could not have brought yourself to suggest that certain bones of the book were unnecessary, and that some of its blood could be let to advantage.

I don't defend each and every one of the three hundred thousand words in "A Man Without Shoes." Many of them are inept, no doubt, and many more are repetitious, and still others are only distinctly related to the central purpose—and before the book is published, they'll be done away with whether an editor orders it or not. But this is a far cry from ordering a book without a face, which I think you're doing when you direct me to take Parts I and II and junk them: they're the face and all that's behind the face of Dan Johnson.

In support of your suggestion, you say, "You would get your reader right into the action of the thing, rather than making him follow a chronological pattern that many readers might find slow going, though, I hasten to add, I don't." Aside from the curious fact that you don't even agree with the suggestion yourself, there's the question here of precisely what kind of 'action' this book has. In the ordinary sense, I think it has none. The only story it tells is the story of the development of a man's character (*toward* action, but rarely *in* action). This I saw fit to do by assembling the main and minor forces that contributed to his growth. There is no plot, no climax, no first or last act, no drama—except insofar as a life can be said to have drama. I happen to believe it has a very great deal, and relying on honest and significant selection, I dropped the usual and conventional forms and made use of the form that life takes merely by being lived. I'm not persuaded that I made an error; the character Dan Johnson has too much body-heat for me to conclude that his only chemicals are the ones you find in ink.

If you believe with me that he has something like physical reality (and you must, because you seem to cotton to him despite the absence of a story to give him literary reality), then you owe that belief almost altogether to Parts I and II. You may not realize this yet, and you'll probably dispute it, but I think in the end you'll have to admit it's true. Indeed, you've already shown your reliance on Parts I and II: you say, "I am certain the majority of my cuts would come in the first two sections, and even if you were to follow this idea out, *much of what you would lose would be brought back in through flashbacks.*" Why? Why cut something out as being of no value only to recognize its value by including it in a flashback? If it has no value, it ought to stay out permanently; if it has value, it ought never to go out, even temporarily. If this book had been submitted to you without the first two sections, if it had opened where you say it ought to open, with the trip across the country, I'm absolutely certain it would never have gone further at Doubleday than your desk. You'd have said, "For Christ's sake, John, do you seriously propose to start a novel with three hundred pages of blank verse, without first showing who in hell the guy is that's thinking it and how in hell he got that way? Why, you must be out of your mind!" But the shoe is on the other foot, Buck: it's Doubleday that's proposing this thing seriously! I too, be sure of it, have a liking for the trip-section, but only as Part III, with two parts ahead of it to draw the reader so fully into Dan Johnson that what Dan Johnson thinks and feels has validity and meaning. As an opening for a novel, as a novel in itself, Part III has nothing.

Now, all this is quite apart from the matter of sales, which I assure you is no down-the-nose concern of mine: I want sales; I want this book to be bought and read as widely as possible; I'm not writing for a couple of thousand half-assed intellectuals. If the people don't read me, all I've done for years is hide myself in a fog of words. Phrig that, brother. I put in my time on the Left Bank, sucking a dry front tit and dreaming that to sell was somehow to be degraded. The real degradation is in *not* selling, because that's when the people give you their verdict on your little old words. So let's say I see eye-to-eye with Doubleday about making a dollar, but, Buck, what kind of sales can be hoped for from a novel that gives the reader the works right from the bell? Three hundred pages of such material as Johnny Appleseed, Debs, Lincoln, Dred Scott, John Brown, the Bisbee Deportations, Sutter and gold, Washington, Custer, Vicksburg, Tuskegee, Sumter, and Appomattox—right smack in the reader's puss before his ass has warmed his armchair! Good God, the poor bastard would drop dead! And we'd *all* be dead.

I have a few things to say about Lee Barker's report. First, he's wrong in assuming that the novel is autobiographical and that I cling to much of the stuff because it happened to me. I don't suppose I figured in more than a dozen of the several hundred scenes: I had the globe-trotting uncle; I was in that Florida jail, not Danny; and I had a few of his more usual experiences; but the great bulk of his life is his own, not mine. The point is inconsequential, though: if the material is high-grade, it can be autobiographical; if it's poor, the fact that it's fiction is no excuse. The test must be excellence.

Barker's next point is vital. He says, "Long sections (of the book) which are important to the author are not important to the reader, for many of them have been covered to death." I take it that he refers here mainly to the first two sections, because in a letter to Bernie Smith he specifically condemns the Sacco-Vanzetti theme, which appears only in Part II. Now, I'm perfectly willing to believe that this monumental injustice has been covered often enough to convince Lee Barker. I have Bernie Smith's word for it that Barker's heart is in the right place, and Bernie's word goes very far with me. But Barker's heart is not the only heart: for every one like his, there are thousands in the *wrong* place, and it's those that I want to reach. I know that they exist, because my own was in the wrong place once. It's the terrible truth that I'd never heard the names Sacco and Vanzetti until the night they died. I was old enough to know—millions all over the world knew—but I sailed along in an ignorance that still, after more than twenty years, seems fantastic. I see that same fantastic ignorance all around me now, as you do and as Barker does—yet he insists that the subject has been covered to death. That might be true if the coverage given to Sacco and Vanzetti had put such injustices, as Lincoln said of slavery, "in the course of ultimate extinction," but I see nothing like it. What hits the eye is Scottsboro, the Un-American committee, and treason-trials—all this long after Sacco and Vanzetti were dust. Barker knows deep down that man is never done in his struggle to better man. If coverage were the sole criterion, it might be said that never after Tolstoy could war be written of. But since his time, we've had such supreme treatment of the subject as you find in "A Red Badge of Courage," Hemingway's Caporette, and "the Last Days of Sevastopol." The test, as I said before, is excellence. If it were only originality, we'd never have had even "War and Peace." The idea was well-covered by the Romans.

Well, I didn't expect to be so long-winded when I started out. I thought I'd get around very quickly to turning down your suggestion as impossible and winding things up between me and Doubleday, but it occurred to me that there was nothing basically irreconcilable between rejecting the suggestion and keeping the relationship alive. That depends less on *my* listening to reason than *Doubleday's*, and therefore the next move is yours.

Please bear in mind that I'm not concerned with my integrity: apart from the book, I don't suppose I have any. But the book, I think, has great integrity, and I intend to preserve it even if Doubleday puts this thing on a take-it-or-leave-it basis. That hasn't scared me in the past, and it won't scare me now. But after a long talk with Bernie Smith, in which he explained the publisher's point-of-view in a way that made me understand it more clearly than I ever had before, I was convinced that I ought to hold myself out as willing to do whatever I can to make this book "a more marketable article." This does not mean that I will eliminate Part I and II or any other section that I regard as indispensable. It does mean that I will listen to and adopt sound advice about cutting and trimming; that within the limits of my purpose of writing the book, I will consent to discard what is not germane; and that I will propose (if we ever reach that stage) certain ideas I've always had for collapsing characters whose functions are similar. In short, I'll polish the book, but I won't polish it off; I'll shrink it, but I won't mutilate it. It's no secret in the trade that it's been turned down twelve times, but I'd sooner see it turned down twelve times more and then burned than kill it and serve it up dead. I'll not knuckle under when I know I'm right.

You will of course show this to Barker. The decision is his to make, and I feel he should have all the evidence before making it. He should also know that Part III, which he likes so well, was the only thing that barred publication at four other houses, and that I've had three different offers for separate publication of Parts I and II, which he has no use for. What I require is somebody with an equal liking for Parts I to IV inclusive.

If Barker sticks to his guns about lopping off Parts I and II, I'm afraid #13 is Doubleday's number, and #14 is my next stop. On the other hand, if I've not yet slammed the door in my own face, and if you believe it's possible to work out a contract for publication based on the type of revisions outlined above, I offer to make an immediate trip to New York to reach an accord and close the deal.

In any case, Buck, let me close with this: whichever way the thing swings from here, I'm grateful to you. You've liked my work, and you've made a sincere effort to put it forward. No man could ask for more, and few could fail to be indebted.

Sincerely.

58. To Marguerite Roberts

(Sanford finds himself in New York, pitching his latest novel, Johnson, Daniel. *Pat Covici was John Steinbeck's editor at Viking. The mention of Fast is left-leaning author Howard Fast. The list of people Sanford mentions having seen in New York include his college buddies George Brounoff, Nat (Robert Lord), Herb Ortman, and a writer and former boxer, Lew Amster, whom Sanford will be instrumental*

in getting published almost thirty years later.)

2.14.49

Dearest and best:

I apologized over the phone a while ago, and you're not going to get mileage out of my failure to write more than one measly letter in two weeks: I'm in one of the famous Sanford fogs (they descend the moment the Chief hits Cajon Pass), and therefore I'm not respon-civil.

Here's the layout. I got the manuscript on Monday, an original and three, making five altogether including the original original, and there was some work to be done that day before I could start passing copies out: I had to indicate italics on the three copies. That took all day. On Tuesday, I had a three-hour lunch with Mrs. Carrick (Appleton), the one editor who had not read the book prior to Volkening's yanking it. She had many good questions to ask, and I think I answered them well because when we parted, she admitted being already much prejudiced in favor of the book. She has no doubt begun her reading by now, and I'm to hear from her at the end of the week. She took two copies, one for herself, and one for Purdy, which is on its way to San Fran. After leaving her, I went up to Wm. Sloane, where I gave Keith Jennison his copy (the old original), and he said he'd have a reaction to me by tomorrow! That's fast even if he doesn't do it. And then today (Wednesday) I managed an appointment with Pat Covici of Viking, who heretofore has been a bogey in all my dealings with the firm. But I think this interview too went off well, and he will read it himself. He rared back when I came to the part about multiple submissions, but I must've had a verbal chain over his nose because he clammed down when I tugged on it. He did say that this was the first time in his life he'd ever read a manuscript in competition. That makes three houses, and I still have a copy that I'm trying to get to a certain Cap Pearce of Duell

Sloan & Pearce. I tried it through Buck Moon, but he doesn't know the guy well, and I tried to get hold of Maria Leiper of S&S, but she's skiing and won't be back till next Wednesday. Tomorrow I have to figure out something else: if it comes to it, I'll call direct. Or maybe try Fast.

Mel has done nothing for me after a friendly start. He's either manic depressive or he doesn't approve submitting to more than one house, and when I spoke to him last night (he's still too busy to see me—he sez), he sounded so lukewarm I told him to forget the whole thing, that I'd turn the trick myself. And damn if I won't. Nobody can do for me along these lines what I can't do for myself, not Mel, not an agent, not Bernie S. I say I'll have a contract in a week (without doubt Appleton's). Mark m'woids.

I've seen Jerry many times, and he's in a terrible funk. He was in one before the Miller play (Max Gordon told me today that Jerry's been dubious about himself for five years), but now it's something pathetic. He won't come right out and admit it, but he simply doesn't think he can write, and he's afraid to go near a typewriter. He has to drive himself. I've tried to buck him up with sane talk, but I seem to make no headway. He puts a lot of faith in some psycho, a guy I hear is an idiot. Don't tell anybody about the kid.

Have you heard from Bernie Smith, and if so to what effect? I haven't had boo out of him.

I've seen Ed's partner Margulies twice about the Boni case, also Heit, Margulies' associate.

I've been at Hat's four times. You better believe me, not her. I've been with Nat at least five times and Herb once. One evening (no, two evenings) I called on Beatrice Buchman. I've seen Blatas twice, once for breakfast at Rump's. I've been at Bergdorf's and Revillon Freres once each, both times looking for something for you. I've seen Brounoff once, Erwin nonce yet, Bernie Hart once, Lenny Tobin once for Lunch at Sardi's, Lew Amster once for lunch at the Waldorf's Men's Bar. I've seen many thousand women in the streets, but I still remember you with love, and I've seen millions of things I could've sworn were dogs, but which on closer inspection turned out to be poodles (oodles of 'em), so I still think Juby's tribe is the greatest. And although Coaltown broke the Hialeah record for a mile and an eighth, I still think Dan-boy will run one so fast, the clockers'll think it was a mile. So I love my horses still, even though I haven't written to them at all.

You're a stinker to punish a poor buffeted about fat slob like me. I'm trying to make you famous back here, and you're withdrawing your immoral support. A good man is hard to find. A good woman—pouf! a dime a dozen.

Love your little old boy who loves you, you fat-assed little bagel.

With Mucho Gusto
for my Porter Mare
meaning you,

59. To Marguerite Roberts

February 19, 1949

Dear best wife:

I just received the note you wrote after hearing about Jennison. Apparently you were so overjoyed at my stirring up another publisher that you gave me carte blanche about such minor matters as fornication. Thanks for the kind permission, babe, but I'm saving my spermanent wave for Encino. In fact, I may say nuts to you.

To keep you up to date. I slapped the book on Jennison late Thursday afternoon, and when he stated that he'd give me his reaction by Thursday, I figured he was only making mouth-music. But, by Christ. At ten Thursday morning the sonofabitch was on the wire 'phoning' at the mouth. 'I like it very very much,' he said, and what are your commitments, and how in the world am I going to get in any more readings before Monday, and would you please not accept any offer without giving me an hour's notice, and can we have lunch tomorrow (Friday) and talk all afternoon? I made the date with him and was ready to keep it when his secretary called to say that an editorial conference had been called, and would I get in touch with Jennison later in the afternoon for another appointment? I said sure, at 2:30, but I most carefully forgot to call and even stayed away from my room to avoid his getting hold of me. I wanted him to sweat out the weekend, if he was still in a sweating mood, and if he wasn't, I wanted to show him I didn't give a damn. My hunch is that after making the lunch-date, he got to thinking about what there was to say to me at that stage of the game, and he realized that he'd only be feeding me with support for being independent with any other house that beat him to the punch—and he called it off. He'd admitted to me that at least two other readings were necessary, and that they couldn't be gotten till over the weekend. As I interpret the guy, he really is heel-over about the book on a most intelligent basis. The only question he asked was whether I had an open mind about picking out the repetitions and trying for a save of pages. I said I thought I'd want to clip about twenty-five thous . . . . and he said, 'That's all I want to hear. That's all I want to hear.' He emphasized that he was after nothing in particular (the politics, the history, etc.), just enough words to make the book more manageable. For my own part, still having one copy, I've read it, and a surprisingly large amount of stuff should go—episodes that have no meaning, no drama, nothing. So that's Jennison, and I'll hear from him on Monday, or I miss my guess by a mile.

Now about Appleton. I have it doped that it'd be fatal to get tough with them just now. I see it that I have to await a hard offer before I can take the chance of jogging them. This Mrs. Carrick has been reading the book since Tuesday, and since there was no particular pressure put on her, aside from the knowledge that other houses had it, I must assume she's giving it a good careful reading, maybe even saving it for the weekend (it's Saturday now). Without much doubt, I'll hear from her too on Monday—or she'll hear from me if Jennison kicks through with something to warrant my tightening the twitch. In the meantime, a copy was flown to Purdy at San Fran. He'll read the book en route, and he's expected back in town come Friday. It's all jelling, and my hopes run high. All this without reckoning on Covici at Viking. He's had the book since Tuesday or Wednesday, and I believe it'll be a while before he rejects it or gets in touch with me. And I've spent three days trying to effect a good contact with Cap Pierce [sic] of Duell S & P, and I finally made it by getting a letter of introduction to him from Louis Kronenberger, an old literary acquaintance. DS&P is to call me. But the battle may be over before they do, and I hope so.

Mel, as I told you, has been a perfect prick, and I'm through with him. I still haven't even gotten a call from him for lunch, although I've tried to make a date with him on at least five occasions. In addition, after one feeble effort to get Farrar & Strauss to read the book in competition, and failing, he showed signs of wanting out on that too, and I let him off the hook. It's the first time I've ever known him to be worried about jeopardizing his own position (and he's wrong, because he wouldn't be if he merely introduced me to these editors; there's no reason why he should be responsible for what I say), and since he feels that way, I'm not going to be beholden. I always thought I'd have to do this job myself, and it seems I was right. But I can't help being disappointed in Mel, not alone for his squirming, but also for his preposterous aloofness, and he can go shit in his hat.

Without meaning to tell you what you should or should not do, I think it might've been a good idea to accept Bernie's invite to that beach-dinner. Not because you needed anyone's company or dinner-treat, but because it would've given you the best possible insight into the man. I condemn pretty quickly, sometimes unjustly, and maybe in this case too I was unfair. I rather think not, but that party might've cleared matters up. It goes without saying that I haven't heard from him or Frances. If she calls me on getting to town, I'll see her and try to get at the bottom of all this.

My constant companions have been John Sanford (a rather good egg once you get to know him), Nat C. (who has called me and seen me not fewer than a dozen of each), Jerry and Rhea (six dinners and two shows), Herb (twice; he was out of town the first week), Sam and Hat, and the Harold Romes (whom I met through Jer; Rome is writing the music and Jer the sketches of a revue for Gordon).

This afternoon, Jerry, Rhea, and I are taking the train to Stamford to spend the day with Midge and Matt. Tomorrow evening the three of us are going to an A.S.P. party for Arthur Miller and the cast. On Monday night, I'm seeing Ed Swann, on Tuesday dinner and a show with Bernie Hart, on Wednesday dinner at the Chods with Danny and Rhea's little sister (that they want Danny to meet). Beyond that, nothing, and I hope it stays nothing—with a contract in my pocket and reservations on the Super.

It was good to talk to you and the family, and I hope all stay well and remember little ole Jabe. I love you, apple-ass, and bear that in mind or I'll make apple-sauce of it when I get home. You're MINE! There's something about your face. . . .

Twelve years of it now,
and, God damn it, you're
sweeter than ever!

60. To Marguerite Roberts

February 24th, 1949

Dearest Baby-doll:

First, let's get one thing straight: I love you more than anything on earth. You're the best wife in the world, and as a woman you're second only to my old love, September Child, with Juno well out of it and up the track, and the rest nowhere. I miss you so much that I walk ten miles a day just to kid myself into thinking I'm walking home toward you and that extraordinarily funny mug you think is a face. Please don't forget me when you're in the seductive company of such great men as man the couches at MGM. You're MINE!

Here's the book-situation as it existed as of 5 p.m. on Friday. I had a lunch-date with Jennison yesterday, but again he broke it, this time sending as his substitute the second editor, Mark Saxton. We talked for three hours, and from the way he spoke I gathered that he liked the book a great deal, possibly not quite so well as Jennison, but he gave me to understand his vote would be for it. He let on that he's a novelist himself, which may account for a certain grudging attitude of his. All the same, I'd call it a good conference. The third editor had finished half of the book, and since the second half hadn't been given to her until Thursday morning, it's not likely that she's finished even now. But I figured the time was ripe to light a fire, and before parting with Saxton, I told him that if Sloane was interested, it had better not think I was unloading a lot of Hollywood shit when I said another house was interested too, and that a notion that I was high-pressuring and selling myself rather than the book might just be fatal to Sloane's chances. Whereupon I left the guy.

On getting back to the hotel, around four yesterday, I thought the setup over for a while and came to the conclusion that the time was also ripe to set fire to Appleton also, there being no sense in putting the squeeze on one end only. So I called the Carrick woman and caught her in the act of making her report to the Boss. What she said was that she "was tremendously impressed." She had found much that she objected to, however, and was incorporating it in her report—nothing, though, that we hadn't already been over together with Purdy—and my all-over guess is that the report said 'take.' I suggested to her that things might get embarrassing very soon, and when she asked how, I told her about the second house. She said Purdy was returning at the end of the week and didn't think anything should be done till he arrived. I agreed with her and said I'd keep her posted.

And then today she called me late in the afternoon to inquire whether anything had turned up at the second house, and I said no, but I looked for action come Friday, and I'd keep her informed, She said she'd talked things over with Rapport (the Boss), and his opinion was that matters be allowed to stand till Monday, when I look for a showdown.

Feeling that I had no business to let the fires go out once they'd been started, I called Jennison after Carrick hung up. I didn't get him, but I left a message, and since he's primed for action from the first house any day, I'll just let the bare fact that I called sink in, hoping he gathers that I did so to tip him off. I should hear from him in the morning. If not, he'll get another dose of the silent treatment.

As I see it, there'll be no action from Appleton till Monday. It's just possible that the third reader (policy-making editor) at Sloane will go for the book hard enough to get them off the dime tomorrow, but I doubt it, so it looks like another long dull weekend of walking from here to Poughkeepsie and back. Naturalich, don't say a word to the Gov. Baby, keep well and think of your stinken ole boy back here once in a while. A lot of kissing and hugging from me to you.

61. To Marguerite Roberts

(Henry Albert and Decky Salina are the names of Maggie's parents. Roberts, by the way, is Maggie's name by her first marriage, which she retained as her professional name. She was christened Smith.)

Sat. Feb. 26 '49

Dearest Wife:

I sent you a letter yesterday morning, telling you what the possibilities were for the day, but nothing happened to change the situation as you know it. Appleton and I had agreed the day before to let things go over until Purdy's return on Monday, and Jennison of Sloane did not rise to the fly I pitched in the form of a phone-call on Thursday afternoon. The Carrick woman at Appleton was 'tremendously impressed', she said, and I know that she's had a conference with Sam Rappaport, the big boss there. As for Sloane, it would be a miracle if the third editor read the last four parts of the book, in the short time she's had so far. And surely there could have been no editors' conference before the weekend began.

So the way it shapes up now, I think Appleton will be the first to act, one way or another, and I look for action on Monday; I have Carrick's word for it. Meanwhile, with time to cool off and think out my chances, I've naturally sunk far below par. I get to remembering all the terrible failures, the near-hits, of the past two years, and what I tell myself is that I'm due for more of the same. I have no doubts about the book, because I never think of it as it is, loaded down with trash, but as it would be before I let it out of my hands—but I have my doubts about publishers, because from all I've ever seen of them, I know them to be selling goods, not books, and if they should come to believe that they can't sell this article, this particular item of merchandise, I'm due for two more kicks in the teeth. I used the word 'naturally' up above. I hope this 'natural' bounce-back is only a leveling off, not a premonition.

I'm letting Covici at Viking take his time. If Sloane and Appleton fail me, I'll have him as a sleeper. I put the heat on him at the start, so I should imagine the book has gotten at least one reading by now, but the guy has kept quiet, and I'm doing the same. Sid Russell's arranging for me to meet Charles Duell, of Duell Sloane & Pearce, on Monday or Tuesday, and even if I'm talking turkey with another house, I'm going to slip him a copy of the book: I'm not going to leave any Sloane unturned.

Frances Smith gave me a call on her arrival last week, and I saw her once, for breakfast at Rump's, as I think I told you. I haven't seen her since, although I've talked to her a time or two on the phone. She's a mighty busy one.

By the way, before I forget, did Mom get the gloves I sent her from Mark Cross two weeks ago?

I spent the day at Woodmere. It was Gladys' birthday (tomorrow is Aunt Rae's), and the whole family was there for a turkey dinner. Got back to the hotel around ten in the evening.

Two nights ago, I saw the opening of Odets' "the Big Knife', and if 'Death of a Salesman' was the best play by an American, then this surely is among the worst. Not only is it one of the most maliciously anti-Semitic jobs ever done, but also its ideas (defeat, despair, decay, and suicide) are those of one kind of man only: a renegade. Dialogue that passed in the day of 'Rocket to the Moon' is now an insult and an outrage, and if it flares up now and then, it's only the popping of a dying fire. This flaneur, this bastard that 'would've been a great composer if he hadn't been a great dramatist,' this vaunting note-taker 'who was born the day Chekov died': he pleads for silence. That's what he has Garfield ask for above all things: the gift of silence. Piss on him.

Well, baby, I've covered four pages with type, and I haven't mentioned the word 'love' once. Consider it implicit, however, in each and all of the other words, but if you must have it barefoot, may I say that I love you better than anything else on earth, including myself. You're the best wife in the whole sonofabitching world, and I wouldn't swap you for two War Admirals, a Bull Lea, and a carload of Porter mares. You're my type—close-coupled, with plenty of drive in the stifle, slick as a buttered eel, full of vinegar but easy-riding, a sweet soft mouth and a clever pair of heels. Mark her paid for! You're for me (br. F. 43, by Henry Albert out of Decky Salina by God himself). I love you, baby, and don't ever think I don't.

Dirty John,

62. To Marguerite Roberts

Late Monday afternoon

February 28, 1949

Best wife:

I'd thought today was to be the day I'd hear from Appleton and Sloane, but with nothing stirring by three in the afternoon, I got annoyed with myself for doing nothing and decided to put the screws on. Accordingly, I called Jennison at Sloane to tell him I'd had an offer for the book and that he had twenty-four hours to get off the dime. He wasn't in, and neither was Saxton, so I sent the message in via secretary to the third editor, a Miss Taylor, whom I hadn't met. She didn't get on the wire, a bad sign, but conveyed word that I'd have Sloane's decision during the morning tomorrow. I don't figure I did any harm (I'd promised Jennison the tip of any action brewing elsewhere), and if they're going to reject the book, nothing I could say or do would affect their decision. On the other hand, if they've been dawdling, my giving them the finger was a good idea. In my opinion, however, Sloane is fading out as fast as it faded in: otherwise, I'd have either been able to get this little Miss Taylor on the line, or Jennison would've called back.

Believe it or not, there was just a knock on the door, and the following wire was given to me:

> TONIGHT OUR ANSWER MUST BE NO. WHAT I COULD DO WITH ANOTHER COUPLE OF WEEKS AM NOT SURE ENOUGH TO HOLD YOU UP. IF ANYTHING GOES WRONG LET ME KNOW KEITH (JENNISON)

So my guess was right: that there was nothing doing at Sloane.

To go back. After the uncomfortable feeling engendered by my contact with Sloane, I decided it would be fatal to tamper with the really solid outfit, Appleton, and I laid off. Now that I think of it, it would've been very unrealistic to expect Purdy down there, back only this morning from two weeks away, to have anything worth talking about. No doubt there was a slew of accumulated stuff that had to be disposed of before he could get together with Rapport and Carrick, and in my case I'm going to give him rope till I scare up interest elsewhere, or he gets in touch with me.

Sid Russell of Liberty arranged a meet for me at 4 this afternoon with Duell of Duell S. & P., and I kept it, had a short talk with the guy, and delivered him copy No. 5. He too knows the book is out elsewhere and will read it as quickly as he can. Covivi at Viking I'm still playing doggo with, and so is he with me, unless the book killed him.

That's my report as of 6:30 Monday evening. It's snowing slush, has been all day, and I'm very gloomy. Rhea is calling for me at 7, and we're meeting Jerry for dinner.

Frances S. called a while ago to ask whether I'd join her and Joe Bromberg for a cup of coffee after the show at the Algonquin, and maybe I will if Jerry and Rhea cast me adrift early enough. Fran mentioned that she'd heard from Bernie this morning and that he'd told her how hard you were to drag out. I merely said, 'Is that so? I wonder why' but she didn't accept the gambit, and I didn't shove it in her face. She says she's having drinks with Harold Strauss of Knopf tomorrow and wants to tell him I'm in town, hoping there's a bit of interest left to kindle. I said go ahead and tell; I'm here to publish a book.

The airplane photo came this morning with your letter. Both of them made me more homesick than ever. I studied that picture like a reconnaissance officer. I don't know what I hoped to find. Maybe you fiddling with a pooch.

Baby-doll, I'm sorry to give you the bum news about Sloane, but that's the way it is, and who should know what's going on if not you? My regret, though, is that I lifted you too far at the start. Now you're the one who may have to get let down. But keep a liff ipper stup, or a stuff upper lup, or whatever it is, and maybe I'll still bring home the lox. The Devil knows.

One thing, though: I do so much love that 120-odd pounds known as Maggie Sanford. More than ever, babe, much more.

Best to the Folks, all of 'em, and that includes Mrs B. and Alva.

Yours but good,

63. To Marguerite Sanford

Tuesday morning

March 1, 1949

Dear wife:

Well, I feel impelled to write my lady a little letter. I sent you a long one last night, just before you called, but today, only twelve hours later, another would seem to be in order. What inspired it was my seventeenth rejection (from Viking) in the morning mail.

I sat around after reading it, suffering the same shame, rage, disappointment, bitterness, and discouragement that my first rejection caused me, but for once, even though vaguely, I understand the malignancy of ambition: in the frustration of my desire to be a fine writer, I've come near overlooking what deep down is far more highly to be prized. I mean you. I mean my most wonderfully loyal and open-handed wife.

At 44 and some change, I think I'm not going to be the Melville or the Stephen Crane of this generation, but whether I ever rise to where I can kiss their feet or not, there's one thing I do know: that from now on, I'm going to see to it that I'm a very great success as a husband. I could never have written half so well as I do if it weren't for you, and if I ever write better than now, you'll be the reason for that too. But one way or another, I'll not lose sight of the fact that the most important moment of my life occurred in a little self-service elevator twelve years ago. I still mean to write, and to write the best way I know how, but the touchable thing will no longer be 'the glory or commodity of life,' as Vanzetti put it, but life itself: you. I love you.

64. To Marguerite Roberts

Wed. p.m. Mar. 2, '49

Well, baby, the Appleton thing blew up in my face this morning. Purdy didn't call or anything; he just shipped the manuscripts out with a regretful note. If you think you've seen me sunk before, it's a good thing you weren't here today to witness this. I simply can't describe my feelings. I think no one could. I'd have called you if I'd had any preparation for such a blow; I'd have called in advance. But getting this kick-out when it was practically my last publishing hope—and when I'd been given grounds for building high on it—I honestly didn't have the heart to hear your sweet voice try to hide your anguish. I tell you the bitter news in this way, therefore, hoping you'll not regard me as unkind. I seldom mean to be that to anyone, and never in my life to you, but I feel I can talk safely right now only to a machine; if I spoke to an organism, especially the one I love more than I do my own, I'd break up and down.

The Viking thing ended yesterday morning with a nasty note from Pascal Covici, and the interest of Wm. Sloane was dead as of the night before last. I've kept on feeding out the manuscripts, and at the moment they're being read by Duell, Harcourt, and Creative Age. The Harcourt submission was an absolutely hopeless stab (Reynal is head of the trade department), but I feel I have to try everybody, even the impossibles. The contact with Duell was arranged by Sid Russell, and I regard my chances as one in a hundred. I was put next to Creative Age, a good small outfit, by Russell too, and I had a long talk with one of the editors this morning. The book is up their alley, but its length is against it, and with seventeen rejections behind me, I have no reason whatever to suppose I'll fare better here. I'm going down to see Russell when I finish this and talk over the possibility of digging up a couple of other houses for the two remaining manuscripts; if that can be done, I'll submit them this week. A reaction [by] Creative Age has been promised for Monday. If nothing is brewing there, then I'll feel justified in leaving for home very soon afterward, for the other four houses will hardly have gotten off the dime by then. In my opinion, Monday either writes the book off finally or it gets taken by an inferior house—death to it in one case or the other.

I won't say anymore except that I'm sorry I couldn't find anyone in the publishing business to justify your unflagging belief in me. As matters stand, only two people in the world have that belief, and, sweetheart, we aren't quite enough. But we're enough for love, just the two of us, without editor-pimps to bring us together, and I'm very deeply grateful to you for being my wife. I love you well.

I've received from you:

1) A horse tooth
2) An air-photo
3) Income-tax forms
4) Letter telling about Ed
(what made you think
I'd be sore, baby?)

65. To T. M. Purdy

(Theodore Purdy was the Appleton editor ultimately responsible for the rejection of Sanford's A Man Without Shoes*—formerly titled* Johnson, Daniel*—manuscript. In 1950 he will begin working for Putnam, and Sanford will have reason to deal with him again.)*

March 7th, 1949

Dear Mr. Purdy:

If you thought I'd be docile about your manner of rejecting A MAN WITHOUT SHOES, think yourself another thought and make it a good one. I don't take kindly to turn-downs of any sort, but when they come by errand-boy, they get my hackles up, and it's time for a little straight back-talk. I've had rejections before, but so far, however they may have rankled, thank Christ no editor but you has pulled the stunt of leaving my manuscript on the doorstep and running for his life. That was blue funk, my friend, and therefore when you took to your heels, you left behind not only my respect, but also (and this is more important) your own self-respect. I don't have to prove that: you know it. But let me go from the manner to the substance: there's even less comfort for you in that. I think your refusal of A MAN WITHOUT SHOES because of "the general feeling that the book might be difficult to sell nowadays" is a bald and disgraceful confession that free speech in this era is strictly a matter of book-keeping. It affirms that if what a writer has to say is a saleable article, all the guarantees of the Constitution are his, even if he's a provable and dollar-hungry liar. On the other hand, if he's "a writer way inside," as your reports state of me, if he has written "a big important novel which deserves serious consideration because of the undoubted impact it will have on reviewers and public alike," if his ideas have resulted in "a powerful book, dominated by a strong social consciousness, a violent hatred for injustice, and a deep compassion for its victims"—if with all this in his favor, he yet lacks the ability to make the cash-register play YANKEE DOODLE, he forfeits his right to speak by default.

It may well be true that A MAN WITHOUT SHOES will not sell like a slick and tailor-made testimonial that this is the best of all possible worlds. I don't know: I wasn't writing merchandise, and up till now, I didn't think you were peddling it. I had the notion that it was my absolute right to express the truth as I saw it, regardless of whether it was in style, and I had the dream that it was your absolute duty to insure that I be heard.

I see now that both notion and the dream were fantastic, and that the right and the duty were only fading words in an old document on the Freedom Train. I see now what my own character Danny Johnson grasped at the age of sixteen: that this cannot forever be a nation of big-say and little-do; that great phrases require to be used, like feet, lest they wither away; and that the white stars of the flag must not all of them be suffered to turn black.

For the better part of a year, you've fought yourself over this book of mine, and whether it was a hard fight or only a little set-to, I think it's a fair conclusion that winning it mattered to you. But you didn't win—you lost—and I pity you, because losing meant that your editorial judgment had to be subordinated to the judgment of salesmen, and so another white star was blacked out, and another fine phrase was dried up.

I charge you with the defeat: a little more courage, and you'd have won. The defeat, of course, was mine too, but I think, despite all my eighteen rejections and my six vain years of effort for this book, that I'm still better off than you: I don't have to go to bed with your conscience.

Yours, etc.

66. To Marguerite Roberts

(Sanford here mentions another new manuscript, The Bandage, *his sixth book, which will later be published by Jonathan Cape in England and by Doubleday in America in 1953 as* The Land That Touches Mine.*)*

March 8th, 1949

Dear Baby-doll:

I promised you a copy of the letter I sent to Purdy, and here it is, enclosed. You'll more than likely feel it was too strong, but remember I wasn't trying to do anything but make the bastard as unhappy as all hell; to have softened what I had to say would've argued that I had some hope of changing his mind, and that would've turned the whole thing into a kind of shyster maneuver. The only way to let fly is to r'ar back.

By the end of this week, I hope to have some reactions to the five submissions outstanding. I'm almost altogether certain that I'll get nowhere except five houses further down the line toward the end. But that's what I came here to do: to turn over every stone. Yesterday, Sid Russell and Howard Fast went over the whole list with me, and we more or less agree that what I've already done just about finishes things for the book in this period. There are half a dozen houses left (Dutton, Lippincott, Putnam, Bobbs-Merrill, Dodd-Mead, Morrow, Holt, MacMillan, etc.), but they're all 100-1 shots, and the sensible way to cover them is through an agent or one by one through Mel, but in no case to wait around here in hopes.

The frame of mind I've moved toward since the Appleton fiasco is this: A MAN WITHOUT SHOES is not going to be published now, and probably it's not going to be published at any time. But I still believe I'm a writer, and therefore I'm going to continue writing. In a way, the trip here was a good thing: it buried what I hadn't realized was a corpse. I think I'll work better now that I definitely know there's nothing to run to the mail-box for but a false hope. THE BANDAGE was only a sort of step-child till now; from here on, it'll be a whole lot closer. And maybe that's all it required in order to be a good book.

I don't mean to discourage you: you seem discouraged enough, what with the way things have been going for you at the studio. But it's like you always say: our misfortunes are joint, not several, and what happens to each other automatically happens to the other, so there'd be no use in my painting a rosy picture. And furthermore, also as you always say, there's still that queer little couple, whey-faced Mag and Chucklehead John, and they can still get a laugh out of each other now and then. Damn my ass if you aren't worth all the phriggen books in heaven or hell.

About returning, I haven't made up my mind yet whether to clear out Saturday or wait till Monday. It'll depend on what turns up in the next two or three days. Accommodations are a cinch to get: I can be on any train I pick. But I don't want to book myself till I know where I stand with a couple of these outfits that're reading the book. I'll let you know.

Tonight is Eddie's and Sade's anniversary, and Hat and Sam are taking us all to see "Mr. Roberts." Believe me, I'd sooner see Miss Roberts.

Best love to you and all, including Ruth B., Alva, the pouches, and the hosses.

Yours,

67. To Ruth Shapiro

March 11, 1949

Dear Sis:

Your letter the other morning reminded me that it'd been a long time since you'd heard from me. Believe it that if I had anything to write worth reading, you'd have been among the first to get the word. But the truth is, I've drawn a blank for my five weeks here, and with less than a week to go (although the manuscript is out at five houses), I feel safe in predicting that the situation will not change. I have only what satisfaction I can derive from the knowledge that I've tried everything and everybody it was possible to try: and that satisfaction is small.

What I seem to run into everywhere is the belief that A MAN WITHOUT SHOES will not sell widely. What's meant by 'widely' I haven't been able to discover, but I suppose these guys mean 'widely enough.' In these days, everyone is looking for a best-seller, because only that will have the house going to the wall. Many a place that I'd have thought absolutely solvent is in a desperate condition, what with the hundred percent rise in manufacturing cost and the (at least) fifty percent drop in sales. In addition, the excuse of unsaleability is often used to cover a basic dislike for the subject-matter, and that's something it's quite impossible to overcome. These are bad times for a liberal.

I've learned one thing from the trip, and that is that if I fail here (and it was foregone that I would), my bet is to bring the book home and forget about it for the time—that, and getting back to work on THE BANDAGE. There's still a desperate hunt on here for good writers, and it's my hunch that only the little book will get the bigger one published.

I've booked reservations on the Broadway and the Chief, leaving here come Wednesday night on the through car; that'll get me to L.A. early Saturday morning. I hardly have to tell you how happy I'll be to return home. I miss, and very keenly, my dear sweet wife, and my loyal sister and Dad; it'll be wonderful to see you all again.

I thought I'd answered your question about Hortie. I did see her for an hour or two between trains. You'd written her that I was coming through on the Chief, and she met that train, but I was on the Super, arriving later, and luckily, when I tried her on the phone, she was at home. She met me at Henrici's, and we had coffee and rolls, and then she accompanied me to the Broadway at Union Station. She told me that three weeks from then, she'd be off on a trip to Mexico, and I presume she went.

As for Ethel, I'd call her under other circumstances, but I'm really not in the mood for seeing people more distantly related to me than Hatty, although I've put in a good deal of time with Herb and Nat, who have been very kind through this long disappointing pull. I suppose I've been with one or the other, or both, on at least ten different nights, and as for 285 CPW, I must've eaten there twenty times. Hat is even more wonderful than ever. Mel has been something of a wash-out, but on the other hand Jerry and Rhea have been thoughtful. And that's about it.

Take care of yourself and don't overwork yourself. My best love to you and Vern and all. See you soon.

Affectionately,

68. To Marguerite Roberts

(More than a year after his last trip to New York City Sanford has returned, this time attempting to place The Land That Touches Mine *with a publisher.)*

May 31st, 1950

Dearest Baby-doll:

I had lunch with Bransten the day before yesterday, and we thrashed out his two big objections, the flashbacks and the pomes. We finished about where we started, both of us sticking to our guns. But you'll note from his letter and his report that changes, so far as he is concerned, are not mandatory, which fact placed the discussion on a high level and allowed me the unusual luxury of being plausible instead of angry. There can be no doubt that Bransten would accept the book as it stands if he were top man at Rhinehart, but he warned me not to take his opinions as typical, and accordingly I'm going ahead just as Rhinehart had given me a turndown.

After leaving Bransten on Monday, I kept my date with fancy Blanche Knopf, and her reception was most cordial until, as I was about to leave, I urged her to read the book with some dispatch. She wanted to know why, and I said, 'Because there are four other copies out among the trade.' She hit the ceiling and stuck there, and from nine feet up in the air she screamed down at me, 'Mr. Sanford, you will take your manuscript under your arm and walk right out of my office.' With the coolness that comes from holding a straight-flush, I tucked the binder up, bowed gracefully but with a trace of mockery (see Raphael Sabatini), and headed for the door. I'll be damned if the lady didn't stop me, make a few moues, and says, 'Well . . . well . . . er . . . LEAVE THE BOOK!' And then she went on, 'But why do you do such things? Don't you know we hate to read books in competition? When did you give out the other four? Why didn't I get mine last Thursday?' I had to laugh in her face, and I did.

I forgot to tell you that when I saw Cameron last week, he asked me for a detailed history of AMWS, which I proceeded to give him. I started, naturally, with Woodburn's chucking the book back in my face, and he stopped me, wanting to know what Woodburn had said. I told him the little I could recall, and he let me finish. Later, after we'd left the office, he said, 'The reason I asked you about Woodburn is that he's now with Little-Brown.' Yow-yow!

I've seen Jerry and Rhea once, as I think I told you, Herb, Nat, Irene, and Miriam at least four times, and for the rest I've been with

Hats and Saml, of whom it's hard to get enough. Twice now, Hats (and on that word the phone rang, and it was Hats wishing me a happy birthday)—twice now, she's been down to the Hotel, and we've had lunch a deux, with gabble-gabble-gabble for dessert, as only us two can go on. Ah, she's a grand dame, almost as nice as you.

Lee mailed me two beautiful coffee-cakes, which got here in time to be attacked at my birthday breakfast. They ARE something, and they reached me perfectly fresh. Thank the gal for me. She sure is thoughtful.

I've been watching the entries and swearing like a fiend at that monster Royden. Not a race carded for anything but stakes-horses and glue-pots. Why, today the louse cards two for maidens, one of them the feature! There mustn't be an allowance horse on the grounds, God damn it. HAS DAMBO [sic] STARTED GALLOPING AGAIN, and WHAT [sic] NEW WITH MESSY? Make a couple of phone-calls, bub.

I'm having lunch today with Georgie Joel of Dial, but I expect a reaction or two during the day, from Buck Moon and possibly Cameron, although the latter's a bit slow from the gate. I'll keep you posted.

In the meantime, my best and only love to my much adored wife (handsomest, smartest, cutest, most-amiable, and so on).

Enclosed is the Rhinehart story.

Lovingly,

69. To Melvin Friedman

(Sanford's first cousin Mel worked for the printers Haddon Craftsman. As a result, he knew many of New York's publishers and acted as an unofficial agent for Sanford and his work, using his contacts to place Sanford's manuscripts in the hands of New York editors. Sanford and Friedman seem to have had many falling outs, as this vituperative letter suggests, but they never experienced a permanent falling-out.)

June 12, 1949

Dear Mel:

Your letter was a cold sheet of paper, no doubt the wrapping off that stiff hunk of meat you call a heart.

But that you piss ice-water is no new thing. What is is your sudden appearance on the side of the publishers, spouting their advice about how to improve a book: cut the balls off, draw the blood, pull the teeth, and strangle it, and we'll be glad to print it.

Get another boy. And while I'm on the subject, I think I'll get another myself. Please return my manuscript.

Sincerely,

70. To Philip D. Shapiro

June 5, 1950

Dear Gov:

Hatty got a big kick out of talking to you on the phone last night. When I handed her the receiver, she had no idea you were on the other end, and you'd have been tickled to see her eyes glisten with pleasure. In case you don't know it, you're her prime favorite. I spend a good deal of time in her company, so I know what I'm talking about.

There's little to report in connection with the book. It was a bad break, getting here just in time to get racked up for the Memorial Day weekend, and although I did arrange to place the book with four houses before the weekend rolled around, I had little belief it'd be read during what amounted to a vacation, and my hunch was right except for a single house, which kicked in early with an excellent report. I thought it best, however, not to use that reaction to goose the other houses, because it's much too early in the game. What I'm hoping for is another good report, either from the same house, or from a different one. Then I'll be in a more commanding position for the squeeze-play. Starting tomorrow, Monday, I'll be looking for further action.

I hate this place. Not only has the weather been punk, with rain on at least five of the ten days I've been here, but also I spit on the kind of life people have to lead in all this stone and filth. It no longer seems human to grub about in droves.

Take it easy, boy, and don't build yourself up to a let-down about either of the books. I'm hopeful of placing the second one, but who knows these frightened bastards who run for cover at a belch and crap in their pants at a sharp word? There's no such thing as editorial judgment anymore—only fear and sales, and those run neck-and-neck in a dead-heat. So count on nothing till I can report a contract firm in hand.

Love to Ruth.

Affectionately,

71. To Marguerite Roberts

(Ad Schulberg worked in 1950 as Sanford's agent trying to place The Land That Touches Mine *with various New York publishing houses and their editors.)*

Wednesday, June 21 '50

Most wife:

There have been no important developments since I spoke to you on the phone the night before last. All the houses that had the book then have it yet, but some time this week at least two of them will be giving me the sign. The one slight change I have to report is that Angus Cameron came in from Boston yesterday for a couple of days at the New York office. Ad Schulberg put in a call for him yesterday morning, but so far he hasn't called back, which she interprets to mean that he has nothing definite to tell her. Since he's in town only very rarely, and since he's had plenty of time to get other readings, I felt that she ought to go after him with all she has, and I told her so, practically warning her not to let him get away without at least confirmation of his earlier statements to her. If she fails to contact him on this trip (or if she does, and the book is rejected), I'll ease her out of the picture without fail and without delay.

Late the day before yesterday, I called the man whose name John Wexley gave me, and we had an hour together. Yesterday he had lunch with Sheila Cudahy of Pellegrini & Cudahy, and it resulted in her calling me right away for a copy of the book. I had none to give her, but promised her the first available copy.

Sid Russell called yesterday to learn how things were going, but would not commit himself regarding making the book a selection till one other person had read it. George Braziller called too, and he said definitely that he would not make the book a selection, but that he would be glad to publish it independently. I'm seeing him for lunch tomorrow to see what such a deal would involve. It has its drawbacks, mainly in the way of distribution, but if nothing else presents itself, it's something to fall back on. Also, maybe somehow I can persuade him to reverse himself about making the book a selection: there can be no doubt that he likes it.

I called Keith Jennison on Monday to find out how the book was faring at Viking, and he told me he'd read it over the weekend, and "it knocked me into a thousand pieces. That's one God-damn explosive book, boy." He passed it on to Pat Covici, my nemesis heretofore, and I ought to have his reaction in a day or two.

Ted Purdy of Putnam's has had the book since last Thursday, and I should be getting that outfit's verdict soon because Purdy promised to take only a week.

The two other copies of the book are with Poole of Thos. Crowell and Stanley Young of Farrar & Strauss, both placed by Ad Shulberg.

I don't want to go into the question of what the chances are. I suppose if I stuck around here long enough, I might dig up somebody (outside of Angus Cameron) who'd undertake to publish it. But I think it would be foolish to show many more people the book under the kind of pressure I have to use on a trip like this, so I'm going to content myself with the decision I get from those who have the book now and then leave it with a good agent (Jerry wired Pat Duggan to wire back to Harold Matson to get hold of me) and go home.

From all you tell me, Decky ran a whale of a race. Her time was two full seconds better than her best previous time for three-quarters, and even if the track's very fast, she must have run better than she ever ran before to stay within smelling distance of Some Gal and Honeymoon and beat Good Excuse. That kind is out of the ordinary, and not even I thought she would do anything but disgrace herself in such company. From the way she performed, it's my opinion that Charley didn't put her in there to give her a needed race; he thought she could cut the mustard, and she came within a hair of paying $180 doing it. At this writing, it would be out of the question to drop her back into a claiming race; she'd get taken at anything up to $7,500, but over and above that, it would seem she definitely belongs in allowances and maybe better.

I can't understand why Danbo isn't breezing. I'm no one to rush matters, but he's been galloping again for months. It may be that Charley is trying to sneak him quietly up on the Haggin without a public performance, or, on the other hand, it may be that the colt's not right, in which case he oughn't even to be galloping. But if you assure me he's okay, I'll take your word for it. As for Messy, I've been hearing she's 'marvelous' for so long I'm beginning to believe it myself.

Thanks for urging me to take in the shows. If I felt like seeing them, I suppose I'd go, but the truth is I'd sooner spend the evenings with Hat, Herb, or Jerry. Aside from the two shows Sam took us to three weeks ago, the only public exhibition I've seen was a ball-game at Ebbets Field last Sunday afternoon. I just had to see that Jackie Robinson play, and he rewarded me by belting a homer with two on. But what astonished me was finding two other Negroes playing on the same team, the whole battery, in fact, on that particular day—Bankhead pitching and Campanella catching. With at least half the customers colored, it was practically their day. It gave me a grand thrill to see those three on the field.

My only other occupation, aside from wandering about in a fog, has been reading—and even that has been confined entirely to Henry James. I've read four of his novels since coming here, plus seven or eight short stories.

I could go on for pages telling you the things I'm not doing, but in all fairness I ought to mention one very important thing I am doing: I'm thinking about you at all times of the day, and I have little doubt that I dream about you most of the night. I love you more than you'd ever believe. Which brings me back to the start of this letter: you're the most wife.

More than ever,

Love to all humans and animals.

72. To Marguerite Roberts

(The reference to "seven men about to go to jail in my behalf" refers to the first wave of blacklisted Hollywood writers and producers, including Dalton Trumbo, who were imprisoned for their political beliefs by the House Un-American Activities Committee (HUAC) led by Senator Joseph McCarthy. These ten, seven of whom were to be incarcerated the very next day, held a meeting in New York's Town Hall to answer questions and plot strategies about further HUAC hearings.)

June 22, 1950

The most:

Here's how it goes as of mid-afternoon Thursday. I made a private check with Little-Brown, through John Woodburn, the New York editor, and I found that Angus Cameron hasn't returned either Ad's or my calls because no decision has yet been reached. I was told that an editorial meeting is scheduled for Monday in Boston, and more than likely it'll be determined there and then whether THE LAND THAT TOUCHES MINE sinks or swims. I made a sneak submission to Pelligrini & Cudahy late yesterday, and the verdict on that too will be handed down on Monday, so there's nothing for it but to stick it out here till then. If nothing else comes in before then (either from Scribner's, Harper's or Putnam's, the three other houses that have the book), I'll await those two actions and make plans for my return: it'd be foolish to keep on hanging around. I've had eight rejections (Viking and Farrar & Strauss have joined the list), and if Little-Brown goes by the board, I expect a lot more.

But I've gotten over the stage of pitying myself (I think that began to end the night I sat on the platform at Town Hall behind seven men about to go to jail in my behalf), and I've taken to adding up my treasures. They come to a simply enormous total: you. I can truthfully say what you said to me, that I love you better than anyone on or under the earth, and, more than that, I always will. You're odd-looking and mean, you're under-sized and devious, you're splintery, short-tempered, sweet-and-sour, and sometimes venomous—but I wouldn't change a hair of your hair or ever do anything to harm one. Now and then when I talk to you, and often when I merely think of you. . . . But why should I admit that a voice or a face can choke me up? Why should I?

Root for me. Erwin and I are going to kill the weekend at his lovely farm. We're going to the ball-game tomorrow night, and after that we'll drive down for two days in the sun. Playing klabyash? Well, maybe. . . .

With all my love.

73. To Albert Maltz

Dec. 5, 1951

Dear Albert:

I have your long letter of November 17, and I'm grateful for the very apparent close study you've given *A Man Without Shoes.* No other writer has ever devoted so much time and thought to my work, and while I have to take issue with much that you say, I do it, I hope, in the spirit that it was offered and in all respect.

You cite certain rules for greatness in a novel, and apart from not caring a great deal about rules of writing, I have little quarrel with them. With the conclusions you reach as those rules are made to apply to *A Man Without Shoes*, I disagree totally.

First, however, before taking up your main arguments, I want to stick my bill into that old pseudo-feud—style vs. content. There's no real antagonism, as you seem to suppose. Stendhal or no Stendhal, style and content are of equal importance, and they're neither hostile to each other nor mutually exclusive. No man knew that better than Stendhal himself. (I think he once boasted that his own style wouldn't be understood for a hundred years), and despite what you quote for him—*Style is the secondary affair of the poet*—I think he was pulling legs, for few writers of the 19th century more perfectly fitted the glove of style to the hand of content. I'm not familiar with the context of the quotation, but standing alone, it hit me hardest with the final word. I venture the guess that when he said style was secondary for the poet, he meant that to the poet style came so naturally that there was no need for dwelling on it, and that for others it was paramount because it had to be striven for.

He is the greatest writer whose ideas and characters are spoken the most eloquently. It's a fallacy that importance of subject lends importance to anything that anyone may say about it. No belief could be worse for a writer—and no belief is responsible for more dull books. You pick four that you do not remember *for individual felicities of expression or for pace and rhythm of dialogue or for anything particularly connected with style.* You astonish me. *Anna Karenina* and *Crime and Punishment* might've been cited by me for style rather than by you for content, because while each is possibly the best writing-as-writing by its author, *War and Peace* and *The Brothers Karamozov* simply tower over them in value. As for *The Seven Who Were Hanged*, your third example, Andreyev is a second-rater alongside Gogol, Chekov, and Turgenev, all of whom you leave out in order to make your point—and any of whom would've ruined it. But it's the fourth example, *The Red Badge of Courage*, that really floored me. The others, oddly enough, are all from the Russian, and beyond hearsay: I have no way of knowing if the translations limp. My own language I do know, and I think there can be little disputing that Crane is one of the three or four first-rank writers ever developed in America, a stylist above all else and a subject-matter man only deep down and thin when you get to it. His content is limited and his range short, but he is powered by one of the most original and poetic talents that ever worked in prose, and all before him (and much since) fades to drab. It's Crane's fine craft that makes him dazzling, very little else, and therefore when you say you don't remember him *for individual felicities*, you force me to wonder whether you remember him at all. Odd choices, the four books you name, but this one is odd beyond belief. For my part, I recall no single character in the novel, not even the name of a character, not even a face, a place, a phrase: I remember only the emotion of fear presented so overwhelmingly as to evoke it in me. When you do that without ever having seen a battle, possibly without ever having experienced fear anywhere else, you do it with your art, with your *writing-instrument*, as you call it, and not with your characterizations and subject-matter—and you may well believe that if these too are memorable, they're so because they were made so by the writer, and not because the people came to life of themselves, and the theme sat up and sang.

To get on to the specific relation of your rules to *A Man Without Shoes*, I have to quote again from your letter. You say *The fundamental need of the great novelist is the ability to present character*, and you dwell on the presentation of character almost constantly, ascribing all the book's defects to my failures in that field. I said before that I disagreed with you; now I want to say why. Primarily, of course, I believe that in Dan Johnson I have a character of very considerable stature, built step by step in his varied aspects and developed logically and with no little passion through his varied stages, the total coming to what I fatuously conceive as a complete man in a vital period. But past that, I might also say that I believe in Dan Johnson because you yourself, in what you say about him, show that you know him so well. You charge me with having omitted all dramatization of his emotional loss in Julia Davis and presenting him to you with a great hole in his face, yet in one bright sharp sentence you quash your own charge by saying *a loss so keen that some years later he would be unfaithful to his wife because of his neurotic need to possess someone like Julia in the person of another woman.* How did you know that? Where did you get your material for that bright sharp sentence? From the World Almanac? from the dictionary? from thin air—or did you get it from the novel itself? from the *defective* characterizations? I put it to you that there *was* no void, first because you drew the full and only inference from Dan's affair with Emma James, and second because I know that there was ample evidence on which to base that understanding. In other words, it was all in the book, and offhand I can support that with at least six explicit references that Dan made to Julia after walking out on her: they were in his actual return to Colorado Springs to look for her, in his impulse to hop a freight in the Hudson River piece, his futile scene at the telephone directory, and three conversations with his wife. Add to these his many low moods, all stemming plainly from his longing for a Julia as he desired her and culminating in his affair with an Emma as he found her, and you have what you so very well summed up for me: *a loss so keen. . . .* The heart wasn't left out of Dan, as you claim; it was all there, and you felt it beat. It would seem to be this, then: that you demand to know of an eighteen-year-old boy *the agony of indecision*, to quote you again, the pulling back and forth, the loneliness and the weeping, the heartsickness, and that you demand to know it here and now and on the nose, as if anyone ever knew the full import of an experience at the time that he had it. Why, Christ, an author can't even know that for himself, let alone for a character out of the vast and imponderable fictions of the mind!

The next illustration that you give of my failure with Dan's character, a much more glaring one in your eyes, is my supposed withholding from the reader of the catastrophic effect of his beating and arrest in Florida. In your view, I went for suspense by concealing decisive information for 150 pages, only to suffer the penalty prescribed under another of your *very sound literary laws*, that of being condemned to surprise, the effect of a moment. A man who understands the totality of the book as well as you do should not be so quick to forget its parts. When you say *The thoughts you give your character are always a careful avoidance of what is evidently troubling him most deeply*, all I can answer is, what else were you doing while you were reading my book? The word *evidently* is a complete giveaway. If something was *evidently* troubling Dan, then you must've gotten wind of it from what I wrote. In short, there must've been *evidence.* I'll go further: there *was* evidence, and a great deal of it. The beating and arrest occur in a section of the book called PASCUA FLORIDA. Right there, in that very section, Dan comes to an understanding of the almost irresistible forces he is up against; right there, lying on his cot in jail, he wilts under his fear of The Big Train, the Forty-eighter from Decatur. It was a long passage, the one dealing with that realization, and I can't account in any way for your having over-looked it. Similarly, I can't account for the way in which you missed the many other passages that followed and elaborated on it. Most of these involved Dan's wife, and little by little he came finally to reveal to her his entire nightmare—but while Dan, in shame and self-disgust, could bring himself to tell her only a part of it at a time, the reader was left in doubt never; he knew what had ridden Dan from the start, and you knew it too. *Evidently,* you say.

I come now to what you call *contributing failures.* One such is mentioned in your rebuke of me for not having pitched Dan into the Scottsboro case. If you had written this book, I think you'd have found an inviolable obligation on you to plunge Dan straight into that fight—and possibly straight into every other, all the way up to the one over the Trenton Six. Your right to do that would've been absolute, on the theory that a writer is entitled to tell whatever story he may desire. You must allow me the same latitude. I simply was not writing about a man who was going to become involved in the Scottsboro case, but even if I had been, I think the Dan Johnson of *A Man Without Shoes* would've disqualified himself. He knew about it, of course (there are too many references to it in Tootsie's letters for you to doubt that), but after his disillusionment over the end that came to Sacco and Vanzetti, his escapist tour of the country, and his awakened fear, he was self-immobilized. A Dan Johnson who was *not* immobilized would've been a Dan Johnson written by someone else, founded on a different conception, and headed toward a different end. You seem to have the notion that because Dan was friendly with two Negroes, he must either have become involved in every struggle for Negro rights, or be charged with insincerity when he held back. If there are no such hard-and-fast rules in life, why should there be any in art, which is only a selective representation of it? Take yourself, for instance. You've just undergone a violent experience (in jail, even as Dan), but you're not at the moment at the heart of every other active resistance to injustice. I suspect you abuse yourself for that, even find yourself unable to do any considerable amount of writing, but I want to make it clear that if my guess is right, you're wrong. You're a writer first, last, and best, and you belong wherever you choose to stay, regardless of fancied duties and a soft conscience. If you don't believe that now, get to believe it fast; otherwise the no-talent boys will drown you in dogma and demands. The point I make through you is valid. The high point of Dan's political life was reached in the Sacco-Vanzetti case, and although he remained class-conscious and vocal, he ceased for the time to be a participant. He was on the long plateau of knowledge-without-action, a common condition for all of us, and although he troubled himself deeply about it, as all do, he managed to live a life that came finally to a promise of flowering. The 150 pages you claim are so Hollywood-thin aren't really thin at all. They're level, they're uneventful, they're normal—and they were deliberate. You were looking for a knight; with regret, I could only give you a man.

A word about Dan's dialogue, which you object to. You say *You have him talk with an emotional profundity and a maturity of which you, John Sanford, are capable, but which doesn't seem true of him.* That's a tough one to knock over. You tell me you don't believe what he says, and there it stands. But in fairness, I think you ought to agree that any dialogue short of the clearly preposterous is acceptable. We don't tell Henry James that his characters, one and all, are capable of writing a treatise on grammar, nor do we tell Hemingway that people in emotion do more than grunt: we demand only that what they say be possible, and we make a literary assumption of educational background, culture absorbed, and ideas digested, unless (which is not Dan's case) such an assumption is plainly unsupportable. We take it for granted that if a man expresses a thought, he does so because he knows something about it. If we didn't, it would be impossible for a writer to get beyond his character's first day on earth: he'd always fear he'd left some essential out of his groundwork. I'm sure you know the old saw about the writer who could never get a character out of a room without having him turn the door-knob.

You say, *I have always believed that the most important part of writing is the work that the writer does before he begins to write.* I don't. The most important part of writing is writing; you get no credit for your preparation; you're judged by what you put on the page. The planning is of course sometimes reflected in the product, but more often than not it's a hindrance. In my case, it certainly is, for I've never prided myself on my ability to think. To make the full admission, I believe I'm quite a lousy thinker. But I don't think I'm a lousy writer—and therefore I have to doubt the invariable validity of your rule. You know as well as I do that a man can think himself right the hell out of writing at all. He can prepare and prepare, like Philip Quarles, and never get a line down worth a quarter. Or, if he doesn't hamstring himself altogether, he can plan with such rigidity that what comes out seems stamped from an inorganic block, from a blank, like a key. As much as anything else, I happen to admire spontaneity, and I thoroughly discount the omniscience you're willing to grant someone just because he calls himself a writer. You assume he's a great hand with the wand and the crystal ball; to me, he's a guy, that's all, and the only magic he has is what flows down his arms to his typewriter. You endow him with the power of divination; all I give the poor slob is humanity. It'll shock you, I suppose, to learn that *A Man Without Shoes* was written with no more preparation than rolling a sheet into this machine, that I didn't know where Dan Johnson was going, how he meant to get there, or why he was trying to—you'll probably say (in fact, you do say) that it shows up in the finished product. Well, maybe it does, and maybe it doesn't, but one way or the other, the way of writing the book was *my* way, and I mean to *keep* it my way. For me, it's the best way, and I can't help adding that it'd quite likely be the best way for many who plot and plan and deal with literature as if it were only another system of weights and measures.

One more point, touching on the presence of the historical prose poems in a novel such as *A Man Without Shoes*. You're quite right when you suppose that many an editor balked at them; you're quite wrong if you suppose they were listened to for a moment. The poems are not stray pieces of chamber music that I sought to inject into a defective symphony, as you put it. *Anything* repeat *anything* belongs in a novel that in any way contributes to it. These poems, all of them representing an unconscious assimilation by Dan of his country's history and meaning, add much to his understanding, stature, direction, and sympathies, and they need no defense whatever. Not if an opera needs no defense for having music.

To wind up, I want to thank you again for your extreme devotion. It's rare—but it's also Albert. Do write again. My best, as always, to you and Margaret.

Affectionately,

74. To Tom Bell

December 31st, 1951

Dear Tom Bell:

I've just finished reading Out of This Furnace, and I must tell you straight off what a warm and deeply moving book I found it. It's full of honest-to-Christ human beings, not the kind that populate the films, the one-or-the-other kind, but the kind that walk and talk and live all around us, mixtures of nobility and meanness, amalgamations of such good and evil as only this particular society can produce. I've read many a novel hailed as proletarian, pictures of killing work, all, and only poverty to show for a lifetime of it, but what the writers didn't know was that backbreak and hunger without more never made people revolt yet. Only people can make people change, with their good will and their good words (Sacco: I love people who labor and work and see better conditions every day develop, makes no more war.)—and that's where your book is so high above the rest. You subordinated the condition of your people to the people themselves, made the work they did only a facet of them, like their taste in clothes and their speech, and proof of this is that all your important scenes were in the home, or at least away from the mill, the so-called conditioning factor (Mike's last living appearance was on his own doorstep; Mary is known almost solely by what she says and does in her two rooms; Dobie's entire relationship at the plant—he is never shown at actual work—is a home-relationship). The result was this, that I became a part of these people, earlier altogether unknown to me, and I ate with them, slept with them, hurt and hoped with them. I can think of no greater compliment than to say you involved me.

I must add a thing about your wonderful economy, a line of words here and there that simply drove my eyes away to dwell on the vistas of the mind that so little had managed to open up to them (P. 119—It had never entered his mind that he himself was all the proof and hope he needed. P. 217—"It takes a long time for the dead to die." P. 258—And when the nurse noticed her the smile was still there. P. 413—"Okay, kid. Any time you're ready."). And I must take my hat off to you for a superb and memorable figure of speech (P. 52—He grabbed Dubik's wrist . . . and felt the skin slide . . . like a wet label on a bottle.).

In short, my gratitude for a very fine book.

Sincerely,

75. To Ruth Shapiro

(After being blacklisted and before having to surrender their passports, John and Maggie embarked for Europe, hoping in England to place The Land That Touches Mine *and* A Man Without Shoes *with an English publishing house and, according to Jack Mearns, to find Maggie screenwriting work.)*

May 25, 1952

Dear Ruth:

Well, we're back from Northern England, have been since Monday evening, and after a day at the Berkeley, we managed, with considerable effort, to locate another hotel. London's jam-packed (first with the British Industries Fair, then with the National Flower Show crowd, and now with the Derby maniacs), and I had to try twenty hotels before grabbing off a room without bath here at Brown's. Once in, we managed to worm a switch, after three days, to a room with a bath, and we expect to remain until around June 1st or 2nd, when we'll pull out for Paris—that is, if we can change our crossing date from June 10th. It'll be pretty hard, because the earlier date is the important Whitsuntide holiday, another of those things that come along to make European living difficult. You have to 'book' for everything, you know—railway travel, ship travel (including cross-channel sailings), hotels, movies, plays, and busy dining-rooms. If you don't, you stay out or off, whichever the case may be. It must be tough to live like that, always queueing up or booking or some kind of planning, and not only for tomorrow or next week but also for next month and next fall! The Automobile Association tells us that some cross-channel sailings, for instance, are full now for October!

Regarding the book, I came back to London to find two turndowns, one from Rupert Hart-Davis and the other from Chatto &

Windus, and within two days a third came in from Collins Publishers, but that one was with a difference, so much so that I'll quote:

> "We have had in a report about your book, enclosed herewith, called 'A Man Without Shoes.' It recognizes the great poetic qualities of the book and says much of the beauty of the writing and of the whole conception. Unfortunately, it is not really the sort of novel in which we, as publishers, specialize. In a word, it is a little too esoteric and our market is, and always has been, the general reader. We must, therefore, with great regret turn down your book but I would like to say that we do so while recognizing the great merit it has. I happen to know that Mr. John Guest, who is Literary Advisor to Longmans Green & Co., would be most interested to see your book if you care to call on him. His standards from the literary angle are higher than ours, and I think he would be particularly interested in 'A Man without Shoes.'
>
> Yours Sincerely,
> Robin Denniston"

Maggie and I interpreted the note to mean that Denniston had taken the liberty of mentioning the book to Guest, and that Guest invited an advance from me. I've written asking for an appointment, and I should have a result tomorrow. Naturally, we both hope it all leads to something, but conditions are none too favorable here, a shade or two better than New York, but not much more, so we pin nothing on kind words. In fact, we're not even delaying our sojourn on the Continent for what may turn up with publishers. We'll be reachable in Paris, and if something important comes up, I can easily grab the Golden Arrow and be here in six or seven hours. And finally, I might add that I've yet to hear from Heinemann and Jonathan Cape, each of whom still has a book. If I've had no word by the end of the week, and we're setting out for Paris, I'll write to tell them where to get hold of me.

It occurs to me that in my last letter, written from the Lake Country, I failed to mention that two or three days after bumping into Brounoff, I got a phone-call from—Nat Cohen! He'd bumped into Brounoff too, and he was eager to have dinner with all four of us. We got together that night at Prunier's—Nat and his wife, George and Bess, and the two of us, and we had a rather pleasant time. Nat was off to Birmingham in the a.m. (to look over the Fair up there), and in the evening Brounoff and Bess and us two had dinner again, this time at Cunningham's, a fish place. Also, it's more than likely we'll all six cross paths in Paris, for both couples wind up their European stay there around the middle of June. I'll keep you posted.

The way we see it, we'll put in some six or seven weeks, after this week, on the Continent, either in France or Switzerland, and sail for home on the 23rd of July, making the trip on the French Line's maiden the 'Flandre,' a brand spanking new 20,000 tonner. It promises a lot of fun, for without doubt the Line will knock itself out to get a good press from the first crossers. That'd get us to NY with the MG about the first of August, and starting for the coast at once, which we intend to do, we ought to be back in California about the 15th, making a grand total of four months away. Naturally the plans are subject to change, but unless I make a ten-strike with a publisher, we'll stick to the above.

Maggie, reading this over my shoulder, reminds me to mention that all those gifts you and Pop gave us before we left, have come in very handy. The Hangers are in constant use, even here at hotels; the diary, of course, is faithfully kept each day; and the traveling kit goes with us where we go in the car, and we always eat lunch along the road after provisioning at some village.

Write us Am. Exp. Co. London till further notice; we'll have the stuff forwarded. Keep well, and much love from the old bag and the old wag.

Affectionately,

76. To Philip D. Shapiro

(One of Sanford's projects while in Europe at this time was trying to get A Man Without Shoes *published. This is the book, which a year earlier he had printed at his own expense by the Plantin Press in Los Angeles, he refers to in this letter as being of interest to Jonathan Cape as "unbound sheets.")*

June 22nd, 1952

Dear Governor:

A word from the most beautiful country in all Europe, bar none, and from a tiny town, Klosters by name, that would make almost anything on earth take a back seat. Till now, we'd thought the Lake Country of England just about par for the course, but this is all that was and ten thousand feet higher all around, with snow everywhere, pines, roaring streams, lovely houses, excellent food (best in Europe, we think), and a friendly atmosphere. Thank goodness we saved Switzerland for after England; if it had been the other way 'round, we'd have come away with a kind of sour taste.

Longmans turned the book down after all (heard about it a few days after we left Paris), but last Wednesday, the day before we left, I called Jonathan Cape on the telephone to find out what was going on, and he floored me by offering to print the book if I could supply him with unbound sheets, so that he could rip the title-page out and tip in his own. Of course, I was in no position to do that, having only 1,800 copies of a bound book made to sell at $10 a copy and costing almost $4, so that even if Cape wanted to take those over, the price would've been prohibitive. I countered with a proposal that he seriously consider getting out a very small fresh edition for the English trade, just to see how it would go, and that in order to help him cut costs, I'd waive all advances and royalties on that edition. He said there were many factors to think about, but that he'd weigh the matter, and he gave me the satisfaction of emphasizing that he heartily approved AMWS and would like to see it under his imprint. As he put it, he approved the book and thought it was real literature; his only doubt was whether a book so specially American would catch on with English readers. I'm to hear from him in a few days—or will by the time I get back to Paris. Don't get your hopes up, though; the situation is a tough one to lick because of the fact that I can't deliver what he wants, those unbound sheets.

Got a letter from Ann Peppers saying that her husband Tom had just undergone an operation for the removal of one lung, but that he was progressing nicely. Probably will be a pretty sick man, though, and we've written to say how sorry we are, because we always liked him.

Enclosing three pictures. The closeup of me was taken in the Bois de Boulogne. The other one of me was taken in the garden of an inn at Provins, France, in the heart of the medieval country; the inn itself was built in 1320. The third picture was taken from our room here at Klosters, Switzerland.

Mag joins me in love to you and Ruth.

Affectionately, as always,

77. To Philip D. Shapiro

July 18th, 1952

Dear Governor:

Well, this letter has the first good news I've been able to write in a long, long time: Jonathan Cape has accepted "The Land That Touches Mine."

Here's the full story. He'd been in possession of "A Man Without Shoes" since the week we landed in England, along about the first of May. The book had been passed to him by his managing-editor, with the recommendation that it be accepted, but Cape took till ten days ago, the week we returned to Paris from Switzerland, to make up his mind to reject it. It was a close thing, though, since at one stage of his thinking, he actually offered to take over a certain number of unbound copies, if I had them, and try the book out on English reviewers. In his rejecting letter, awaiting us on our return to Paris, he stated he'd always be willing to look at anything else I might submit, and I replied, although with a heavy heart, that I had an unpublished manuscript which I wasn't ready to show him, and that he'd see it when I was satisfied with it. And that was how matters stood for some days, with Mag and I counting all as lost in the way of European publication as well as American. But just one week ago, Mag said she felt like reading the new book, so I dragged it out of the bottom of one of the trunks, and we crossed the street to the Tuileries Gardens, and she got to work. She made no comment till she finished the last page, some three hours later, and then she looked up at me and said, "If you don't show this to Cape right now, you're crazy. It's a good novel, and if he doesn't like it now, he won't after another revision. Mail it to London today." But I didn't; instead, I read it myself that night, from page one to the end. In the morning, I called Cape and told him I was going to be in London over the weekend, and would he see me? He said certainly, my boy (what he always calls me), and on Sunday last I took the Golden Arrow, the Paris-Calais-Dover-London flyer, getting there in the early evening. I stayed at Brown's again (Mag remained here at the Lotti), and on Monday, I had an hour and a half with Cape and his editor. By Tuesday morning, the editor had finished the book and sent it on to Cape with another recommendation to accept, and Cape got to work himself. There was no verdict by Thursday morning (yesterday), so I grabbed a plane—hell, I couldn't sit a train in the frame of mind I was wearing—and returned to Paris, with the understanding that I was to call Cape this afternoon for the news. I got him on the wire only a couple of hours ago, and when he began talking to me in French and kidding at that, I had the feeling I was in—and, sure enough, he finally broke it to me that he was taking the book, with "A Man Without Shoes" waiting on the results.

Mag and I celebrated by having dinner at the best restaurant in Paris, the Tour d'Argent, and a half-bottle of Chateau Margaux 1928, at five bucks the half-bottle. It was a twenty-buck meal, but you never saw two people enjoy squandering dough like us tonight. And, we think, with good reason. You know, those words of Cape's this evening were the first words of acceptance I've heard in seven years, ever since Taylor of Reynal took my half-done "AMWS", only to drop me two years later.

Now, in return for having told you the whole story, I want you to do me this great favor. Read this letter to Ruth and then forget the whole matter without another word. You may indicate to Pearl that the book was accepted, but you don't know any details, particularly the publisher's name, and you're not to discuss it any further. As for Ruth, she is to communicate the news to NO ONE! In explanation, I simply want nobody to know, that's all. There's too much loose talk, and I don't want anybody to queer this deal, however, inadvertently. This is of the utmost importance, and you're smart enough to know what I'm referring to. I was going to phone you the good news, but I felt I couldn't make all this clear in a short call. Remember, I'm counting on you and Ruth, and you might even suggest to Pearl that there's many a ship, etc., and that she'd serve us best by saying nothing too.

I wrote a note to Tootsie expressing our sorrow over Aunt Minnie (your letter with the news came while I was in London.)

We're immensely pleased with Messy's coming back to form and look to a win or two from the grand old mare. Every time she's in the money, we get a quarter of her share, and already it comes to about a grand this year, without any expenses. Glad you and Ruth won a neat bet.

Don't write to us here any more. We leave Paris on Tuesday (this is Friday) and sail on Wednesday from LeHavre. I intend to phone you on our arrival at New York, where we'll remain for a couple of days. Letters to the St. Regis (55th & 5th) will reach us if they arrive there not later than August 1st, on which day we expect to start for the coast in the MG. Ask the hotel to hold.

Remember, no talk about the book—and keep well, and think cheerfully now and then of your devoted son and his converted bagel.

With all affection,

78. To Philip D. Shapiro

23 July 1952

Dear Governor:

In my final letter from Paris, I broke the news that Jonathan Cape has taken "The Land That Touches Mine." In case that went astray, I'll add that his acceptance came by phone just about two days before we quit the Lotti to drive to Le Havre. Both Maggie and I had given up all hope, despite the fact that I'd left the book with Cape on my departure from London, and that Cape's editor had recommended publication. It just didn't seem possible for 1952 to be our year.

Now for more good news. I received the following telegram the night before we left Paris:

> "Have heard some exciting news about your new novel for Jonathan Cape, and since I was one of the editors who reluctantly declined 'A Man Without Shoes,' I hope very much that Doubleday can have a chance at the new book. Jonathan tells me you are sailing for America this week, hence I have asked John Sargent of our New York office to contact you at the St. Regis. I hope you will be willing to give him a look at the manuscript. Regards, Lee Barker."

For your entertainment, let me add that Lee Barker is the President of Doubleday in the States, and at present traveling in Europe. It's easy to see what happened. Cape and Barker must've been together on Monday, the 21st, and Cape, who knows the trouble I've had getting American publication (29 rejections on AMWS, etc.), probably twitted Barker, asking him what the hell was going on, that American writers had to travel to England to get publication. Barker, of course, knew who I was—in fact, it's a joke that he gives as a qualification for getting a crack at the new book that he turned down (reluctantly!) the old—and now he's on my tail. Hoho! So maybe the tide's turning. At any rate, I've written to Cape, telling him about the feeler and asking if I still have the American rights to dispose of. He's to answer by mail to the St. Regis, so I'll know how to act with John Sargent. If you like, you can write to me there, telling us how you like this news. See that your letter gets to N.Y. before August 1st, that's all.

We've gotten some general news of the big quake, but no more, and we're wondering how our families and houses stood the shock. If you can give us any details, please do, first as to how the people we care about weathered the event, and next, if you have any dope, how the buildings, pool, etc., fared. Chet might know.

Want to get this off the Flander at Southampton for air mail, so won't say more now, except the ship's a beauty, lovely cabins, superb food, and so on.

Mag joins me in sending love to you and Ruth.

ONCE MORE, GOV: TELL NO ONE REPEAT NO ONE ABOUT THE BOOK DEALS, ONLY RUTH AND PEARL—AND EMPHASIZE TO THEM TO KEEP IT TO THEMSELVES!

As ever, with love,

79. To John Sargent

(John Sargent was the Doubleday editor assigned to bringing out Sanford's The Land That Touches Mine *in 1953.)*

Feb. 13, 1953

Dear John:

I stuck to the job—like a galley-slave, oddly enough—and just finished.

When you get the proofs, you'll find that I've made practically no author's changes (half a dozen, at the outside) and that I've acceded to your man's suggestions almost wholly—capitalization, decapitalization, spelling, etc.

Where the trouble will lie is in the matter of hyphenation and dehyphenation—and there, frankly, I've held the line with great tenacity. Of the nearly six hundred removals and/or elisions, I've restored my pattern in no fewer than five hundred places. What the recomposition will set you chaps back I've no idea, but you could've saved it all by asking in advance, and I'm sorry you didn't, because I hate to see even a single needless buck go into cost. I know you'll be sore at me for being insistent in this, but I'm equally sure you're fair enough to admit that the fault isn't mine.

As I said in my note yesterday, the matter of hyphenation (of all punctuation) is important. Aside from the words themselves, which don't always fall naturally into rhythms, punctuation is one of the rare ways you have to indicate a reading in prose. In poetry, you can get a good deal out of word-arrangement, but that's denied to you in prose, and you can well use something else. Beyond the reading, though, there's often the consideration of sense, and when you travel light, without hyphens, you sometimes lose that. Take a few examples from my own stuff:

Galley 4 : "You made a bell-sound that only you could

hear." Without the hyphen, you'd have an actual striking of an actual bell.

Galley 8 : "rag-head" This is a local name for a Hindu field-worker. Without the hyphen, you get nothing I know except a head made of rags.

Galley 18 : "punk-sticks of cattail" Without the hyphen, punk relates only to sticks, and you get sticks that're punky, instead of cattail that looks like sticks of punk.

Galley 18 : "steering-wheel" Without the hyphen, you get a wheel that's steering, not a wheel for steering.

Enough of that shit, though: I'm not up a stump, and I'm not trying to give you or anyone an English-lesson. I've set down enough to show you what's on my crazy little writer's mind—I must be crazy; otherwise I'd be at the furlong-pole hollering home an 8-1 shot instead of fucking around with hyphens, no less!

Of course, if you're all out of hyphens, that's another matter. Say so, and I'll send you a case. They're grown here, you know. Man name of Hyman Phen. . . .

Let's hear from you—I don't mean that roar you just let out; I heard that. I mean a nice cheerful little billet-doux, saying, Sanford, you can have your way. I'll be sending you the galleys after one more run-through. Maybe I missed sticking back some hyphens.

As Ever,

80. To John Sargent

(The Bradbury mentioned in this next letter is Walter Bradbury, managing-editor at Doubleday at this time. Every Island Fled Away *would not be published until 1964, by Norton & Co. deKay is either another Doubleday editor or an editor at Jonathan Cape, the English publishers of* The Land That Touches Mine.*)*

2.27.53

John:

You sounded as rascally as ever on the phone the other day, a good way to be—the world needs more catamounts, God damn it, and fewer mice. This deKay and I seem to be getting along, which is a pissen wonder, because I don't generally get very far with editors before they lie awake nights cooking up ways of sending me to my maker (General Motors, man, and what's good for me is good for you).

I write to remind you of the change I want in the dedication (I'd like it to read: This book is for my mother). Confirm it back to me, will you, so I'll have it off my mind.

Been looking for a call from Bradbury, but so far nothing. I think he got lost.

Took the wrong train out of Chicago and wound up in Skagway. Who slaves for Doubleday up there, for Christ's sake? Only inhabitants are old sourdoughs and Chilkoot Indians. Not a book in a tribe.

Well, back to work on a book called "Every Island Fled Away"—to be referred to henceforth as EIFA.

As Ever,

81. To John Sargent

March 2, 1953

John:

Had a call from Mr. Bradbury (it's Brad and John at his request, suh) and met him at his hotel for a couple-hour meet. From where I sat (on my ass), it looked good. What he thought you'll find out when he gets back to town and says, "Where's that fucker's contract?"

The main course was what comes after TLTTM, and I was dee (teeth-showing) lighted to learn that Doubleday is singleminded about A Man Without Shoes. Do that book next, pal, and you can have my awl (and, man, that's a real gone pun!).

In England, they have nice publishers. Got a letter from Michael Howard (Cape) today asking (said asking) what kind of jacket do I want. Copy to Barker.

Tell me this, kid, how you been feeling?

Yours,

82. To Walter Bradbury, Esq.

(Marguerite Roberts had been on the HUAC and Hollywood blacklists for approximately two years at this time. Unable to continue her career as a screenwriter, she turned her attention to turning The Land That Touches Mine *into a screenplay titled* The Hero Suit.*)*

March 20, 1953

Dear Mr. Bradbury:

When you were here a couple of weeks ago, I spoke of the dramatization that my wife was making of THE LAND THAT TOUCHES MINE. It turns out that the work is moving ahead a bit more rapidly than I expected, so much so that another few weeks will see the finished version.

We've been anticipating that time by discussing the best way to proceed, and while we have contacts of our own and could doubtless get sympathetic readings, we feel that in view of our community of interest with Doubleday, it might be better to follow your suggestion and let the Company effect the connection. What I suggest, therefore, is that as soon as the novel comes off the press—now, if the book is ready—a few copies be placed with such producers as you may have in mind. If any of these shows a belief in the stage-possibilities of the book, you'll be in a position to reveal that a dramatization of it is on the way; you might, in fact, even have it in your possession at the moment.

The above, as I say, is a suggestion, and of course you're at liberty to proceed otherwise and as you think best. What I'm after with this is mainly to start the wheels turning.

A word about the merit of the dramatization. I've read two of the three acts revised, and I can only say I'm enormously pleased—and I'm far from a pushover. An astonishing job of staging the entire action in one room has been done, and my wife has written lines to loop the various scenes that I'd very much like to have thought of myself. In short, she has made a play that does more than just realize the novel; she has added to it. When you read it, I think you'll agree.

Please be good enough to let me have your views. Meanwhile, the best to you.

Sincerely,

83. To John Sargent

3.30.53

Dear John:

By now, you'll have gotten my comment on the jacket, which I liked a great deal. This is to say I've tried it out on a dozen people since, and all of them thought it most effective. Another score for Sargent, the man who can do no wrong.

Since your catalogue came out, I've had letters about Swedish serial rights; Scandanavian, French, German, and Italian book rights; and Chinese Wall rights.

What did you say in that catalogue? Send me one, will you?

Good about Bradbury and the dramatization. With Doubleday having a real money-interest in any play, it's only sense to let Doubleday crank the motor; the dramatic version'll do the rest, or I miss my guess.

Ask Miss Sylvester to ask you to write.

As ever,

84. To David Cape

May 16, 1953

Dear Mr. Cape:

I have your note, the first English review, and the royalty statement—for all of which, thanks.

The review seemed to me intelligent. It was based on the book written, not on what the reviewer would've had me write if he stood with a pistol at my head. What we so often get over on this side is the reviewer's opinions, and to hell with what the writer had to say. As for Mr. Paul's appraisal ("these two novels may well have been the best to have appeared so far this year."), innate American modesty prevents me from commentary. Let's hope the reviews to come are but half as good.

Your royalty statement shows 650 copies to have been sold up to publication. While that figure may be disappointing to you, it's quite the reverse to me. After all, I'm absolutely unknown even in my own country. I could go further: I'm not even known to some members of my family! 650 copies till now suits me. For the future, it all depends on the book itself, and may it catch on.

I've had no word from Doubleday for a couple of weeks, anyhow. A few bookseller friends keep me posted, and they tell me one review has appeared so far, and that one excellent (they say). I haven't seen it.

Have you had any comment regarding the play?

With all good wishes.

Yours sincerely,

85. To Sid Russell

(Sid Russell of Russell and Volkening, Sanford's one-time New York agents. The review Sanford mentions of A Man Without Shoes *was published in the July, 1952 issue of* Masses & Mainstream, *page 58.)*

14 June 1956

Dear Sid Russell:

Your note chased me from Carmel through Hollywood to here, where I now live.

Sure I'd like A MAN WITHOUT SHOES more widely read, and I'd tick an ear at any reasonable suggestion. What you mean by my putting "Unnecessary obstacles" in the way is, I suppose, m-on-e-y. Let's mention it by name, Sid.

I have in storage about 1,700 copies. According to records I hate to look at, each copy cost me exactly $3.34 to make, and I'm in the hole for something over 5 g's on the venture. I could've done a lot better at a slot-machine.

Only one review appeared, in Masses & Mainstream, and it was written by Charles Humboldt. A good part of the review was favorable in regard to specific aims, but the whole of it missed the boat (I think), and it did me no good. I haven't looked at the review in some years, though, and possibly I'd have a different attitude toward it. Several other copies went to such periodicals as The Nation, The New Republic, etc., but if a review was written, I missed it. All the stack is bound, meaning that if I sent you 25 copies, I'd be out a hundred bucks in cash. I might consider it if we had a satisfactory deal, but merely on spec it's no go. So what I think you ought to do is make me a proposition, so that I know where I stand. I can't be shipping out copies for promotion and review before I have a publisher and a deal.

Your list is impressive, and I'd like to be a part of it. If this book of mine were still in manuscript, I'd string along with you and take my chances, but my position is vastly different, having a printed and bound book to put up.

So—what's the deal?

Best regards, as always.

Sincerely,

86. To Angus Cameron

(Angus Cameron was formerly an editor for Little, Brown when Sanford submitted The People From Heaven *and eventually joined The Liberty Book Club, where he was responsible for the re-publication of Sanford's* The People From Heaven.*)*

10 July 1957

Dear Angus:

Well, your letter certainly didn't give me much to go on, but it's worth another six cents to find out whether Liberty would help me if it could.

You say A MAN WITHOUT SHOES has done better than most progressive books even as things stand. If you think so, you're the first publisher I've ever known who was satisfied with a sale of 200. As a writer, I'm not at all satisfied, even if my book is no BROTHERS KARAMOZOV. It deserves better than that, and Liberty could help put it further in a way something like this.

Suppose Liberty got up a blurb and sent it out along with its monthly mailings, its bills, its circulars. If it were made part of the club's bulletin, it wouldn't cost you a cent to announce the book to your entire list of subscribers. I tried to sell it for $10, as you know, and a very foolish price it was, as I know, but this time it could be offered at, say, $4.95 direct from the author. In return for circularization, I'd send you $1.50 for each copy sold, in addition to which I'd stand the cost of shipping and the sales tax. You'd be out nothing, and by the time I was through, I'd be getting less than the actual cost of the book, which was $3.34 per copy.

There's a deal you couldn't possibly lose on, and if you're worried about losing face by sort of sponsoring the book, I can supply you with quotes from the blurb from letters written to me by Dalton Trumbo and Al Maltz which might serve to quell your qualms. I wouldn't expect you to take my word about the book.

What do you say?

Sincerely,

87. To Jim Light

Sunday, 18 June 1961

Dear Jim Light:

Your book on Pep West came a weekend ago, but my wife got hold of it first and took it away to Hollywood. She brought it back this past Friday, and I read it through at a sitting.

I'd only be a faker if I criticized the literary side of your interpretation. I'd be pretending to know a lot more than I do about Symbolism, Dadaism, Surrealism, and most of the other movements that influenced Pep. They did not influence me, and I'm willing to set that down to a second-rate mind, a patchwork education, and uninspired taste. At any rate, it wasn't Pep's fault that his Paris-school lectures left me cold, and looking back, as your book made me do, I can only wonder why he spent so much time on a dope. I'm less than half-joking when I say that Pep ruined me. I met him too late in life, as Robert Cohn met W.H. Hudson; I could've been a dope and a crack lawyer, but I couldn't be a dope and write. I didn't know that at the time; I thought any number could play. Beyond my difficulty of ignorance, there's the fact that I knew Pep so long and in some areas so well that I find it nearly impossible to split the man and the books. I don't really read him, even today; I hear him. As one of my two prime teachers (George Brounoff was the other), he's just as alive for me now as he was at Viele Pond in the summer of '31. I have now, and I had then, an enormous respect for him as a writer, but I read your book for Pep, for Slabsides, for One-Punch Weinstein, for the guy who, to me, was always blank in hearts—

for the teacher who cared for the teaching so much more than the thought.

The personal picture your book gives of Pep is that of a man with about four teeth left from a set of thirty-two. The mayhem was not committed by you, of course, but by the people of mean spirit who refused you the facts. If they'd been free with their knowledge, they'd not thereby have become large in spirit; they'd only have been doing what decency required. I deplore the omissions because they made it impossible for you to choose from a mass of evidence, and as one of the few whose name appears often in your book, I feel a very great sense of responsibility. I tried to be honest, but here and there could I not have been honestly wrong? I'd hate to think that because others failed to speak, my limitations may have been lastingly imposed on a man I deeply admired, a man able and original in a way I do not hope to equal. It had never occurred to me that I'd ever be in a position to pronounce upon Pep West even as a person, and I earnestly hope I've done him no harm. Christ knows I never meant to.

I hope your book does well, friend, and I thank you for sending it to me. I prize it.

All good wishes to you.

Sincerely,

88. To George Brounoff

8 November 1962

Dear George:

First of all, Maggie and I rejoice in the knowledge that you aren't seriously ill. If that little heart flutter is all you have, you'll live to be a hundred—and in truth I hope you do.

But, George, dear old friend, you'll be a sad old man, I'm afraid.

Indeed, you're sad right now, and I'm as sorry for your soul's sickness as I was at your body's.

You're wrong. What we believed in in our youth was not an illusion. It was the realest thing we ever knew, and those that let it go for something else dropped the actuality for the shadow, and what they're left with is the image, not the grapes.

It was no illusion to believe in the perfectibility of man. Even the imperfect knew that once, and it was that knowledge, that faith, that the old wife-beater Dostoevsky took into that shabby little house with him in Piazza Pitti—and he came out with "The Idiot."

It is an illusion, though, to believe in the "impossibility of spiritual communication in this age," as you say. I don't care how many modern writers you can cite to support you, because they're all as wrong as you are. They've given up, let go of the grapes, and they've gone over (in their despair) to the side they should have stood against until the end. These matters get borne in on you in a city like Rome. You stand under the Sistine ceiling, as I did this morning, and you tell yourself (or the paint above you tells you) that when you lose faith, you lose hope, and when you lose hope, you die.

I'm not a religious man. I don't believe in God. But I do, I still do as I've long done, believe in man. You started me off in that belief, and it's a great grief to the pupil to find the teacher gone. I deeply wish you could find your way back some day.

* * *

We leave for New York from Naples on the Leonardo da Vinci on Nov. 21. I'll call you in town, if I may.

Love to you and Virginia from Maggie and

89. To Jim Light

17 June 63

Dear Jim:

Thanks for the note—and for requesting a review copy of "Every Island Fled Away." I've written to Norton about it, and you're on the list. Since the Fall catalogues are out or in the making, I don't think I'll get publication before the Spring of '64. Norton is arranging simultaneous publication in England with Jonathan Cape, so it's quite likely you'll see the book over there too—in Hatchett's window as you pass along Piccadilly (or is Hatchett's a restaurant?)

I'm interested in the De Forest book, but that one I want to buy (assuming it's about John William and not Lee). I got onto him twenty years ago, and I've got three of his books: "Miss Ravenel," "A Volunteer's Adventures," and "A Union Officer." A very real writer for the 1860s—or any other time. I put him with one other writer of the period, Rebecca Harding Davis, whose "Life in the Iron Hills" you're surely acquainted with. But only that one book; I tried others, and they're bad romances. Let me know what success you have with the book when you start submitting it. In fact, why not start with Norton? Send it to Eric Swenson (55 Fifth Ave., N.Y.C.) and say you're a friend of mine. That might help—and, again, it might kill you.

You must be quite a guy to get a Fulbright. My best congratulations—and my envy. No, I'll not be in England while you're there unless my wife, who is a screen-writer for Columbia Pictures, is sent there on an assignment. Right now, by the way, she's revising her script of an old and lousy novel of mine called "The Old Man's Place," which Columbia bought for her last year. First time that's ever happened, a studio buying a guy's book and assigning his wife to the script. All I can say is, I wish I had in the novel some of the ideas she's working into the script: it wouldn't've been a lousy novel.

I regret that you didn't reply to the unjustifiable criticism in the

Minnesota Quarterly. Nothing like that should be allowed to get by, never. Hit back always. In fact, God damn it, hit first!

Glad the West book will appear in paperback. I know an editor at McGraw-Hill, a man named of William Decker. He came damn close to taking my book a couple of months ago and only got stopped by the Brass—ordered to stop, to be exact. He's in the trade book dept., but if you think he can help you with the paperback, write to him and tell him too we're friends.

Keep in touch. It's good to hear from you. Meanwhile, the best.

Sincerely,

90. To Herb and Irene Ortman

14 Dec. 63

Dear Herb and Irene:

Thanks for the Christmas card. You were thoughtful, and you'll soon find out we were not: we don't send cards, even to those we love. But if we offer greetings of the season (Chanukah), here they are, two full portions. I'd've written much sooner, but to tell the truth the shots fired on November 22 are still ringing in my ears, and I'm still very deeply disturbed. Oddly enough, Kennedy wasn't my man—I'd written Stevenson in, only to find that after The Bay of Pigs, he was a pig himself, as far short of White House stature as I am. But even so, Kennedy never seemed to me a Jefferson, a Jackson, a Lincoln, a Wilson, an FDR, the five greats that stick out of the crowd. So why, Maggie and I have asked ourselves again and again, did Kennedy's death hit us so hard?

We can only conclude that, in this world that has shadows, he represented Everyman's deep desire. Concentrated in his person were all the favors fortune can rain down on a man—youth, riches, intelligence, looks, position, and a future—and I think, through him, we all enjoyed those favors in our dreams. We were all of us President. And when he was killed, a sense of mortality flooded over all of us. We knew that, great or small, we all would die, and therefore Kennedy's death was the enactment for all to see of The Great Tragedy. Hemingway once said that all stories, if continued long enough, end in death. When Kennedy ended, we knew that we'd end too, that that was the future of all.

That's the sobering thing, and I've been sober ever since.

I'll write again soon. Love to you both.

Affectionately,

91. To Patricia Neal

(This is one of many letters Sanford wrote to test the Oscar-winning actress's receptivity to taking the role of Eugenia in the film version of The Hero Suit, *written by Marguerite Roberts and based on Sanford's* The Land That Touches Mine. *The movie was never made.)*

9 March 1964

Dear Miss Neal:

I heard from Joe Losey four days ago. I'd been pressing him for a decision for weeks, and he finally wired from N.Y. that he'd read the script of *The Land That Touches Mine*—and liked it. I called him right away, thinking everything was falling nicely into place, but I learned that each of us had been counting on the other to supply the vital missing element: the production set-up. He was willing to direct the picture, he said, but he supposed I had an organization behind me panting with eagerness to start shelling out a million bucks. Green horn had met green horn, for I'd imagined the organization was in back of Joe.

We were both disappointed, of course, but even so I'm to hear from somebody called Robin Fox (agent? money-man?) as soon as he reaches Beverly Hills, which should be in a day or two. Not knowing this Fox, I got something moving through my wife's agents, and last Friday they put the Neal-Losey-Sanford-script package up to Mike Frankovitch at Columbia. There should be some reaction to the proposal shortly. (My wife, by the way, is the screenwriter Marguerite Roberts, and her contract lot is Columbia.).

Where to go and what to do if Columbia loves us not—I wish, Miss Neal, I knew. As I told you far back, I'm a writer—a novelist, really, despite my screenplay—and the ways of the world, especially the part that disburses money, fill me with dismay: no one has ever disbursed it in my direction. In view of your continuing interest in the script, I take the liberty of suggesting that if you know a producer who might be interested too, you put the venture before him. Be sure I'll do all I possibly can on this end—and be sure too that you're Eugenia until you say otherwise.

Brando has never seen the script.

As long as I have the least word from anyone, I'll send it along to you.

I send another copy of the script—with pleasure. I send you also, with my compliments, a copy of a novel of mine called A MAN WITHOUT SHOES. If you can bear to read it through, I hope you enjoy it.

Please be good enough to tell me whether you have any ideas for turning our plans into reality. I'm open to any suggestion.

Meanwhile, all good wishes to a person it would be a great satisfaction to know.

Sincerely,

P.S. In answer to your question, "Being a writer is not easy, is it?" may I say this—being a writer is impossible! I call myself a writer, but I'm really a horse's ass. Who else (or what else) would devote his life to screaming at the deaf and trying to show the way to the blind?

92. To Norman Rosten

14 February 1965

Dear Norman:

I caught you on Channel 2 this morning. Unfortunately, I also caught Uta Hagen and Robert Elston, and whatever they read they ruined. Better, but no world-beater at speaking poetry, were you, wherefore I'd've gotten far more if I read the poem myself. It's no easy thing to decipher a poem when it's coming at you with no regard for your best speed—slow. But if I had to put a value on what I heard, or think I heard, I'd say you're a clear-seeing and thus a lucid poet, Norman, but much too gentle and jocular to suit me. You're on the right side always, but always with regret and amusement instead of anger and an iron rod. You've got to beat the bastards to death—you can't joke, you can't laugh, you can't have pity, you can't be cool. You've got to kill—and it isn't in you. It wasn't in Ed Rolfe, either, and maybe the lack of it helped to kill him.

You asked.

Love to you and Hedda.

93. To Norman Rosten

(Rosten responded to the above-letter in a letter dated February 17, 1965 that if someone can't laugh and be kind, he isn't whole. He then cites a Brecht poem, includes his own poem "Harry" and tells Sanford, "It is a fantasy to think the iron rod will win; it is a totalitarian syndrome." Rosten then compares Sanford to the African-American poet and activist Leroi Jones (later Amira Baraka).)

24 Feb. 65

Norman

Who's Leroi Jones?

I couldn't agree with you less about joking, laughter, and pity. Those are the things that you have; they've got the guns. Worse, they're using them—and on you. The Lincolns never shoot; they just get shot. I think with John Brown: nits grow to be lice.

What do you mean—the iron rod won't win? Where you been looking, son? What else has ever won? Jesus? Now, come on, chile!

You and your stocada, your rinverso, your punctaversa—while Harry drops the bomb. En garde!

As for Brecht, we both know why he who wished to lay the foundations of kindness could not himself be kind. Because, if he'd been kind, he'd've been run down. You don't get kind watching injustice, not if you want to end it. And you can tell that to Honest Abe Miller, the silly cock! So it's the blooded Prussian who surrenders his ticket? What loose shit!

A kiss for Hedda. For you, the finger.

94. To Norman Rosten

(The book mentioned at the end of this letter is probably the manuscript of The $300 Man.*)*

11 January 1966

Dear Norman:

We've read THRIVE UPON THE ROCK, and for Maggie I'm to say that she liked many of the poems, and AUTOBIOGRAPHY best. An odd choice for a Nebraskan Christian. After all, I'm the one who was born in Harlem and shivered in the schules, trailing tephilin and dribbling rheum. Of course, I too like the poem—how could I not? It made me hear the old rebukes, the old warnings, it made me see the old dismay (Why couldn't you write on Sundays?), and it reminded me of the old estrangement. Who has not violated the generation that made him?

Still, I admired another poem even more, much more, the one to Hart Crane. I've read most of your poetry now, and I doubt that in comparable length you've ever beaten THE BRIDGE REVISITED.

The jazz harp (*), a lovely phrase.

Mouths as united as water, another.

But in FACE ON THE DAGUERREOTYPE, you may have the finest line in the book: *with your one-stringed instrument, our desperate glory.*

You're a very good poet, with the courage to choose clarity and the gifts to be clear with. I'm altogether at home with what you say and how you say it—and even more, how you feel it. Your imagery appeals to me, your mildness is a relief from myself (I'm mean), and I often think you say what I feel about my own daughter, which is remarkable, for I have no daughter.

Thanks for the book. I'll send you mine if it's ever published (it went to Norton yesterday).

Our love to you and Hedda.

95. To Norman Rosten

21 January 1966

Dear Norman:

Yesterday I answered all the questions you asked about me, but there was one obliquely asked about yourself, and I let that one go. THRIVE UPON THE ROCK was transitional, you said, and wondered out loud: what next?

Next, if you listen to a fool, you get tough. In my letter about the poems a couple of weeks back, I said something about your mildness being a relief from my own meanness. That wasn't pure praise of you any more than it was pure blame of me. A soft word does not turn away wrath; that's for the birds. Wrath turns away wrath, and until we realize it, the Lincolns will keep getting shot.

Rebel, man! Don't rebuke, don't chide, don't scorn—rebel!

I have one excuse for all that: you seemed to ask for a bearing. Wait, though; I have another. It matters what you do next.

Love to the Rostens.

As ever

96. To Eli Jaffe

16 June 1966

Dear Eli:

I have to write you about your book while my own is making the rounds with no takers. I get form rejections from fifty-year-old editorial cunt, I get printed no-dice cards, and twice the book came back with no word at all. I'm sick and sore, but I have to write about your book in a way that won't make you think I'm trying to get even with the world through you. If you prefer to think otherwise, go ahead. You may be right.

I know how important this book is to you—who the hell writes one that isn't—but I don't like Moccasin because, in all its length, there's no living person, no dramatic page, no line that was written, meaning wrought. The book, therefore, is only 185 pages of notes for a book still to be done.

You're a most intelligent man, Eli, and that's why I've always been stumped by your reckless run at creative writing. You'd never tackle any other thing in the world without plan and preparation, but you go at writing as if it were a stuck door—buck it hard enough and sooner or later it'll open. Well, sir, it won't. I told you the same thing years ago, after reading your book about the fund-raising racket, and either I didn't say it well enough, or you thought what I said was so much shit, but the fact is that what was true of that book is equally true of this: it's a string of statements. In your mind, they may add up to drama, but if they do, it's a drama you've staged nowhere else.

What undoes you is the assumption that what moves and has meaning for you must move and have meaning for all. As a writer, you could not possibly make a bigger mistake. You have been profoundly hurt by the death of your son, and though not a father myself, I think I can understand and even partly feel your grief. I can't feel all of it though, Eli, or even enough of it to convert it from a fact into a tragedy. When you use it in a book, the obligation is upon you to make the conversion. Lives are separate, and one of the few ways we have of joining them is with words, carefully chosen and correctly used. You were in too much of a hurry for that, so you simply made a statement—my son was killed because I gave him a bicycle—gambling that the fact, which so wracks you, would also wrack me. It could've done that only if the boy, who lived and died before your eyes, had been made to live and die before mine. You didn't accomplish that, you never even tried to, and I'm sorry.

The defect pervades the two main relationships in the book—the one between you and your wife and the one between you and the Iroquois. Not having been made to experience your sense of guilt in the former, I couldn't share your sense of expiation in the latter. There's more to it than that, though. I had the feeling that you had two separate themes all the way—a family breakup over the death of a son and, second, the objective cause of the Indians. One never seemed to lead inevitably to the other, and they knotted insecurely, like different thicknesses of rope. Force was used to bring these themes together, and when the force failed you, you fell back on coincidence—lo, Walter Sundown too lost a son!

Sundown of course is the best character in the book, but even he falls short of being animate. I learned little of him during his long silences, and I learned little of the Indian when he spoke. He spoke—and so did the other Iroquois—as if he were being interviewed. All of them seemed to be merely answering questions; they rarely got to talk as people have to do to stop being names and start being warm.

I think you'd've realized much of all this if you hadn't chosen to write in the first person. The form locked you inside the characters, and you seem never to have really seen or heard them. The third person would've let you get outside, and you'd've known you were putting in material that wasn't scoring or that simply didn't belong. Didn't it occur to you, for instance, that it's preposterous to set a Yiddish expression alongside an Iroquoian? Further, your

Depression and Oklahoma background have nothing to do with the Dam. And furthest, the scene with Sally in the Washington bedroom must've been written by an enemy of yours. Manhood, joystick—for God's sake, Eli, burn that embarrassing crap! This guy is in Washington on a job he hopes will purge him of guilt for the death of his son. If he forgets for fifteen minutes, let him not spend that time gloating over a stiff prick. Let him use it (without referring to it, damn it, as a joystick!) and then regret his having done even as you and I.

Somewhere in the book, you refer to a time in Hollywood when you were wandering around with a couple of unpublished novels. Those novels, plus others now, are still unpublished, and I wonder whether you've ever wondered why. They're all about serious matters, I'm sure, and they've all been personally experienced, even personally suffered—but they're still in manuscript. The reason is that you've never paid any attention to your craft. The man who keeps on experiencing twenty-four hours a day obviously has no time to spend on his craft; he's running, afraid to stop living long enough to reduce his life to language. A man has to miss something in order to acquire something else: it becomes a question of which something is more valuable to him. Most writers believe it's better to stop from time to time and write down what they've learned than to keep on endlessly learning. You've elected to let the craft go, and your lack of it speaks louder than anything else on any page. Your great desire is to be a writer, but you've never taken writing seriously; you're a surgeon who never bothered to study anatomy.

What was I to do, Eli? Lie to you? Faint-praise you? Refuse to read you at all? I don't think so. I think you came to a long-time friend for what the friend believed to be the truth. As I see it, what I've said is the truth. There are other ways of seeing it, though, and from first to last I could be wrong. I hope so. I hope you prove me to be less a critic than a foolish and disappointed old man. You'll never prove, though, that I'm not your friend.

Affectionately,

97. To Eli Jaffe

28 June 1966

Dear Eli:

Your letter pleased me. You please me. I simply couldn't say anything different about MOCCASIN, I couldn't even say the same thing in another way, as Maggie urged me to do—I couldn't only say what I said and take the chance that you wouldn't turn out to be a pissant. You didn't, and I'm glad.

You say I wrote to you as one of God's angry men. Maybe, but when you rewrite MOCCASIN, you be even angrier. There's nothing in this soft touch that some writers use, only more Lincolns to be shot, only more Vanzettis to wind up with 2,000 volts through the balls. The Indian (and the man who elects to write of him) ought to be angrier than Moses down off Sinai. We took the Indian's world away and gave him smog, syphilis, and shoddy. He knows it, and you better learn to know how he feels about it. If he's satisfied, or even cooperative, he ain't no Indian. He's got to feel as if it might still be a good idea to drive us white shits back into the sea.

Good luck, kid, and call on me anytime. I'm always good for a bum steer.

As ever,

98. To Eli Jaffe

3 Sept 67

Dear Eli:

Somehow the idea has gotten around that I'm sore about your borrowing the galleys of THE $300 MAN from Norman. I'm not sore at anybody, but if I were, I'd be sore at Norman for letting you have them.

Your "murmurings of discontent with the book," as you put it, are something else, and while I'm still not sore, I can't fathom your persistent foot-dragging. I'm slightly prejudiced in my favor, but the book is as good a one as you're likely to see all year, and I'm impatient with such reservations as the charge that the characters all talk like Sanford. That's one of those loosely-thought condemnations that don't amount to a damn when you pick them apart or ask what they mean. All characters written by anybody talk alike, and if they don't, then more than one man wrote the book. Who should they talk like, if not the man who made them? Would you have the writer be so careful to differentiate that he made one character an Uncle Remus, another an Indian with an Ugh and a How, and also dragged in some vaudeville kike—just to make sure nobody would say they all spoke alike? Your quibble is bullshit, Eli, and in one of your mellower moments you might admit it. Another charge—not necessarily made by you—is that something or other doesn't "come off." Mister, what comes off is a cock in heat, not a book, and I groan when I hear or see the thoughtless phrase. A writer goes to unbelievable lengths to be exact—and some obtuse chump will be sure to tell him the work didn't come off! Well, enough of that.

Sorry about Mickey Uris. We were never close friends, but I knew him well enough to be sure he was on the right side, which is the left, and if there's a heaven, which I doubt, he'll be there. And he'll be on the left side of heaven, which I don't doubt at all.

Mag joins me in sending you the best.

Affectionately,

99. To Herb and Irene Ortman

(The movie mentioned in this letter to be directed by Henry Hathaway is 5 Card Stud. *The RPL mentioned in the letter's last line refers to Ortman and Sanford's fellow college buddy Robert Lord.)*

13 September 1967

Dear Irene and Herb

We haven't heard from you since your letter from The Netherlands in May. We answered through Irene's sister in N Y, but we have no way of knowing whether she sent the message on. You had us upset for a while, you know, but we finally realized that you'd've written again if things hadn't improved, so we figured that your trip had only been interrupted briefly.

You'll want to know how matters stand with us, and I'm happy to tell you that Maggie has had a very good year, her best since coming back to pictures in '60. She finished the job for Wallis a couple of months ago, and he was so pleased with it that he offered her another assignment, doing the screenplay on Neil Simon's "The Star Spangled Girl." She read the play, but didn't care for its one-joke story too much, and then Wallis asked her to write the pilot for a TV series he means to do with his wife, Martha Hyer, in the lead. That's still pending. Meanwhile, Maggie's doing another screenplay, this one for an outfit called National General, owned by Fox West Coast Theatres. Wallis called her the other day to ask her to give him a few weeks of rewrites, and she's arranging it with her employer. Wallis told her he'd signed Henry Hathaway to direct her script, and Dean Martin and Robert Mitchum for the two male leads. So—she's doing well, and I couldn't be happier if it were happening to me.

Of course, it isn't happening to me. THE $300 MAN has been out for about six weeks, and the reviews that count have gone against me. The N Y Times and the Chicago Tribune gave the book a mean pasting, and their power outweighs all the rest put together. Everywhere else, the reviews have been excellent, from small town to first-class city, but without the Times, you've only written another unsuccessful book. Here are some quotes, the kind I try in vain to get warm on:

> LOS ANGELES HERALD-EXAMINER—"Sanford, a master of word imagery, has been called one of the most important of American writers. THE $300 MAN would justify that reputation if he wrote nothing else."
>
> ST LOUIS GLOBE-DEMOCRAT—"His other novels charmed many of the critics, but the book-buying public seems never to have gotten the word. The author should make it this time."
>
> PITTSBURGH POST-GAZETTE—"Here is a novel that gives joy to the heart of a writing craftsman. All through this novel, the writing is superb; if only other authors could learn to be so crisp, so sparkling with their prose, so imaginative. Here is a rich artist at work."
>
> KANSAS CITY STAR—"Reading THE $300 MAN, you soon understand why Sanford's work has been so highly evaluated. He is that rare sort of novelist capable of creating and sustaining such an intensity of emotion in the working out of the relations of his characters that while you are reading about them, they become the only people alive in the world."

DENVER ROCKY MOUNTAIN NEWS—"Using a basic theme of literature, man's inhumanity to man, Sanford has written a fast-reading and interesting novel. It has deep philosophical connotations."

SACRAMENTO BEE—"John Sanford writes with power, feeling, and depth; he writes with understanding and with truth; and he writes about facets of character which most of us would prefer to ignore."

FORT WORTH STAR-TELEGRAM—"Sanford's new novel, THE $300 MAN, is worthy of high praise. His style is lyrical, yet off-beat. It has a discipline, an authority that might win the praise of critics and awaken appreciative envy in other writers."

SANTA BARBARA NEWS-PRESS—"This novel is brutal, yet it is poetic. It is as well written as any novel you've ever read."

NASHVILLE BANNER—"THE $300 MAN is one of the finest novels written anywhere in the last 25 years."

SATURDAY REVIEW SYNDICATE—"John Sanford is possibly the best unknown novelist in the country."

SAN FRANCISCO CHRONICLE—"John Sanford is one of those dedicated writers who refuse to accept failure in the marketplace. THE $300 MAN may remind you of Robinson Jeffers' rock-ribbed poems."

> BRIDGEPORT POST—"John Sanford ranks with the very best of contemporary American novelists."
>
> HOLLYWOOD DAILY NEWS—"Sanford writes in sharp focus, with a penetrating understanding of human nature. His skill with words to express his ironic message is biting satire at its best, for he has done it all with the simplicity of artistry."
>
> WASHINGTON D C STAR—"A book far above average."
>
> NATIONAL GUARDIAN—"Poets are the glory of English, and Sanford, writing stories and histories in prose, is one of our best poets, from Melville and Whitman and Twain to Jack London, Nathanael West, and the John Steinbeck of THE GRAPES OF WRATH. John Sanford is the best American poet we have writing today. He has his own work to do, and it is not much like anyone else's work, and he does it superbly. . . ."

A great fire, you may think, but to me it's only a picture of fire, and it fails to heat the room. Some of the biggest cities in the country are with me, and some of the biggest are still to be heard from (Philadelphia, Detroit, New Orleans, Atlanta, Boston, Cleveland, Cincinnati, Baltimore, Buffalo, Miami, Portland, Seattle, Birmingham, Houston, Oklahoma City, Omaha, Louisville, Milwaukee, Minneapolis, etc)—but nothing counts in this profession if the N Y Establishment is against you.

As I say, though, Maggie does well, and I rejoice.

My Dad, knock wood, now in his 90th year, is enjoying himself within the limitations (as he puts it) of his twenty-odd ailments great and small. His wit is a marvel, his good cheer too, and I love to be with him. His wife was away for four days just before Labor Day, and I went to stay with him and had a grand time of it. He likes me quite a bit, I've discovered; he even thinks I'm a good son. I deny the allegation and defy the alligator.

We'd very much like to know what your plans are. If you find a moment, a rainy fall afternoon in London, drop us a line and tell us all about it. We haven't forgotten that your furniture is stored in California. You'll find, if you try to sneak it out of the state, that we've slapped a lien on it.

Maggie joins me in sending love to both of you, along with the hope that we may see you very soon. Keep well.

Affectionately,

No word from RPL since a birthday note last May.

100. To Naomi and Jesse Greenstein

(Jay Martin is the author of a biography of Nathanael West. The letters mentioned herein are included earlier in this collection. See letters number 2 and 34. The previous letter from the Greensteins must have included the originals as they now reside in the Boston University archive.)

13 November 1966

Dear Nonie and Jesse:

The two letters you sent me, like the two days with Jay Martin, were harrowing reminders of the past. You say you wish you were younger; I'm glad I'm not. I went through this thing once, and once is enough. I recall that on a long-ago day, a cab-driver observed to me like so: "Life is a beggarly game." He hadn't gone to Harvard, nor even to Fordham Law, but I often think he knew whereof he spoke.

The letter about Pep, which you think beautiful, is not really beautiful at all. As I read it, it's more about me and my regrets than about Pep and his work. My calling him "a respectable writer just beginning to grow" is praise so faint that it must've been meant to damn.

The letter from England, dated ten years earlier, was written on stationery come by quite honestly: a cousin was staying at the hotel, and I was her guest and therefore lawfully on the premises. Did you note that I spelled it "honours"? That, at least, was illegally obtained. As to having been turned off by both Eliot and Joyce on the same day, some sort of record must've been set there. Christ held the previous record: Thrice denied before cockcrow by Peter.

Next time we're together, and may it be soon, we'll talk of the séances with Martin; there's much to say.

Maggie and I send love to you two, whom we love much.

Affectionately,

101. To Russell Ames

(The content of this letter concerns a review Ames had written of Sanford's The $300 Man.*)*

2 Apr 67

Dear Russell

In your letter of 28 Mch, you said my editing of your review was okay except for "one lonely sentence I'd leave out." I studied the review as edited, and my guess is that this is the lonely sentence: My good liberal friends don't like Sanford's dramas.

I think your good liberal friends are pretty much my good liberal friends, and I say fuck our good liberal friends! They were, for the most part, shits when they became liberals, and as good liberals, they'll still be shits when they die. I fancy you've gotten very much the same kind of reaming from them as I have, and I respect them these days about as much as I do a pinch of owl-puke. My dear wife took a nine-year blacklisting in their behalf, and their reward was to suspect that she'd done the dirty to get off it.

I won't ask who your good liberal friends are. I never want to hear their names again. I'm a good hater.

Russ, once again, I hardly know how to thank you for your great generosity to me and my work. It's unprecedented in my experience, and I'll never forget it. I hope you and Jean get everything out of Spain you're going there for (avoid the black patent leather!), and of course I mean to write to you while you're there. I'll try to follow your itinerary, but just to be safe, keep me informed from time to time, even if only with a card with your address.

Here's the latest couple of reviews that've come my way. I seem to do well with the teaching profession. I'll send more as I get them.

Meanwhile, much love to you and Jean from me and Maggie.

Affectionately,

102. To Norman Rosten

7 Apr 67

Dear Norm

Oh, this Mailer!

I'm in the drugstore this p.m., and I go over to take a look at the good things on the bookrack. I pick up a little gem called "Welcome to Hard Times" because I dimly remember the name of the author, some bard name of Ed Doctorow (Dial Press?). Anyway, a glance at page 1 reveals that I'm holding in my hands 170 pages of garbage, and I'm about to stick it back when my little old eye lights on a blurb. So help me, here's how it reads:

"... A superb novel. ..."

Norman Mailer.

I hasten to tell you that if he's getting up a piece about "The $300 Man," he can quit right now. He's naked, and he's dead.

Mag joins me, etc.

103. To The Editors, *The National Guardian*

12 August 1967

Dear Sirs

Four months ago, Russell Ames wrote a review of my new novel THE $300 MAN, for the Guardian. Knowing it to be overlong, he asked me to cut it for him. I did so, taking care to submit my version to him; he approved it fully. When the cut version reached Miss Brooks, however, she cut it still further—with a cleaver. She turned the best review I ever had into a bloodless statement of the story. When she sent me a proof, I kicked, asking that she run the version endorsed by Ames.

So far, The Guardian has run nothing at all, and it's plain by now that you intend to give the book a pass.

I want you people to know that I'm God damn sore about that kind of treatment. It hardly seems better than the treatment writers received from the House Committee. My wife and I got ten years on the blacklist from that quarter, and now, for Christ's sake, I'm on your blacklist of the left!

Cancel my subscription at once, and to hell with you all.

Yours, etc.,

104. To Cedric Belfrage

(Belfrage was another co-editor of The Clipper *with Sanford.)*

15 September 1967

Dear Cedric

Since a NYTimes review either makes or breaks a book, of course THE $300 MAN is now broken—Humpty Dumpty broken. All the good notices the book got elsewhere won't put it together again: one New York beats fifty from the sticks.

Your furious letter did much to kill the pain. Only a very just and warmhearted man would've troubled himself to write it. I might say it was one of but two such (the other was from Norman Rosten), and I'll owe you both love as long as I live.

I learned today from my publisher that C.D. B. Bryan, the Times reviewer, is a son of John O'Hara. At first, that seemed to explain a great deal, but after a while, I found that it really explained nothing. Maggie and I send our gratitude and love to you and Mary. Yes, we must meet again—for that abrazo—before the sun goes down.

Affectionately,

105. To Norman Rosten

19 Sept 67

There once was a gentle bard named Norman
Who at an awful review got sore, man,
So he drew out his quill
And used it to kill
But lawful, like a good guy, a law man.

...... John Done....
(Done John)

Normie!

You're about as good a guy as I ever met in my life. I wish I were halfway up to your level. Again, thanks.

Dumb John

106. To Herb and Irene Ortman

(The Wallis script and "John Wayne commitment" Sanford mentions here refer to Marguerite Roberts' screenplay for True Grit, *released in 1969. The book Sanford mentions writing, the "little history-book," is probably what would eventually become* A More Goodly Country, *published by Horizon Press in 1975.)*

29 May 1968

Dear Herb and Irene

Thanks for your long letter from Munich and Vienna. I'm glad my pair finally caught up with you, though the duplication of news must've been boring. The Governor at 90 was marvelous. We threw him a dinner-party for eight at the Beverly Hills Brown Derby, where a couple of brandies down his hatch increased the size of the party to 150, all the rest of the people in the place. They enjoyed him as much as we did. Afterward the management somehow caught on early and served him up a cake, we went to Ruthie's apartment, where, guess what?, she too served up a cake. To cap it all, he handed me a birthday card—me on his birthday!—and on it he'd written "You cared!"

As for my birthday (#64), you were early. The date is May 31. However, thanks. In order to avoid being remiss, I congratulate you, Herb, for last February 26, and you, Irene, for next November 7, and both of you for your anniversary on August 9.

Meg and I went to Beverly Hills yesterday (she was delivering some script to Wallis), and going into Linny's Bagel Shop, we ran into Ed Rose.

It's good of you to keep on saying I'm a good writer, but the fact is practically no one agrees with you. My wife, of course, and even myself at times, and about a dozen aficionados scattered about the world, but aside from us chickens, there's nobody in here. But there's no fruit to be picked by agreeing I'm worthless. That way, discussion ends quickly. It has to be assumed that I can write, but that for some reason I can't make a breakthrough. When you suggest that I have offended some of the powerful in the Establishment, you're only too close to the truth, for

I've insulted the shit out of several of the most influential editors of my time, and in red and blue ink. All the same, however vindictive they may be, I don't think they could kill a writer even if they were so minded. They could delay him, make it tough for him, exclude him for a while—but in the end he'd surface. We've got to look further, and so far only Maggie has come up with a good theory, one I'm very much inclined to accept. She says that my writing from first to last is preaching, and the preaching of a particularly hard doctrine, angry, scornful, intolerant, harsh, and inlaid with broken glass. She says most people don't like to be preached to, that the only way they'll take the iron hand is in the kid glove. She says I alienate the very audience I'm writing for. She says it's the rare few who grow better under the lash—and she says, kid, you sure can lash!

What do you think?

I think she's smart.

She expects to finish the first draft of her latest for Wallis in two-three weeks. After that, by contract, he'll have seventeen weeks of her time for revisions, but I don't think he'll be able to use them all, since the John Wayne commitment makes it necessary to start shooting very early in September. However, if Wallis turns her loose then, she goes back to Henry Hathaway-ABC for three months of rewriting owing to them. Which about takes her to the end of the year.

Me, I'm working hard on FUCK'EM ALL, my new little history-book for ages 6–13. I hope to see it in every classroom.

Mag joins me in sending love. We miss you.

Affectionately,

107. To George Brounoff

29 November 1969

Dear George

No need to be surprised about Martin's failure to use the material I gave him; I told him to leave it out. Here's a copy of the last letter I wrote to him:

> 11 March 1968
>
> Dear Jay Martin
>
> I've now read both halves of your book on Pep West. I find it neither a biography nor a work of literary criticism. It's a canonization, and an apt title for it would be "St. Nathan."
>
> The book is all laurel. For you, apparently, Christ came a second time, and he came as Lithuanian landed gentry, good through and through. The bad and the inbetween, both of which are known to you, have either been written out or fumigated and written in. The result is no man I ever knew. This Pep West is some wish of yours. For me, unfortunately, it doesn't come true.
>
> I'm sorry, but I must withdraw. Please remove my name from the book wherever used, and delete as well any information or material I may have put in your way.
>
> Yours
> John Sanford

I've seen no later versions of the book, of course, so I have no way of knowing whether Martin improved it; he could hardly have made it worse. In any case, if the early version went through without an overhaul, God help Pep.

You don't speak directly about being sick or well, but I'm a little disturbed by the indirection. You say you travel a little and rest a lot, which in itself can be taken several ways, but coupling it with other things (no music, no poetry, and, as you put it, "what's left is not a great deal"), I come up with the notion that things could be better. I'd be very sorry to be right. If I hit you at the wrong time with that Hemingway panache, I regret it; I was being gay without having a look at the clock.

Mag and I haven't done any traveling for a few years now. She's had a fine streak going for four years, and at this stage of her career (and the biz), she's reluctant to refuse decent assignments; they get scarcer in direct proportion to age. As for me, I write every day for hours, and the result is anonymity, as usual. The new book, an odd one, is now seventy thousand words long. It will be rejected, I predict confidently, at least twenty-five times before some incautious editor goes crazy and costs his firm about seventy-five hundred dollars on my number 9.

Mag joins in best regards, as does Ruth, who's here for the holiday. And if my father knew I'd heard from you, he'd add his best. He's coming up 92.

Write again soon and tell me about your home in Paumanok. How can you say you live without poetry? You live in it.

Affectionately,

108. To William A. Koshland

(Always For Erie *is one of the first working titles for* A More Goodly Country.)

17 May 1970

Dear Bill Koshland

We haven't been in touch with each other since Knopf turned down my novel, The Hero Suit, a few years back. It was put out, by the way, in '67 by Prentice-Hall as The $300 Man.

I have a new book ready now (non-fiction this time), and as yet nobody has seen it. I call it Always for Erie, and I have the obligation of telling you in advance that your house would go for it only if some miracle has come to pass. That's bad selling, of course, but I've known you too long to let you waste your time—unless you choose to.

The book is my interpretation of American history from Leif Ericson to the Enola Gay, and it's one damn angry thing pretty near all the way. There are 140 chronological sections, of which I send you two—"Rip Van Winkle" and "Illinois Central Caboose"—for tenor and treatment. They must certainly be the mildest pieces in the book. The tone gets hotter when I touch on Joe Hill, Mooney, and Vanzetti.

The miracle, I suppose, would be this: that Knopf was willing to publish dissent (or anything else) provided only it qualified as literature. If you want to read more, I've got more—450 pages of it—and I think it is literature.

Well?

Sincerely,

109. To Harvey Satenstein

6 January 1971

Dear Harvey

I've been trying to find a publisher for my new book, and in going through Literary Market Place—1969–70, I came across the house of H & B, with yourself listed as Production Manager.

I know you're not the right person in the outfit to apply to for a reading, but I thought it might be a good idea to sound you out on the kind of books put out by H & B, which, frankly, is unknown to me.

The book I speak of is called Always for Erie, and for once in my career, I've done a work of non-fiction. In describing it beyond that, though, the going is rougher. It wouldn't be inaccurate, I suppose, to say that it's my interpretation of the history of America from the time of its discovery by Leif Ericson to the dropping of the Bomb by the "Enola Gay." It's no Nixon-Agnew interpretation, you can bet your ass on that; in fact, it's far over on the other side of center and as liberal as all hell. There are 170 sections dealing with what I regard as salient forces, figures, and events of nearly ten centuries, and starting out hot, it only keeps on getting hotter—too damn much so, I guess, for the name-houses along Madison and Third Avenues, because they've turned the book down one and all, and fuck 'em.

If H & B is the same kind, fuck it too. But if it happens to have nerve and brains (it'll need both), you'd better hand this over to the Editor-in-Chief and tell him to ask me for the book. Or, if you prefer to keep out of it, drop me a line and tell me who to write to.

How are you, Boombala?

As Ever
(Cousin Julian)

In the event you decide to pass this along, you'll want to know the names of my previous books and publishers:

The Water Wheel : Dragon Press
The Old Man's Place : A & C Boni
Seventy Times Seven : Alfred Knopf
The People From Heaven : Harcourt, Brace
A Man Without Shoes : Plantin Press
The Land That Touches Mine : Doubleday
Every Island Fled Away : W W Norton
The $300 Man : Prentice-Hall

110. To T. Tobin

8 Apr 71

Dear Mr Tobin

I have your letter of 1 Apr.

Payment on the check was stopped when you failed to present it in the normal course. I don't have to carry an outstanding till you're ready to cash it.

Unhappily, your delay has given me time to get sore about having been asked for postage in the first place. You guys are in business because us guys write, and if we pay to ship you the stuff, you ought to pay to ship it back. It's small of you to stick us for the round-trip.

Tell you what I'll do, though. You get Lippincott to publish the book, and I'll allow the house a $5 credit on the advance.

Sincerely,

111. To Ben Raeburn

(Ben Raeburn was an editor at Horizon Press, the eventual publisher of Sanford's first work of non-fiction, eventually titled A More Goodly Country.*)*

26 May 1971

Dear Mr. Raeburn

Thanks for your letter of the 21st.

I believe you when you say you're giving up Always For Erie with much reluctance. Your liking for the book has been plain from the start. It has been equally plain that the book would probably stumble on the economic stone.

I feel I have to ask this question: why can't Always For Erie make its original appearance as a paperback?

The readers I'm aiming at are on the American campus or near-about, and there are millions of them. If a book costs twice as much as it has to, they're not going to buy half as many; they're going to buy none. It's the one group that can be priced right out of the market. I suggest that a publisher would see daylight if he got ten paperback copies into every college bookstore in the country. But I suppose I'm just being stupid.

All the Best.

Sincerely

112. To Ben Raeburn

27 May 1971

Dear Mr. Raeburn

This is a Royal Standard rigged with Great Primer type. My trouble is that I don't write primers on it.

In ESPIRITU SANTO, yes, that *the* ought to be a to. In ELIXIR VITAE, the *them* was consciously used as an archaicism, but I could switch to *they* and lose nothing.

A film is due to open at the Baronet in New York on June 30. It's called GLORY BOY, and it's based on a novel of mine, THE OLD MAN'S PLACE. I sold the picture rights several months back, and yesterday the producer asked my wife and me to drive down to Hollywood for a special showing of the final cut. It simply knocked our blocks off. In our opinion, it's as good an anti-war film as any ever made and a mile better than most. Neither I nor my wife, who happens to be a crack screenwriter herself, had anything to do with the script, but we take our hats off to this job, and maybe you will too. Why not see it and let me know what you think?

It won't be easy to keep you au courant with ALWAYS FOR ERIE from now on. My agent has notified me that he's taking over the submission of the book and that I won't be told a thing till he sells it. He has the nerve of a thief, but he usually gets results, so I do what he says.

I await your answer to my suggestion about a paperback ALWAYS FOR ERIE.

The best.

Sincerely

113. To Mel Friedman

19 February 1972

Dear Mel

I'm troubled by the phone-call I made to you yesterday, and I don't know why or where it went sour. Maybe I said the wrong thing, or maybe I failed to say the right thing, but whatever I may have done or not done, I'm left with a sense of failure. That's not the way I wanted it to be, not at all what I had in mind. On the contrary, I called you with good will, hoping you'd gather from the act that I was interested, that I regretted our misunderstandings of other days, that I felt I'd said unwarrantable things on occasion, injured you when you well deserved gratitude and praise. Instead, I hung up feeling I'd somehow managed to make things worse.

I write this to make myself clear, to say I'm ashamed of my poor behavior toward you through the years. I'd have it all otherwise if I could call back the actions, the hot words. As it is, owing you much and having ill-repaid you, I can only ask that you believe more in the spirit that makes me write this than the one that made me offend you in the past.

I wish you well, and Maggie joins me.

Affectionately

114. To Ben Raeburn

(Here, Always for Erie *has been abandoned for* The American Room, *the book finally published as* A More Goodly Country.*)*

17 April 1972

Dear Mr Raeburn

My agent has returned my book to me, and in part this is what he reports:

> ". . . During the past several months, I've tried THE AMERICAN ROOM (*) at enough of the big-name house to know what all of them are going to say—no dice. The surprising thing is their candor about why. Almost without exception, they shy away from the book's liberalism, and they make no bones about saying so. None of the usual phrases they use in the trade. They come right out and say they don't intend to publish a book that attacks what they stand for. I'm going to be blunt and say you may never find a taker for THE AMERICAN ROOM, but if you ever do, he won't be part of a conglomerate. He'll be a born independent with ideals, and you're going to have to find him for yourself. You were born in the wrong time, or in the right time with the wrong point of view. Sorry, but I can't help you with this piece of goods. . . ."

Well, what do I do, Mr Raeburn? Do I put the book away, as I had in mind a year ago, or do I reapply to someone like you, who once expressed appreciation? Eventually you turned the book down, but was that your final word on the matter, or is there any chance at all that you'll reconsider? I have to take it as true that no Doubleday, no S & S, will accept THE AMERICAN ROOM. That leaves only the poor independent with ideals, a handful at most. Are you among them, Mr. Raeburn? If there's any room for hope, please let me know.

Believing that your taste for the book remains, I'd like to say that since you saw it, I've added about fifty sections. Here's a partial list of the new subjects:

Sinclair Lewis	Nathaniel Hawthorne
Eugene O'Neill	Hart Crane
Edgar Allen Poe	F Scott Fitzgerald
Henry James	Mary Lincoln
The King Ranch	Emily Dickinson
The Leo Frank Case	Ralph Blakelock
Mary Baker Eddy	Cotton Mather
Tin Pan Alley	Judge Webster Thayer
Emma Goldman	Peter Zenger
Isadore Duncan	Robert Ingersoll
Alfred Stieglitz	Billy Sunday
Randolph Bourne	J.J. Audubon
Willa Cather	Sarah Orne Jewett
Margaret Fuller	

I ask you to give my questions the thought I think they deserve—because the book is deserving. It can't be right that anything as good as THE AMERICAN ROOM should be prevented from reaching the people. It can't be right, and it isn't right!

Best Wishes

Sincerely

115. To Mr. and Mrs. Samuel L. Shapiro

(Sanford responds to a letter of sympathy from his cousins regarding the death of his father, the Governor.)

30 August 1972

Dear Hatty and Sam

I haven't wanted to write to anyone, and I really don't want to now, but it wouldn't do to get that fine picture of Dad and Sam and say nothing. So far as I know, I'd never seen it before, and it's a sight, the two of them smiling out at this Indian-guru world of ours.

So many things came back to me from the sixty-eight years I knew my father that I'd have to live another sixty-eight to re-experience them all. I find myself thinking of him when I don't know I've been doing it, in the middle of the night, while I'm working on my book, or out of a clear or clouded sky. Today, for instance, I happened to take a drink, and suddenly I remembered what pop used to say sometimes after a shot of good brandy: "The man who invented that should never have died." And he should never have died, either. There was none better, anywhere or ever.

I keep saying to Maggie, "I never knew I loved him so much," and it's the truth. I simply didn't understand the extent of the hold he had on me, I didn't think I was capable of the emotion. I learn now, after he's gone, that his going has diminished life by a very great deal.

Much love to both of you. Thanks for the picture and thanks for the letters and the calls.

Affectionately

116. To Angus Cameron

(An early admirer of Sanford's novels, Cameron was a proponent of The People From Heaven *in the early Forties, and arranged for the republication of that novel with the Liberty Book Club. When Sanford wrote this letter, Cameron was an editor for Alfred A. Knopf.)*

26 November 1972

Dear Angus

It was kind of Albert Erskine to try the book out on you again; I'm sorry it made no greater impression on you than it did the first time.

There must be something the matter with me. I keep on believing I've written a good book, maybe as good a one as many a season has seen around. To me, it doesn't seem a matter of stubbornly holding onto a wrong notion; if you allow me to say so, I think the wrong notion is held by every editor who's turned the book down. They're numerous by now, but still I say that they're in the wrong, not I. That the book comes in a poor climate, I of course agree (my God, only Maine and the District of Columbia for such a man as McGovern!), but doesn't a book like mine always show up when the political chill is on? In a generous day, it wouldn't have to be written.

There's no point in badgering you, though, Angus. You know what I'm talking about quite as well as I do: the penalty for going against the grain is exile.

You made the offer, and I'll take you up. Do you know any publisher in this country, big or small, commercial or college, left or right, that might consider the book for publication? If so, pass the book on; if not, kindly send it home.

Good wishes always.

Sincerely

117. To Eli Jaffe

13 December 1972

Dear Eli

Over the past forty years, eight of my books have been published, a fact that might tempt one to believe I'm a writer and so regarded by the editors of the country. I'm five years into my ninth book, though, and it still goes begging after sixty-three rejections. I'm not a writer yet, it would seem, just as you are not, but there's this difference between us, Eli: I know the requirements, and you don't.

When you ask me to criticize a book you've written, criticism is what you're going to get, not the fob-off your eastern friends seem to have been giving you—jibber-jabber about "architecture" when there is no architecture and about "style" when your writing is simply a denial of style. They've ill-served you with such foolishness; they should've told you what I have to tell you now.

As I read it, A Seat In Heaven is a failure. There's no way to soften that short of not saying it at all. The book doesn't succeed here and there, it isn't a near miss, it doesn't give promise: it's a failure from end to end. The reason is plain—you're insensitive to the medium you're trying to work in. You couldn't be more handicapped if you were a color-blind painter, a deaf musician.

Ten years ago you sent me Moccasin, and I told you quite the same thing then, hoping you'd understand what I was getting at and do something about perfecting your craft. The only thing you've done is grow ten years older. You certainly are no further along in your knowledge of what happens when words are strung out in a line.

Writing isn't street-talk, toilet-talk, bed-talk, table-talk, idle in the main, formless, pointless, ephemeral—it isn't conversation carried on by other means. The guy who tells the best story lying down or over a beer had better stick to beer and fucking. Writing is solemn, solitary, draining work that in the making of a single sentence tests your total experience up to that moment. If it doesn't do that, you aren't writing, and if it doesn't do it significantly, you aren't a writer—at any rate, not the kind I care about, not the kind I'd like to be.

What kind you care about is a mystery to me at this stage of the game. We've know each other for over thirty years, and while you've always wanted to be a writer, I've never found you to do anything about it except collect words on paper. That isn't enough. You've never troubled to listen to the language you've been using for sixteen hours a day for better than half a century. The language doesn't seem to count for beans with you beyond a way to get the salt, or a certain brand of cigarettes, or another can of that God damn beer. Words—that's all writing is to you, and since that's so, anybody's words will do, expressions like "phonus-balonus," catchphrases, the jargon of the hour, clever toasts and parting shots, anything that comes to mind. Anything but the fresh, the personal, the made-to-order. You settle for the ready-to-wear, though, Eli,-and what comes to on the page has no force, no substance, no rhythm, no novelty, yes, and no architecture or style—in short, it has no reason for having been written, page after page giving off the dreary sounds of everyman.

You speak of making one more revision before turning the book over to your agent. One revision won't do it, Eli, twenty won't do it. What has to be revised is you—you have to make yourself over into someone who treats language with the care and devotion and comprehension it deserves. If you can't do that, every minute you devote to revising the book will be thrown away. I'll say it again. You must revise you, and that may well be the one new thing I say in this letter.

If you should succeed in revising yourself, and of course I hope you do, consider these two specific suggestions when you tackle the revision of the book:

1) Stop using your books (I've read three, and they all do the same) to erect an Eli Jaffe bigger than life. You seem driven to doing that all the time, particularly in regard to sexual prowess. I'm weary of reading that Buck (Eli) Stone is six feet tall with a cock to match—it simply doesn't matter to me how good you are straddling anything but a typewriter. And while you're about it, stop calling your cock "the pork," which is hardly better than your earlier love, "joy-stick," and I beg of you, Eli, to abandon such emetics as "crotch-juice." For Christ's sake, Eli, listen to yourself!

2) Try writing in the third person for once. The first person is bad medicine for you. It ties you up inside yourself so that the rest of the world becomes only talk dimly heard, blurred faces, descriptions that cover motion only. There are in fact no realities outside your "I," only names that you extract responses from. That won't do; it isn't writing.

I have no apologies to make. You asked for an opinion, and I've given an opinion. It may be wrong, but it's the one I hold. Doubtless it'll be hard to take. Be sure, though, that none of the sixty-three I've had to read has been easier.

As ever

118. To Eli Jaffe

23 December 1972

Dear Eli

You're wrong. I didn't hate you for asking me to read a book I'd have to cut up as I did SEAT. But I did rather despise the people who read it before it got to me: they left it to someone else to do what they cannot have failed to know had to be done. They're published men, the ones you mentioned, and while that doesn't make them Proust or Joyce, it does mean they had to pass editorial boards, meet some kind of standards, however academic—qualify, if you will. But they didn't make you qualify, though they had to know you wouldn't wherever you submitted the book. I don't like anyone who fobs a man off: he asks for bread, and he gets buttered!

I stick to the opinion I gave you, and I add this. I don't object to you writing a book from the point-of-view of a man in the fund-raising game, I don't object to you jumping inside him and speaking with his mouth, settling for his vulgarity, accepting his aims. I do strongly object, though, to your acceptance of his literary limitations. What you seem to be saying is that you wrote the book badly because that's how Buck Stone would've written it. I don't go for that at all. Earlier I told you the first person was bad for you, and now I say so again. You occupy a man, thinking to know him better from within, and you wind up being dominated by him: once you get in there, once you set down that first I, you forget how to get out again. And you must get out at times, to see your character, to hear him as others hear him, to objectify him, so that you can walk all around the sonofabitch before it's time to dive back in. You can't do that: once you get in, you stay in, and you're his man. It's got to be the other way 'round: you've got to run him.

Yes, Maggie will read the book. She's of course absolutely independent of me in her judgments, and I have no idea in the world what she'll say about SEAT. I hope she disagrees with me. It has happened before.

As ever

119. To James S. Allen

(James S. Allen was at the time of this letter an editor at International Publishing Company, Inc.)

5 February 1973

Dear Mr. Allen

Recently I queried you about reading my new book, The American Room. I described its nature, and to make quite clear what it was all about, I sent along a Table of Contents with explanations typed in after many of the headings which might not be self-revealing. To be frank, I rather took it for granted that a mere glance at the Table of Contents would cause you to call for the manuscript itself. It was a surprise, therefore, to get Mr Diskin's two-line note telling me that the book (as he put it) did not seem to fit your publishing program. I refuse to let it go at that.

What is your publishing program that it can't include a book dealing with the injustices wrought in America from the time of its discovery to the dropping of the bomb on Hiroshima? What are you interested in if not Tom Mooney, Debs, Sacco and Vanzetti, the Molly Maguires, the Haymarket, the Homestead strike, and John Reed? My book treats of all those events and people and damn-all more. It's concerned with the Pullman strike, the Depression, and the course of empire, with American wars, women, science, literature, and art; it's about Poe, Emma Goldman, Frank Lloyd Wright, Big Bill Haywood, the Quakers, the Jesuits, the Jews, the blacks, and the Indians. But you guys—for Christ's sake, what are you concerned with?

I think you owe people more than two lines from Mr Lou Diskin for five years of hard work—and good work, too, as good as any you've ever seen. You're supposed to be a liberal press, one of the handful in all America, but your Mr Lou Diskin refused to read material with all the easy arrogance of a man working for Doubleday.

I'm sore about his refusal to read The American Room. It's as good a book as you're likely to see in all the rest of your publishing life, but it'll never find a home along the upper reaches of Madison Avenue. If it can't even get read downtown, it's going to stay in the trunk—and the responsibility for that is squarely with the Left.

Yours, etc.

120. To Ben Raeburn

29 April 1973

Dear Mr Raeburn

I've just been reading over our correspondence, and if it weren't for your letter of rejection, nobody would believe the book failed to wind up on Horizon's list. Everything preceding the turndown indicated eventual acceptance. You were impressed with the work as a whole, you said, and you were impressed with its various parts; in fact, you even named the parts that impressed you most. You used heady words for the insights the book afforded, for the writing, the intention, the point of view. Your hesitation, you said, was solely on the score of sales, but even that problem you held out hope of solving. . . . All that—and the book is still on my desk!

The original, that is. Copies have never stopped circulating. I've stayed away from the big houses, though, feeling that in such places the book would be judged in one way only—politically. Instead, I've been concentrating on the university presses, only to learn that there too the situation is deplorable. Only about one in four colleges that I query consents to read the book, and of the handful I've managed to reach, every single one warns me in advance that slashed funds make my chances poor—and then of course the poor chance becomes no chance when the book's content gets to be known.

So here I am, Mr. Raeburn, with my hat in one hand and my book in the other, asking you to give this serious matter one more round of thought. It isn't serious simply for me. It's serious for the country as well, I think, when a book as worthy as mine goes begging because it contains dangerous thoughts. I have something important to say, particularly so in this time of national disgrace, and the disgrace is merely compounded when a rebellious voice is silenced.

Everywhere I see publishers putting out safe books—books that're books only in the sense that they're black print on white paper. They protest nothing, teach nothing, change nothing—they're safe politically, and therefore, the thinking seems to go, they're safe bets, sure to sell in the thousands. Something must be wrong, though, because they don't sell. I see them on shelves of every bookstore. Month after month, that first and only edition waits for a buyer who never comes—a sure thing that went sour.

Out of any ten books in his catalogue (omitting the Frank Yerbys and the John Updikes), it would be a poor publisher who couldn't predict at least one success—but it'd be a rash one who tried to name it. The fact is, a publisher doesn't really know whether a given book will do well or badly. He relies on his best judgment, he seeks sound advice, he goes by the writer's record—but in the end, he's merely guessing. If he's a winning publisher, he guesses right more often than wrong. But there's no way to avoid the conclusion that in choosing one book to publish instead of another, the odds favor error. If they didn't, the publishers would own the earth.

What I'm driving at is this. Why not go against better judgment for once, why not refuse advice, why not disregard the record—why not, for this one time, put aside all thought of the safe venture, the cinch bet? Why not publish The American Room, a book which in your own hand-written words is "a work unique and full of marvelous things, masterly language, moving rhythms"? Why not publish it for this reason alone—that you know it deserves to see the light?

Why not give it to the people it's meant for, the many who have no say and for whom it speaks? They might just take it to their hearts and cry it in the streets, you know—they just might make it go!

Will you, being as I think a just and generous-spirited man, call for another look at the manuscript? I urge that you do.

My best regards.

Sincerely

P S I enclose the complete Table of Contents, with a few words of explanation typed alongside many of the headings. As noted, an * indicates material that you've never seen.

121. To Angus Cameron

2 November 1973

Dear Angus

Thanks for the good wishes, but I crowed too soon.

The publisher was Kennikat Press (man name of Cornell Jaray), and when the manuscript was returned to me for approval of their editing job, I found that the book had been cut in two—from 679 pp to 350.

The claim was that at full size the book would have to bring the impossible price of $20, and no argument of mine—more words per page, cheap paper, soft cover—could knock it down. It was either half a book or none. What could I do but what I did. I asked for a cancellation of the contract, and I coughed up a nice advance. I had to do it, and I'd do it again.

You know a good publisher? A sour sonofabitch, like me, an experimental type, a nut, an idealist, a real fuck-you-Jack who happens to like words? Know one like that, Angus? Oh, yes. I nearly forgot—he better be rich.

Always warm regards.

Sincerely

122. To Eli Jaffe

6 February 1974

Dear Eli

The blind leading the blind: you send me your books to appraise, and I can't get my own into print. Why you want my comment I don't understand. What can it be that it wasn't before? Is it likely my rejections will change my tune? I'd say the same thing if I never got printed again.

We're far apart in the way we look at writing. You're willing to put anything on paper that comes down off your arm; I'm not. Ink isn't language. You think that if you have something to say, all you have to do is spit it out; I don't. Spit isn't language, either. The ability to say something is more than merely saying it; it's saying it in a way that makes it part of the person you're saying it to, saying it so that what you've said is him, his. That takes art. If you have none of that . . . well, a man can be worthy without it, but he can't be a writer.

I told you this years ago, Eli, and I'm going to tell it to you again now, and that'll end it: all your life you've wanted greatly to become a writer, but you've never taken the first step toward becoming one. The step is the acquisition of a feel for the language. It was something that wouldn't come easy, I said, and if it came at all, it'd be a long time coming. You've never taken that step, and I'm afraid you never will.

I have no reaction at all to this latest version of Walk In His Moccasins except this—it isn't a book. To tell you why would be to rewrite an old letter and repeat an old lecture. I invite you instead to go your own way with the book. Nothing I've ever urged on you has had any effect; nothing has changed. So go your own way, Eli; maybe it's a better way than mine. I've had no success, God knows. Why should you listen to me?

Best to you, Wilma, and the fine little lad.

Sincerely

123. To Stephen Whitney

(Mr. Whitney was at this time the editor of the Sierra Club "Bulletin." Sanford had already placed "Sequoia Gigantea" in the 1974 November/December issue under the title "The Bark Was Three Feet Thick.")

21 October 1974

Dear Mr. Whitney

I have your letter of the 16th, telling me why you were rejecting the Paul Bunyan piece. I'm disappointed, of course. I understand and sympathize with the aims of the Sierra Club, but I'm not quite sure the piece violates them.

Certainly the tall tale as usually told celebrates the American individual's feats performed at the expense of the American wilderness, but unless I'm much mistaken, PAUL BUNYAN IN OREGON doesn't do that. The title it'll carry in my book is LEGEND WITH ADDED MATERIAL—which indicates my notion that the Great Logger lies no longer sway. My joining of the John Henry and Paul Bunyan myths was meant to do more than point up the need for black and white cooperation; it was meant to end the myth of individualism altogether and therefore to slow the devastation that individualism produces. But, as I say, I may be wrong in my thought of what the piece achieves, and I accept its rejection with the good nature that writers are famous for.

Thanks for inviting me to try again. I'll do so soon, with a third piece from the same book. It's called BUCKEYE JOHNNY APPLE-SEED. It may be more to your liking.

With all good wishes

124. To Robert Lord

14 March 75

Dear Nat

Thanks for your letter, and thanks as well for taking two chances on A MORE GOODLY COUNTRY. I hope it turns out to have been worth the price.

In reading it, maybe you'll want to bear in mind that it took me five years to write and another three to find a publisher. Along the way, it was rejected 111 times, another 85 publishers refused to read the manuscript, and 46 more didn't even trouble to answer my query about it. It went out under four different titles, sometimes to a publisher who'd already rejected it, so that occasionally I had the honor of being turned down twice by the same outfit. Usually the book was kept a long time, seven months once, but there were times when it was fired back at me the day after receipt. I lost friends on account of the book, but I was also lucky enough to make friends—indeed, it was only because the book was well-liked by an editor at a turn-down house that I ultimately got home with it at Horizon. It has, in short, been a rare experience in a career filled with rare experiences. And to cap it all, this, my ninth book, is appearing at a time in the nation's economy that just about parallels the time my first book appeared in 1933: The very week that F.D.R. closed the banks.

Let me know what you think of the work, and if you come across any reviews of it, send them along—even if they're good.

Mag joins me in sending love to you and Stelli. We hope you've been well.

Affectionately

* I began a new book last November. I haven't hit on a title as yet. The subtitle will be "A Personal History of American Literature."

125. To Tom Dardis

(Dardis wrote a chapter about Pep West in a book called Some Time in the Sun, *published by Scribner's in 1976. Earlier, in the 1950s, Dardis, working for Avon Books, published Sanford's* Seventy Times Seven *in paperback under the title* Make My Bed in Hell. *Dardis later became a Professor at the City University of New York and published several more academic studies on American writers, publishers, and silent film stars.)*

16 April 1975

Dear Mr. Dardis

I have your letter of 11 April concerning your proposed book SOME TIME IN THE SUN.

As to Fitzgerald, I never really knew him and saw him only twice, once at M G M during his lifetime and once in a funeral parlor when he was dead. What I know about him comes from what I've read, and it doesn't lead me to believe that his Hollywood years were the best of his life, as you seem to think. Before you commit yourself to that theory, you'd better do some more digging; you might change your mind. His work as a screenwriter was well short of the best that was being done in Hollywood at the time, and in my opinion Sheila Graham was hardly the sort to help him find "those lost talents" you speak of. I'm not one of those who celebrate THE LAST TYCOON; I've always thought it inept and derivative, a long way down from TENDER and GATSBY. If Fitzgerald found anything in Hollywood, it was only a place to die, and, damn it, very little stir was made when he did.

You ask about Nat West. Most of the mystery is in your head. Many people out here knew him about as well as most people get to be known, and if he had secret places, so does everyone else. Jay Martin's biography was the so-called authorized one, a eulogy rather than a study, a book for the family, and it fails even at that. He wrote of a Nat West who never did a wrong thing, and no such man ever lived. It wasn't that Martin ran too much tape; it was that he believed certain people as against certain others. That's quite all right, but the anti-votes weren't even registered. West was an excellent writer and a less than excellent person. Few of us are the former; all of us are the latter. I offered Martin many examples of West's humanity, but he used none of them.

I think it would be wrong to say that West held Hollywood in contempt. Many of its people, yes, and also a few of its aims, but he was no fool, and he knew the possibilities of the medium. He did much of his screenwriting for Republic, and outfit with the rep of never having made a good film, but even so West took his work quite seriously. Of course he was more deeply committed to books than to pictures, and it's true too that he used what he made in pictures to buy him time for books. But the fact is, he never drew a top salary and was never able to buy complete freedom for himself, assuming that he wanted it. On what he earned, he never could've salted enough away to quit. He didn't live lavishly, as you seem to think. He owned a thousand-dollar Ford, he rented a modest house, he kept a dog, he wore Brooks clothes, and he shot doves on the cheap in Baja California. If he was another Hemingway, he was the economy-size. It's easy to call his old studio Cheapsville, but that's not how any Hollywood writer ever saw it. Those who were simply making a living by writing scripts were much more respectful; those, like West, who were buying time for other things, were rightly grateful for the chance that Cheapsville gave them.

EVERY ISLAND FLED AWAY is two books back. My eighth novel, THE $300 MAN, was published by Prentice-Hall in '67, and Horizon Press is just now issuing my latest, a book of nonfiction called A MORE GOODLY COUNTRY. As yet, no reviews have appeared.

Regards.

Sincerely

126. To Tom Dardis

30 August 1975

Here are the two pictures of Pep West I said I'd send you. They were taken in the summer of 1931 at the cabin we'd rented on Viele Pond, near Warrensburg, N.Y. As I told you, you may leave me in or out, as you choose.

In your letter of 22 August, you ask me to add to my remarks about your prose. With encouragement like that, I could easily become didactic, because I take writing seriously. Instead, though, I'll let you instruct yourself with your own words. You say I'm probably right about the prose "but it'll be better in the next book." What next book? There is no next book!

There is only one book that any good writer ever writes—the book he's writing now. There's no past for him and no future. This chapter, this page, God damn it, this very line—that's all he has. Let him slight it, and he stops being a writer then and there. I'm not saying no worthy writer ever writes a bad line, a bad book—I say he never knowingly does.

So it isn't your tone or your attitude I stop short of admiring, and it isn't that you sound amateurish, for you don't. Your writing (in the West chapter, which is all I know of it) is orderly and serviceable—but if that's all there were to prose, I'd be for burning books instead of coal. The composition of prose is a high art, and the conditions of that art are not met by work that's orderly, serviceable. You've settled for that in this book, I gather, and if you're honorable, as I believe you to be, you'll regret it.

Good Wishes.

Sincerely,

127. To Dr. Matthew Bruccoli

(Dr. Bruccoli taught at the University of South Carolina. The O.B. mentioned as The Water Wheel*'s dedicatee was Olga Brounoff, sister of Sanford's good childhood friend George Brounoff.)*

6 September 1975

Dear Dr. Bruccoli

It pleases me that you intend to recommend The Water Wheel for the Lost American Fiction series. You ask for some information about the book's publication and what I hoped to accomplish when I wrote it.

For my people, the Jews, there's no intercessor, no surrogate, no one to propitiate for the sins of man: each of us must suffer and each in that way atone. The writing of The Water Wheel was self-punishment deliberately undertaken in order to lighten a burden of guilt I felt in relation to O.B., to whom the book is dedicated. There's no confession for a Jew, there's no symbolic penance or outside absolution: A Jew must suffer for such of his acts as he knows to have been wrong, and his suffering lasts until his heart informs him that his God has relented—and a worthy Jew, I might add, never lets himself off lightly.

Far from my mind, therefore, was any intention of sparing myself in The Water Wheel, of justifying my conduct, explaining each error until I'd explained it away. On the contrary, I exposed every villainy I could find in myself, every lack, every meanness, and so far from wanting pity, I courted scorn and odium. In large measure, judging by reviews, I got them both.

But while writing the book, somewhere along the way I began to perceive (or apprehend) that I was doing more than putting myself in a pillory. I saw, not very clearly, that I was somehow doing the same to the class I came from—to a certain extent even to the society responsible for that class. I hadn't planned anything like that; it just seemed, after a while, to be there on the page. I didn't know enough at the time, or I'd've realized that I'd stumbled onto the right track. I had to grow some in the mind before I knew that I was a product, not a phenomenon. I had to get rid of the notion that I was all in order to see the shape of the world. The world was dim for me when I wrote The Water Wheel, but the man I wrote about was very plain, and very plainly I stoned him, and I made him suffer much before I left him alone.

I started writing the book in 1928, and as nearly as I can now recall, I completed it some time in 1932. A cousin of mine, later the designer of the book, took the manuscript around for me, and it was he, after several rejections, who showed it to Angel Flores, proprietor of Dragon Press. Flores was a language instructor at Cornell, and so far as I know, he published only two books: one was The Knife of the Times, by William Carlos Williams, and the other was The Water Wheel. The latter came out in March 1933, during the Depression week when all the banks were closed. Fewer than 500 copies were sold, and the book earned me nothing—there'd been no advance, and I received no royalties.

Along with this, I send you excerpts from the reviews. On the whole, they were unfavorable. Here and there, someone credited me with skill, passion, vividness, or what he called a way with words, and I had to be content with such faint praise because the rest of it was hardly praise at all. Kindest of all was Dr. Williams, whom I met not through Flores but through my friend Nathanael West. Williams found flaws in The Water Wheel, as his enclosed letter shows, but he seemed to think he could descry the makings of a writer in the book, and he was kind enough to put me forward more than once through the years.

Sincerely

128. To Paul Mariani

*(Professor, scholar, and poet Paul Mariani wrote introductions to two of Sanford's books—*A View From This Wilderness *and* William Carlos Williams/John Sanford: A Correspondence. *The reference in this letter's opening sentence is to the terrorist act at the 1976 Munich Olympics.)*

13 July 1976

Dear Paul

If you're one of the Chosen, even part of one, join me in a toast to the Commandos. Shalom!

I received TIMING DEVICES yesterday afternoon, and I read all the poems in a single rush; then I ran upstairs and read many aloud to Maggie. One, "Rite of Passage," broke me down, and I had to try a second time before I could get through it to the end. I like the poems a very great deal. Their quiet, their unassuming, their private and yet documentary quality (lights in strange houses), their personal history suggesting other histories—these things brought me into the poems, and though we're very different, we seemed very much the same. I knew what you were talking about, and if I hadn't met the people, I'd met other people who were in the same fix: life. You love the people you've written about—there's a warm eye in you and a warm heart—and in celebrating the few triumphs and many defeats, in not forgetting the poor of Parma, you show how deeply you feel for all. These are elegies, many of them. You have much somber music in you: you are sad for the world's sadness and therefore good. I found myself thinking of the shoemaker and the seller of eels. It would not be possible for me to pay you a higher compliment. I will think more about the poems, and I will take them up again when you get back. Meanwhile, you might consider one suggestion. Except for the last few poems, your theme is the Marianis, past, now, and to come. In adding the others, especially the ones written after your trip to Italy, I believe you take something away from the drive. Tough times, dump-trucks, death, disappointment, the skinny little snare-drum boy, college, Eileen, the babies, the babies growing, the history of the past becoming the history on the way—that's what you started with, and that's what you should give to the end. All this, of course, is without reference to the merit of the concluding pieces; they should be saved, I think, for another book. You may not agree, in which case you may be the one who's right.

Keep well. All the best to the Mariani Five (poor kids, wait till they find out they're also related to Christ on their father's side!).

Since you read VOICES, I've added pieces on James Agee, James Otis, Edw Taylor (glad you liked that one; I wrote it in a trance, or, as my Grandma Nevins used to say, in a trench), Samuel Adams, Joel Chandler Harris, and Thos Jefferson, and I'm working on Davy Crockett. In the offing are Jemmy Madison and Johnny Woolman.

It's been the better part of a week since I sent the W C Williams stuff to Gallup at Beinecke. There were 26 pieces and a new annotation I prepared for him. It's on deposit in contemplation of a gift, and it belongs there. I'm glad you made the suggestion.

129. To Mrs. Dalton Trumbo

12 September 1976

Dear Cleo

Maggie and I had known of Dalton's serious illness for a long time, but even so we were unprepared for his death. Always a dauntless man, he seems somehow to have made us feel that he'd find a way to triumph again. Nothing had ever defeated him before, we must've thought, and nothing could defeat him now.

In every sense but the physical, though, he is still a living man. His work will outlast us all, and his honor, his susceptible heart, his love of justice—his love of the world, really—these are the things that make the world itself last.

We weren't lucky enough to have been among Dalton's intimates, but even from far off we were aware of his fine quality, and to have known him at all, simply to have been on earth in his time, has raised the level of our lives.

We send you our sympathy and our love.

130. To Hui-Meng Wang

(Mr. Wang was a Professor at the University of Massachusetts and a translator of Mao's poetry. Voices of the People *was Sanford's original working title for* A View From This Wilderness, *which was eventually published by Capra, "one of the small presses." "Wigwams of the People" was at this time the working title of* To Feed Our Hopes.*)*

18 November 1976

Dear Mr. Wang

If you've run across Peter Farb recently, he may have told you that his submission of VOICES OF THE PEOPLE to Houghton Mifflin resulted in a refusal. If not, perhaps you'd care to know what was said by the editor, Robert Cowley:

> "John Sanford's book VOICES OF THE PEOPLE is a difficult book to classify. You think of Williams, you think of Dos Passos, but Sanford is an original, no doubt about it. His writing is fine and so are his perceptions. There are bits, such as the Emerson or the Richard Wright, that are truly powerful. And as a recreation of American literary experience (McMurtry's phrase), the book, unexpectedly, does begin to add up. But how in hell could you sell it? I hate to bring up that sticky question, but I must. I don't see any way around it. . . .

Farb is giving the book to Dutton, but I fear the only difference between Dutton and Houghton-Mifflin is the name. That "sticky" question is asked everywhere.

You're right. I do know whose poetry you wrote the "after" poem for: W C Williams, and your poem is what I believe is called imagist. It's lovely.

I'm at work on a new book, to be called THE WIGWAMS OF HER PEOPLE (a phrase from IN THE AMERICAN GRAIN). It's about American women.

One of the small presses has made me an offer of publication of VOICES, and if Dutton turns it down, I may accept it. I'm just tired enough of the so-called prestige houses to throw my lot in with people who still like books.

I invite you to write again. It's a pleasure to hear from you.

Sincerely

131. To Mrs. Joseph Moncure March

(Peggy March was the wife of Joseph Moncure March, Sanford's second writing partner at Paramount pictures in 1936 and the man who introduced Sanford and Roberts. March is more widely known for his books The Wild Party *and* The Set Up, *both published in 1928.)*

27 April 1977

Dear Peggy

I've had your letter of the 22nd for a couple of days, but I've saved it in order to give myself a chance to go through the new book once more before sending it off to the press. It's on the press now.

Jim Farrell says some good things in his two columns in the N Y Times, but I think Joe deserved much more than Farrell chose to give him. I've known Farrell for nearly fifty years (of which I haven't spoken to him for 45), and he's something of a begrudger. It hurts him to give the palm to another writer, hurts him in the body and hurts him in the mind. What he says, therefore, falls far short of what he might've said had he been a different sort of guy. . . . .

1 May (after talking to you)

But he isn't a different sort of guy. He's Farrell, and that's why, in the part where he quotes from Joe, he gets off his "If that's poetry, I'll eat my hat." That's nonsense, Peggy; Farrell simply doesn't understand what Joe was doing in that passage and throughout the two books. Joe was quite deliberately writing his verses, blank and rhymed, in the jargon of the day, in the cadences of ordinary speech. The "poetry" Farrell was referring to would've been absurd in the context of a murdered prize-fighter and the Arbuckle case; such things called for rhythms and the idiom of the man in the street. Which, by the way, Farrell pretends to know better than any man. His trouble, however, is that he has a tin ear. And another thing: he's wrong in saying Joe is barely known. I've always been proud of the fact that Joe was my friend, and therefore I spoke of him often, to writers, critics, editors, and publishers—and never was there one who wasn't familiar with Joe's work. Those two books of his were landmarks, and my wish, when we first met in 1936, was that he write more of the same, and I told him so.

My new book went to press about the middle of last week, and, if nothing else, it'll be a good-looking job. I've seen the jacket, and it's a real beauty, plain, typographical, and in excellent taste. We should be having bound copies in another sixty days. One will go to you—with my love.

My little (5 feet!) love sends her best to you, and so do I. It was great to hear from you. We hope you keep well.

As always affectionately

132. To Mrs. Joseph Moncure March

15 July 1977

Dear Peggy

I have the fragment from Joe's DEATH AND THE UNDERTAKER sent to me by Lori, and I've read it through, read it twice, and I wish I could say I think something can be done with it. The truth is otherwise. I believe that showing these pages to a publisher would be a disservice to Joe's earned reputation. His place in literature is established, and it would be a pity to weaken it with work below his best.

Both THE WILD PARTY and THE SET UP had vigor and surge, but those qualities aren't present in the fragment. Lacking too, or so obscure that I can't perceive it, is character definition. The people here are hardly people at all, a serious fault. Joe was writing a book about Death, and at least this much is plain, that he meant to dramatize many of the ways in which it pays its visit. But where the people it calls on are not quite people, where they're merely recipients, targets, the emotion Joe must've wanted to arouse isn't there: Death has come to people who have no lives.

I've tried to stand back from the work and judge it as I think a publisher would, but I have to suppose these 55 pages would leave him as much in the dark as they do me. They contain two episodes, the one in the bar and the one with the undertaker. If they're connected, they're connected only in the sense that they occur in sequence. It's impossible to tell whether the work actually opens there in the bar or whether other scenes precede it; it's equally impossible to guess where the book was meant to go after the undertaker scene. In short, no clear purpose is evinced in either scene or both taken together.

There's a chance, certainly, that some publisher would read these pages and wish to see more, a chance that he'd call for whatever of the unrevised material is readable. I'm inclined to believe, though, that the chance is small: there isn't enough to go on in the fragment. That would not be so, I feel, if it held any considerable number of lines as effective as the first one: "Death lit a cigar." If that line were one of many, surely anybody would expect buried treasure in the rest of the manuscript. But no other line in the 55 pages matches that one. It stands alone as an example of that enviable Joe March jauntiness, of the special Joe March approach.

God knows why Joe was so long at the work—and when I say God knows, I think I use the right words, because Joe wasn't the man to talk anything over with others, certainly not his writing. I wish he'd spoken out, not that anyone could've shown him the way—no one can do that—but maybe if he'd heard himself state his plan and his problems with it, he'd've found the way himself. That article in the Amherst Alumni News had Joe right: he was the world's champion private man.

I hope you'll believe it's almost as painful to write this as it is to read it. I loved your Joe, and it would've been one of the delights of a lifetime to find his late work equal of his early. In my opinion, it isn't. That's only my opinion, and I invite, even urge you to consult someone else. I may be wrong. I'll go further: it'd make me happy to be wrong.

Shall I hold on to the Xerox or return it?

Maggie joins me in sending you love.

Affectionately

133. To Robert Lord

3 Aug 1977

Dear Nat

This is to thank you for your telegram, asking how we fared in the recent fire. It was good of you to be concerned.

And I must thank you too for your fine letter about "The Water Wheel." I have fluctuating feelings about the book, always have had. There are times when I'm a little ashamed of it, and there are others when I wish I'd put off the writing of it for a few years, and there are still others when I'm sure it can stand as it is on its own. I've come away from the kind of writing I did there, but now and then I wish I'd brought some of it with me. I'm glad you think it a good book, though, and I'll not quarrel with you. It was a start for me, and not too shabby a start, and if it's ever reprinted, it'll go without a change.

I had a fine letter from Be, full of writing remembrance, and Maggie and I, reading it together, several times laughed out loud. She omitted recollection, of course, of my negative characteristics—and unless I'm much mistaken, I had some.

Here are nine pictures, scrapped from an album. Look at them, examine them under a glass, copy them, if you like, but return them!

Love to you and Stelli d'Oro (I like them cookies!) from Maggie and Yonk.

Affectionately

134. To Thomas McGrath

(McGrath was a U.S. poet residing primarily in and associated with the Dakotas and Minnesota. Like Sanford, McGrath was a "fellow traveler." Norton published Every Island Fled Away *in 1964, not 1967.)*

4 Sept 77

Dear Tom

You have a perfect right to resist editing. That's what I've done for 45 years, and I owe all my success to it. Time and again, editors have told me I'm their favorite writer under contract elsewhere.

Talking about elsewhere, how about my writing on your behalf to a man name of Eric Swanson? He's up at W W Norton & Co, and in 67 he put out a book of mine called Every Island Fled Away. We have nevertheless remained friends. Would you wish me to drop him a line and say that a book of poems by a hammerheaded mick named McWrath is available? You'd find him as pleasant a guy as you ever met—barring me, of course.

Let me know as soon as possible. Maybe Swenson has no lady-editors.

View will be out this week.

Maggie joins me in love to you and Genya.

As Ever

135. To Lou Harris

23 March '81

Dear Lou

I'm afraid you picked the wrong guy for a comment on *The Gadfly*. I know little of ancient Greece (or modern, for that matter) and nothing at all of philosophy (or anything else, for that matter). As to the content of your play, I'm the last man to venture an opinion.

I spot you your knowledge of the time and the subject, and for how well you handle them, it'd be far better for you to apply to someone with equal knowledge. I ought to say a word, though, about one particular impression I was left with: there's a lack of drama in your presentation. There are comings and goings, of course, there are portents, and danger and conflict are promised—and even I could gather that for Sophocles the ice was growing thin. But all that was for the most part "said;" it was in the words, not in the air; nothing was fated, nothing (and this is bad in a play about the Greeks) inevitable.

It makes no difference whether an idea is trivial or, as here, consequential: it will live only as the people live who put it forward. They've got to be more than "sayers," because sayers are only other names for you. They must be independent of you; they must be made, through the writer's talent, to live on their own.

Maggie joins in the best to you and Vera.

Affectionately

136. To Thomas Andrews

(At the time of this writing, Thomas Andrews was on the faculty of Santa Barbara's Westmount College; later, he became the Director of U.S.C.'s Master of Liberal Arts Program.)

15 June 1981

Dear Dr. Andrews

So far from being an intrusion, your letter of 12 June was a welcome surprise.

For me, the worst part of writing is the silence that follows the act: it's as though the whole damn world hadn't heard a word. Maybe that's because I'm unknown, but I have a notion that even the famous feel at times that they've been speaking in an empty room.

You've proved that the room wasn't empty at all, and I thank you.

Sincerely

137. To John Martin

(John Martin was founding editor and publisher of Black Sparrow Press, who began a relationship with Sanford by redistributing a few of his earlier books, including The Old Man's Place, A More Goodly Country, *and* A Man Without Shoes, *with the last two including new introductions by the author. Martin went on to publish Sanford's five-volume autobiography and* The Winters of That Country, *the final volume [at that time] of Sanford's reinterpretations of American history.)*

29 July 1982

Dear John Martin

This is what you said a few months back: "There isn't a publisher in the trade who hasn't built his house on unpaid royalties."

That was certainly on my mind when an unsigned copy of *Shoes* turned up in Washington; my notion was that Black Sparrow had sold all the signed copies and, without telling me, was now distributing blanks. Through the course of many publications over a fifty-year career, I've been so indecently treated by publishers that I really hate to deal with the breed. I've been storing away a lot of unstable material, and when I heard about that unsigned copy, the stuff went up in your face. I'd hoped, I'd even believed, that you were going to be different from the rest, and I'll allow that it didn't take much to make me think I'd been had again. Your recent report on sales and earnings has gone a long way toward restoring my confidence in you, and I'll not demean you—or myself—by challenging your account.

I have your check for $769.50, paying me to date for my share in the proceeds of THE OLD MAN'S PLACE, as represented in your recent statement. I ask that you continue to account at the agreed intervals.

As to my share in the proceeds from *Shoes* (469 copies at $7.50 to date), I'll look to payment in August or September, as you promise to try for.

As to rights in *Goodly*, *Winters*, and any other work of mine, I must tell you that the time has come for me to be paid in advance for anything I may sign away. Without asking for sympathy, I say that at a guess a lifetime of work has brought me less than Ten Thousand dollars. That's a long way short of what they pay for making license-plates at Folsom. A royalty basis alone will never again be sufficient. I've donated too much writing, much too much, so you may say the buck starts here.

To sum up. You got what was really due to a slew of other publishers. It wasn't just, but think how you'd feel if you'd written

Goodly and never made a dime off it—a property you call the most valuable in literature.

I suggest we go on as we have till now, with one little variation: you sell the books, and I'll stay away from your stoop.

Yours, etc.

138. To Morris Dickstein

29 July 1982

Dear Mr. Dickstein

It would give me pleasure to share information I may have for your book on the 30s. There won't be too much, unfortunately, because I was one of those writers who steered clear of other writers, and therefore I'm familiar with only a few. The man I knew best was Pep West, all the way from our Harlem days to those of Hollywood wine and Stanley Rose's. I was fairly well acquainted with Jim Farrell, and though I met Dr Williams only once, at a hotel managed by West, I did have some correspondence with him over a dozen or fifteen years. Richard Johns, the director of *Pagany*, wasn't a writer himself, but I suppose he must've known every writer living at the time; I came to know him through stories of mine that he published in his magazine. There was also Henry Bamford Parkes, a very good historian, but apart from those I've cited, my encounters with writers were rare: I really didn't care for the breed. Still, for what I may be worth, I invite you to draw on me at will. I'll answer all queries and give you my best.

And if I may, I have a question or two of my own. Why am I regarded (when regarded at all) as a proletarian writer? My background is professional; no one I can think of has ever worked for wages. My sympathies lie of course with the working class, but they got there from without. Nor have I ever written as a proletarian;

there are no industrial disputes in my work, no sons of toil, no barricades.

Another thing that mystifies me is the label I wear like a star of David: "a writer of the 30s." It happens that I'm a writer of the 20s as well, and the 40s, 50s, 60s, 70s, and 80s. I've been published in seven decades, not bad for "a writer of the 30s." For my part, I've never thought of myself as belonging to any period short of my lifetime. Unlike the proletarians, unless I flatter myself, I don't play a one-string lute. They did, and that's why they aren't writing any more; to me, people were always more than factors in a cause.

As to books that might be helpful, I'm sure you know of all that I do, with this possible exception. In 1969, Beacon Press put out a book called A Return to Pagany, by Stephen Halpert and Richard Johns. It details the history and correspondence of Johns' magazine, and it contains many selections. For a broad view of writing in the 30s, I think the book may be invaluable.

More when and if you call on me. Meanwhile, my best.

Sincerely

139. To Robert Smith

17 September 1982

I didn't take this up with you when you were here some weeks ago, but before you go any further with what you're writing about me, if anything, I'd like your assurance that I'll have approval of content before publication. I waived the right once, to my sorrow. Have I your promise?

Here are my answers to your questions in your letter of September 10th:

1—re the stories: I wrote only those that comprise *Adirondack Stories* because even then, back in the 30s, I thought there might be more in me than I'd shown or could ever show in the short form. Whatever that was, it appeared in *The Water Wheel*, my first novel, and thereafter I regarded my five or six stories as exercise. I had no models for them that I was aware of, but who in that time had not been exposed to Hemingway?

2—re Nat West. He and I were only acquaintances in our Harlem days of 1914–16, but when we met again in 1925, we became friends, and our friendship, on a fairly steady basis, lasted for seven or eight years. At the time of his death, I'm sorry to say, we were estranged, but I'll not go into the reasons for the break, nor will I comment on him personally. You're not, however, to interpret this unfavorably to him. Suffice it that we had differences, and I hold them to be our business. As to his work, which you ask my opinion of, I regard *Miss Lonelyhearts* as his most perfect, and I don't mean to limit the comparison to his other three books. *Miss Lonelyhearts* is a novel that anyone of his time must've envied deeply, and had he written nothing else, it alone would've gained him a high place in American literature.

3—re Maggie. She has been more than merely helpful to my writing; she has been indispensable. For more than forty years now, she has read every word I've written, and her contributions, in suggestions and judgment, have been enormous. Before our meeting in 1936, the only one who ever read my work prior to publication was Nat West. While we were in the Adirondacks in the summer of 1931, he asked me to let him read *The Water Wheel*, then nearly complete. In a day or so, he handed back the manuscript with a single comment that concerned a character whose real identity I'd made no attempt to hide: "This simply isn't done, Julian," he said.

4—re informers. A fink is a fink. They don't come in sizes, classes, degrees, or kinds. I hate them now, and I always will. No excuse moves me, no reason persuades, and as for forgiveness, even after thirty years, I hope they burn as brightly as the Mathers hoped for a witch. As for their having done what they did out of weakness, I piss on their weakness. What kind of weakness gives people the strength to save themselves by sacrificing others? If my feeling for them still isn't plain, let me make it plainer: it's hatred.

Best regards, and I look forward to having your assurance of approval.

As Ever

140. To Richard Wentworth

(The recipient of this letter was the Director of the University of Illinois Press, which had, in 1980, published Sanford's To Feed Their Hopes: A Book of American Women.*)*

22 October 1982

Dear Dick

Here's a Xerox of *A Very Good Land To Fall With*. I might add that no one but Maggie has ever read it.

Of course, I'd prefer your covering the book yourself, but for the benefit of any editor to whom you may assign it, let me repeat what I told you on the phone.

A Very Good Land is the first part of a three-part relation, and it covers the years 1–16 of my life. The work was undertaken in response to certain queries put to me by my wife. How did someone like you, from a middle-class professional background of lawyers, accountants, doctors, and so on, ever manage to wind up before the House Committee of UnAmerican [sic] Activities? None of your people ever worked for a wage or ploughed a furrow, you had every educational and social advantage, and you never missed a meal—

how did you ever come by a belief in Socialism? My answer was this: I don't know, m'love, but tomorrow morning I'll start to explain. This book (or Part 1 of it) begins the explanation. I'm 78, and if I live long enough Maggie will get her answers.

I'm very eager to have an opinion of the book a little further from home, so drop whatever you're doing and start reading.

You didn't know I was a Jew, you say? What did you take me for—a white man?

Best as ever,

141. To Robert Smith

22 February 1983

Dear Bob

Thanks for your letter of the 18th. Have no fear that I'll doubt your praise. Think of the Lincoln story—as a boy, he said, no one liked gingerbread more than he did and got less of it. So praise on, if you must.

Yes, I've read *Call It Sleep.* Did so when it was reissued, must be a dozen years back.

I had nothing to do with the preparation of the brochure Prentice-Hall got out for *The $300 Man.* When I saw it, I cringed. It seemed like such a begging little job that it made me feel ashamed. But what it says about my earnings up till then is true:

The Water Wheel	-- advance	$ 0	royalties	$ 0
Old Man's Place	-- advance	200	royalties	0
70 x 7	-- advance	500	royalties	0
People	-- advance	500	royalties	0
Shoes	-- advance	750	royalties	0
(from Reynal & Hitchcock, no publication)				
Land (U S)	-- advance	750	royalties	0
(Eng)	-- advance	0	royalties	250

Every Island	-- advance	500	royalties	0
		-------		--------
		$ 3,200		$ 250
$300 Man	-- advance	2,500	royalties	0
Goodly Country	-- advance	1,000	royalties	0
Wilderness	-- advance	1,500	royalties	0
Hopes	-- advance	500	royalties	800
Stories	-- advance	100	royalties	400
		--------		-------
		$ 5,600		$ 1,200
		Grand Total		$10,250

That figure works out to $200 a year for 50 years, give or take a ruble. Or, to reduce it still further, to $4 a week—considered low pay even in Bangladesh. But what the hell, Bob—I had Maggie.

And that's why you're wrong if you think my odd career dictated the mood of my work. I write as I do because I don't like what I see and long to change it. I know I never will, but I'll have had my say. Personally, I'm rather a cheerful guy, hard to get along with, but always up. Ask anybody. Joyless is no description of me at all, nor does it describe my view of life. At 79, I love it well. If I treat my characters badly, it's because I'm deep down a preacher, which Maggie has always called me, and if you gather that, you'll have me. My worst fault is wanting to make Christians out of a lot of unchristian sons-of-bitches.

Maggie says when I get to the part about your coming out here again, be sure to say he'll be more than welcome. I say it for both of us.

Goodly was originally published by Horizon. It was remaindered to Capra, which sold it with a new jacket advertising itself. Answer: the Horizon is the first edition—the only edition.

Always best.

Sincerely

142. To Joe Kahn

(This recipient was the brother of Gordon Kahn, who co-edited, along with Sanford and Cedric Belfrage, The Clipper *magazine, and later became the editor of SUNY's Bilingual Press.)*

11 April 1983

Dear Joe Kahn

I wish it were possible to thank you for the book and let it go at that. Unfortunately, the one you chose to send was Hollywood Red, a wretched screed by that third-rate hack, Lester Cole. I'm sure you were unaware of this, but on p. 400, there appears by implication a contemptible slur upon my dear wife, an offense for which I'll never forgive him.

He's a base man, a cheap blow-hard whose lifelong work has been in the field of calumny, where he excels. In linking Gordon's good name with his on the flyleaf, you did your brother a great disservice. On Lester's best day, Gordon was the better man.

You'll understand, I'm sure, why the book has been sent to the city dump.

Sincerely,

143. To Louise Sorel

27 April 1983

Dear Louise

Thanks for your note of the 25th about *A Man Without Shoes.* I understand your position, and I sympathize with it, hoping you'll be equally sympathetic with mine.

Over the past several years, I've been involved in three option deals. One was with producer Phil Waxman, who paid $5,000 for a one-year option on a novel twenty years older than *Shoes*. Another was with English producer James Woolf, who put up $5,000 for a three-month option on an original screenplay. And the third was with producer Hal Wallis, who paid $3,000 for a three-month option on a screenplay based on one of my novels.

From these numbers, which I can document, you'll gather that I'm not likely to be tempted by your offer of $500 for a six-month option on *Shoes*. Nor is the figure you name a selling price—$50,000—any more appealing. *Shoes* and I have been companions in neglect for over 30 years, and we're not to be requited for it at the sum you offer.

You have a right to know the terms I would accept, and they are these:

a) a selling price of $100,000 for the book with the usual spin-off and collateral rights to be negotiated for at the time of sale;

b) a six-month option for $2,500, renewable once at same figure.

Please believe I have nothing but pleasure in the knowledge that after all these years, you still have regard for *Shoes*. Far back, when I first began to write, I wanted it all—reviews, royalties, awards, fame. At this end, I settle for the few expressions of esteem that come my way. They make obscurity easier to bear.

If what I've said here puts you off, I regret it, but it stands. Maggie joins me in best regards.

Sincerely

144. To Einar Raedergard

4 June 1983

Dear Mr Raedergard

Your kind letter of 20 May has been sent on to me by my publisher, Black Sparrow Press. It was good of you to take the trouble to write to me about *A Man Without Shoes*; I'm rarely the object of such generosity of spirit, and I'm grateful for it.

It would be a repetition to tell you of my difficulties as a writer—the introduction to *A Man Without Shoes*, with only a few changes, could serve for every book I've ever written. I had to smile when you told me you couldn't find me in the Encyclopedia Britanica. My friend, I have trouble getting listed in the telephone directory. It would take a long search to find a reference to me in any book on American Literature. In fact, when an English Professor at the University of Massachusetts wanted to do an article on me, he had to call me for material: in the two-million-volume library at the university, he couldn't turn up my name.

I blame no one for all this but myself. The subjects I've chosen to write about go against the conservative grain. They always will, and therefore I'll remain obscure. But I'm still writing at 79, and to hell with fame!

You'll have trouble finding other books of mine. A dozen have been published since 1933, but only one or two remain in print. So far as I know, none has been translated except *The People From Heaven* (1943), and that into Danish.

You may care to know that Black Sparrow will issue my latest in January '84. It will be called *The Winters of that Country*—meaning the country of mine.

Warmest greetings to you and the good people of Norway, whom I much admire.

Sincerely

145. To Noel Young

(Mr. Young is the founding editor and publisher of Santa Barbara's Capra Press.)

16 September 1983

Dear Noel

Here are the four pieces by Lew Amster:

1. Clever with Confectionary
2. Center of Gravity
3. The Killer Instinct: an anecdote
4. Mama Eu Quero

(the last, he tells me, means *Mama, I want you* in Portuguese)

I've tried to put forward the work of others on occasion, but never with the sense of elation that these stories give me. Maggie has read them too, and I say for both of us that they have our high regard. They're so simply written that they seem to have been spun off, spoken, almost, as though to kill an hour in a waiting-room. For all that, they're carefully told, and they stay in the mind. They're about the lower depths, of course, but Amster beholds what we tend to forget, that there are people down there as well as up here, and he loves them though he knows them well. He's wry, witty, keen-sighted, and inside what he's writing about—and I'll miss my guess if you don't agree. He's entitled to publication, Noel, and the publisher ought to be you. For myself, I can only say I wish I were able to write a story like Mama Eu Quero: it's a beauty.

Please read with great care. If you should decide in Amster's favor, I'd be only too happy to help in any way I could. If called on, I'd gladly write you a foreword. Maggie suggests, as an illustration for a cover, Eakins' Stag Night at Sharkey's. Do you know the painting? It has all the sleaziness of a $50 main.

Let me hear, eh?

Sincerely

146. To John Parke

5 December 1983

Dear Mr Parke

Thanks for your letter of the 1st. I'm glad you found stuff in *Goodly* suitable for the delicate air.

You say that in reading my work, you can't always tell whether it's fiction, fact, or stretcher. In truth, it's each at times and at other times all three. The Bunyun/Henry piece of course is clearly a tall tale told to make a social point. A piece on Davy Crockett, in *View From This Wilderness*, is a tall tale told to outdo tall tales; another, that merely looks like a tall tale, one on Mike Fink in *Winters*, is altogether true. As for the black schoolboy piece (correct title: A Voice From Harlem), it is fiction end to end and it was reprinted entire from where it first appeared, in my novel *A Man Without Shoes*. Fiction, I say, but the point was and is that, in view of our treatment of the blacks since the beginning, Pollard's was a wholly possible paper and therefore more authentic than invented.

As a writer yourself, surely you know of the writer's many stances—the participant, the observer, the commentator, the critic, the interpreter, the inventor. In the nearly seven hundred pieces I've written for the books we're talking about, I've stood in many places, but I've always been armed with research.

If you believe *Winters* to be solely about the enormity of nuclear bombing, then of course you're right about the flyer: it does *not* convey the nature of the book. Its title is the fourth I've taken from Bradford's *History*, all off the same page: "For the season it was winter," he says in his marvelous prose, "and they that know the winters of that country knew them to be sharp and violent, and subject to cruell and feirce stormes."

His winters were those in which the noonday sun shone most obliquely; mine are social, racial, political, economic, military. As in *Goodly*, the range is long—from Vikings earlier than Leif to Vietnam and Nixon. In 150-some sections, I try to present our "winters" in a way even more "cruell and fierce" than I showed them in *Winters [sic–Sanford probably meant to have written, "than I showed them in* Goodly*"].* There are strikes, riots, lynchings, bombings, wars, discriminations, and other assorted injustices. I might add, though I don't suppose I have to, that always I'm on the side of the people and therefore always against their rulers. That got me before H U A C in 1951, and well it may do so again.

You ask why I call these pieces "tales." As the word is defined, tale embraces all three of your categories, fact, fiction, stretcher: an account of some event or sequence of events, actual, legendary, or fictitious, usually imaginatively composed or adorned.

Re: your editing of *Goodly* for Kennikat. I did have a contract with Jaray for its publication, and of course you did go through it and make your recommendations about publication. He sent them on to me at the time, but I believed that if I followed them, I'd be putting out two halves of a book that would never add up to a whole one: the book was whole as it stood, I thought, and I told Jaray that it had to be issued that way or not at all. He said not at all, and I returned his advance, and the contract was cancelled.

You say that you think the book, as finally published, *was* cut in half. It was cut by me when Horizon agreed to do it, but only to the extent of some 90 pages. Those pages didn't seem to me to be of equal value compared with the rest, and I took them out. At a guess, I'd say they came to about 15% of the manuscript. After much revision, a few of the pieces were used in other books.

Yes, I think it is fair to claim Kennikat as a rejection along with all the rest. Jaray did not want to publish *my* book; he wanted to publish *his*. Certainly a publisher may suggest some editing, but when it comes to halving a book, I think he's making a proposal that a serious writer is bound to regard as a refusal to publish what the writer has written: in short, a rejection.

We should've been writing to each other far more often than twice in ten years. Let's not make that mistake again. I'd welcome word from you.

Sincerely—and just as warmly

147. To Joe Napora

(Joe Napora is a teacher, writer, poet. Fink *was eventually published by Wind Publications in 2010.)*

17 Dec 1984

Dear Joe Napora

I'm hard at work getting a new book ready for the press, but I can't let a letter like yours go unanswered. What with that book and eye-problems, I haven't read more than the *Fink*, which I must say I liked very much, and skimmed the rest enough to turn up the name of Tom McGrath, to whom you dedicated one of your poems.

I've known Tom for a long while and regard him as one of our best poets—absolutely Grade-A. If you too know him, you're lucky.

You're doing a good thing, letting the essence of America evoke your poetry. Too few care a shit for the country, as if they sprang from space, not a place with a history. And best of all, you're not dazzled by the history they taught you at school; you get at the real history, and that, I've found, is enough to provide a lifetime of material for work.

Keep at it, and the best of luck to you.

Sincerely

148. To Master Thomas Andrews

28 February 1985

Dear Tom Andrews (the younger)

Your good father, Tom Andrews the elder, has permitted me to read your story, *The Trial of Brian Banter*, and I must say that I'm glad he did. I wish that when I was 15, I'd been able to write as well. I urge you to try your hand again; it would be a pity to abandon something you seem to have a talent for. I was particularly struck by your construction. You open with action—that is, the setting out of the explorers—and having gotten them under way, you drop back easily to characterize the town and supply the reason for the journey. From there, you move forward swiftly to the description of the terrain, the finding of the shaft, the descent to the "Pit," or Hell, as I suppose the place to be, and then the trial and acquittal of Brian.

You accomplish this *telling* very surely. It's an art that few acquire after long practice—and its secret lies in the artlessness of the art, that is, in its natural quality. You seem to have that; don't lose it, don't (as they say) get arty.

I'd like to add a word about your imaginative observation. It takes a good mind to capture a place with two adjectives (*fading, rugged town of Danby*), and I liked too the personification in *his legs searched for the courage to move.* I was taken also by your metaphor *demonic cartoons* to describe the reflection of the flames.

And as much as anything, I admire the story's teaching: greed is a sin. I didn't know that at 15; you do.

And to conclude, Tom the elder has reason to be proud of Tom the younger.

Sincerely

149. To Per Petterson

(Mr. Petterson is a Norwegian novelist best known, perhaps, for Out Stealing Horses *and* To Siberia.*)*

17 April 1986

Dear Mr. Petterson

First, my congratulations on having your stories published. It's a great hurdle, finding a sponsor for early work, and you've cleared it. Now, Avanti!

Here are the answers to your questionnaire. You didn't number the questions, but I've taken them in order, and you ought to have no difficulty in making the match-up. I hope I've covered the ground as you wished; if not, call on me again. And you need have no fear of invading privacy; I haven't much to hide.

Color has won two awards in a week! John Martin doubtless will tell you about them. They're not Nobels or Pulitzers, but they're better than "Best Book Written by a Left-handed Man of 82."

All good wishes.
Sincerely

For Per Petterson, Tromo Bokhandel, Oslo

1.—

Yes, being called a writer's writer does mean that my books sell poorly. It has a deeper meaning, though, and that is this—what I write about doesn't catch the fancy of the general, or non-professional, reader. There are other elements—the *way* I write, for instance—that help me earn the faintly sneering designation—but primarily I sell poorly because of my choice of subject. I do not deal with the rich or romance, I do not glorify war, I do not make light of injustice, I do not write of zany antics. I'm hardly the one to ask whether my books are easy reading. They're experimental in form, which may put off the reader at home only with the traditional. I might say that *I* don't find them difficult.

2.—

If my writing had taken a new turn with every publisher, I'd've turned twelve times since my first publication. No, the only novelty for me with Black Sparrow is that it's the first publisher to have published me twice. I've never seen fit to ask John Martin what he thinks of my work: he publishes only what he likes (repeat, *only*), and after five of my books under his imprint, he'd just stare at me if I put the question. Let me add that I've never been asked to change a line.

3.—

Sooner or later, every writer who acts as his own publisher makes the same discovery: he cannot sell the book. He has no sales-force, he can't afford to advertise, and it's impossible to get reviews, this last because the reviewing media calls self-publication the work of "the vanity press" and ignore it. I'm greatly pleased that Norwegian readers regard *Shoes* as a good book; perhaps Americans would've thought so too had they been able to get their hands on it; it was never brought to their attention. In my introduction to the Black Sparrow reissue, I wrote of the book's original failure to see the light. From the Norwegian response, I take it that the book did not fail as literature.

4.—

For what my opinion of my own work may be worth, I think *Shoes* is the best of my first five books, but even so, it was only a stage in a developing career. Except for the autobiographical *Water Wheel*, I hadn't until then dealt with what I'd had the most experience of—people I'd known in a known locale, the Jews of New York. In writing of the Adirondack Mountains in my next three books, I was not quite in undiscovered country. I was fairly well acquainted with the district, in upper New York state [sic], but it had never been my home for more than a few months at a time. The stories I laid there in my second, third, and fourth novels were imagined elsewhere, and the attitudes they expressed came not from the particular place but from me. They were brought in from the outside, and they may or may not have caught the nature of the region. At any rate, I've never been fully satisfied with those fictions, and I tend to regard them as exercises for later things.

5.—

It's true that at the time *Color* ends, I've shown no signs of becoming a writer; at the age of 23, I still hadn't written a line. But I'd just then become reacquainted with Nathanael West, through whom literature entered my awareness; and in addition, I was carrying a sense of guilt over my ignorance of the Sacco-Vanzetti case. Within a year or so, these two factors began to work on each other, as you'll perceive, I hope, in the second volume of the autobiography, *The Waters of Darkness*, now on the press.

6.—

I've always regretted my change of name. It was never objected to by my father, whom I adored, but it must've pained him that his only son, for snobbish reasons, forsook his name.

7.—

I was exposed to anti-semitism as far back as I can remember, but it did not make me stop considering myself primarily an American and only secondarily a Jew. I was of course familiar with all things Jewish; raised by an orthodox grandmother, I could hardly have been otherwise. But my mother, though modestly religious herself, very early imbued me with a love of country that has never left me, indeed, that has only grown. I may say, however, that it was a mistake to go so far afield with my stories and their characters; I had all I needed in my very household, but I foolishly reached past it into another sphere. Perhaps, I sometimes think, I might've fared better if I'd stuck to my last. Still, when I came to write the autobiography, my Jewish experience simply poured out, as if it had been stored up too long.

8.—

I belonged to no particular school of writers in the Thirties, and I belong to none now, certainly not to the proletarians. Granted, I lean far to the Left, but my background and upbringing were those of the professional class, and I never knew (and have never written of) a single member of the proletariat. How could I honestly have handled a class I knew nothing of? I'd never worked in a mill or a mine, I'd never sold my life for an hourly wage, I'd never walked in a picket-line; instead, I'd dressed in the best, squandered my summers at the beach, and eaten well in dining-cars while I watched the hungry walk. My wife was born in a tar-paper shack on the plains of Nebraska, daughter of a plasterer, and to her it has always been a mystery how one such as I ever found the way to the left side of the road. It's a mystery to me too, but whether I understand it or not, that's where my heart is.

9.—

For one who has been writing for well over fifty years, I've known very few writers in my own field. After coming to California in the mid-Thirties, those I knew wrote almost exclusively for the screen, and since my wife was one of them, I quite naturally fell in with her associates, many of whom became my friends. When McCarthyism came to Hollywood at the close of the war, the fate such people met with was also my own: they, my wife among them, were blacklisted by the studios, and so was I by my publishers in New York. I was in fact on a blacklist even earlier. At the beginning of 1942, I was summoned to Washington by director Frank Capra (then a Colonel in the Signal Corps) to write training and indoctrination films for his unit. I wrote two of these, after which Colonel Capra offered me a commission in the Army, which of course I accepted. I soon learned from him, however, that I was unacceptable to G2 (Army Intelligence), and the offer was withdrawn. Thereafter I made four more efforts to enter the service—the Navy, the Officers' Candidate School, the Wright Field Signal Corps unit, and finally a film unit headed by Captain (Director) William Wyler. All these failed; I was always refused. The Hollywood Blacklist did not begin for another four or five years.

10.—

The development of a style is particularly difficult to explain. I can't account for my presence on the Left, let alone the manner in which I wrote about it. I can see a vast difference between my writing of the Thirties and my writing today, but its evolution has been the result of no conscious process. To a certain extent, I suppose, style is suggested, even compelled, by subject, but it would be a most unimaginative and mechanical writer who continually subordinated his style to the content; one affects the other, true, but the writer himself must control both. A good writer will take off, fly, no matter what he's writing about; a poor one never leaves the ground. A good writer, whether he's dealing with a book, a letter, an answer to a question—will be trying for his best. He will stamp his work with himself always. I hope I do that, but it's for others to say.

11.—

William Carlos Williams makes much of "writing like an American," but I've never been certain what that is. I'm reminded of the identification testimony given by a prosecution witness in the Sacco-Vanzetti trial: "They ran like Italians," he said. For me, American writing is simply writing by an American.

12.—

As far back as *Seventy Times Seven* in 1939, I began to intersperse the narrative with commentaries on American history, providing the story with "the color of the air." With *A More Goodly Country* in 1975, I dropped the story and concentrated on the commentary. It has been so ever since—and, yes, I did feel that I'd said all I had to say in the novel form.

13.—

My four books of historical commentary will, I hope, be published some day as *The American Quartet*. They constitute, I think, a form developed by me, and it may turn out to be a new field in literature. The four are made up of some 600 vignettes, and their burden is a collective indictment of injustice and inequality found everywhere in America since the time of its discovery. They were written in outrage over the ways in which a paradise was plundered by whites whom the Indians in their simplicity welcomed as "the people from heaven."

14.—

A sense of responsibility takes in more than responsibility for self; one must also be responsible for others. The teaching is Dostoevsky's, Christ's, and that of many another good man in history. If we ignore it—and we do ignore it!—we're left with a world like the one we live in.

15.—

The difference between Woody Guthrie and Ronald Reagan is this: When Guthrie says "This land is my land," he means it's his and mine; when Reagan says it, he means it's his, and I can go fuck myself!

16.—

I met W C Williams once and then for only fifteen minutes, but he was of unlimited importance to me through his superb book *In the American Grain*. It had a catalytic effect on me, resolving my entire American experience and thus pointing to where I must go on my own. Norwegian readers should know him better—he's held to be one of the three or four greatest poets of the century. Read his biography by Paul Mariani.

17.—

Many a contemporary was affected by Hemingway—by his remarkable suppression, his complete control—but those who let themselves be so influenced that they sought to emulate his style are no longer around to tell the tale of their folly. He wrote well, very well, enviably well, but the language needed just one of him, not a James Cain and the long train of others.

150. To Robert Gorham Davis

(Author of the article "God, My Grandson, and Me.")

9 May 1986

Dear Prof. Davis

When your Boston Review article came, I happened to be writing a scene involving my beloved father, and I felt all over again how deeply I must've injured him when I forsook his name and took up Sanford. The example had been set by Weinstein/West, but he wasn't to blame because I followed suit; for a contemptible piece of snobbery, I always blamed myself, and I'll never let myself off. West used to inveigh against the "professional Jew," more *fromm* than a rabbi, argumentative, loud in public, in short the stereotype, and my impression of him over a long period was that it troubled him to be a Jew, even an amateur (*teraphah*, conciliatory, quiet, you'd never guess etc.). I didn't feel that way about my Jewishness. I didn't care a pinch of owl-shit about being anything else, not even when Shapiro stupidly became Sanford: the opposite, rather, for I greatly enjoy being a Jew. We're a fine people—but a people, mind you, and therefore we have eyes, ears, dimensions, fault. Sometimes I think it isn't the Jew's sense of superiority that gets him in Dutch; it's the Dutchman's agreement.

You needn't have worried about how I'd take your article; I spot you good will, and my hackles are as flat as yours would be after reading my screeds on Alvin Fuller and Webster Thayer. I wasn't asked, but if you care for a Jew's opinion on your grandchild problem, here it is: I agree with your three Harvard pals. Let the kid choose when he grows up, or, if he chooses, choose not at all. Maybe he'll want to sit on the fence and watch both parades of We-know-we're-right. If there's a God, he'll understand—but why bring him in when, as you say, the great problem of the day is to preserve the planet for further debate as to whether there's a God?

Always a pleasure to hear from you. Volume 2 of the autobiography, by the way, contains nearly a hundred pages on my association with Pep West. It'll be out soon.

Yours

151. To Per Petterson

16 May 1986

Dear Per Petterson

The two copies of Klassekampen have arrived, and I thank you for them. This time, knowing what I said, there'll be no need for a translation—but I must confess to being curious about how you rendered the final line. Did you really say in Norwegian what I said in English? I hope so, for I surely meant it. So intensely do I dislike what Reagan stands for that I'm inclined to rank him as one of the most reactionary figures in American history—a saga of reaction, despite what we like to call the American Revolution. My only hope, and it's a slim one, is that the people will learn in time that the Reagan policy leads to war—and that war leads to the end of the planet. So far, nothing seems to have been learned from the Chernobyl disaster. The Administration has used it for propaganda purposes and not to teach the dangers of radioactivity. We're the good guys, the White House says; the other guys are the bad guys. Well, where can that lead except to a shootout?

You're certainly giving this old man some unexpected publicity, and I'm most grateful for it. I fully endorse your submitting the interview for Swedish publication as well; I'm absolutely unknown in the country. But, hell, I'm unknown in my own!

I heard only this morning from Black Sparrow that bound copies of Volume 2 of the autobiography will be shipped from the binder (In Michigan) within three weeks. If the book should come your way, I hope you like it. And I hope too that you're making progress with your own writing. Let me know what success you have.

With best regards.

Sincerely

152. To The Jewish Publication Society

17 August 1986

Dear Sirs

I write to express surprise over the failure of your publication(s) to take notice of the first two volumes of my autobiography, entitled: *The Color of the Air* and *The Waters of Darkness*—Scenes from the Life of an American Jew. You are not alone in the failure. No other Jewish publication in the United States has reviewed the book! Copies were sent to at least fifty such publications, and not one, *not one!*, reviewed the book.

My publisher, Black Sparrow Press of Santa Rosa, Cal., is wholly owned and operated by Christians, and yet they have sponsored these books by and about Jews. They are more than surprised that Jews have not supported their ventures—they are astounded! They simply cannot understand why Jews don't seem to care a rap about their own.

It will do no good, I suppose, to tell you that these books have been reviewed with favor by the N Y Times, the L A Times, the Cleveland

Plain Dealer, the Boston Globe, the Kansas City Star, and assorted magazines and weeklies. It will also do no good to acquaint you with the fact that *Color* was given an award by P.E.N. for being the best book of nonfiction in 1985 and the author was given a Distinguished Writer Award by the Santa Barbara Writers Congress. Such things don't count with us Jews.

I know we're stiffnecked (Exodus 32.9), but why against our own?

Sincerely

153. To John Martin

20 August 1986

Dear John

> Every publisher exists by reason of unpaid royalties—
> John Martin

You said *every*, and make no mistake. You said it in your driveway, and I repeated it to Maggie when I got home, and now and then we trot it out for a laugh.

I did not mean to imply that I felt cheated, however, and if that was your inference, I correct it. But I do feel squeezed by your insistence on retaining earned royalties as long as you do—it smacks of the foreclosure, of the Yankee trader, the Alger villain. I do not admire you for the position you take; in truth, I disesteem you.

A point now that you must think I'm too dumb to understand: you have not paid me $12,000 in royalties since we began. On the contrary. *I* have paid *you*. If I made $10,000 or so on *Shoes*, you made the same, dollar for dollar, on *my* book, handed over complete. If I made a grand on The Old Man's Place, so did you—on my manufactured book. That leaves some $1,500 for Winters—the only money I've ever gotten from you that you earned as a publisher, that is, laid out the costs for. And as for the two volumes of the Autobiography, I have yet to see a cent.

Say what you like, mister, but don't try to shit me.

You bet your ass I'm an author of distinction. A lot more so than that God damn anti-semite and Hitler-lover, Wyndam Lewis. You shame yourself by having him on your list.

And again, you said *every*.

154. To Per Petterson

25 March 1987

Dear Per

I have your letter of the 13th, and I was distressed to learn that your wife has been ill. I do hope that she has been responding and will soon be well.

I hear from Black Sparrow that Volume 3 is in the hands of the typesetter; doubtless I'll be reading galleys early in the coming month. Meanwhile, I've been at work daily on Volume 4, to be called "A Walk in the Fire," and it goes well—in my opinion, at least. It will cover the period 1945-51, that is, from Nagasaki to the House committee hearings at which my wife and I were blacklisted. The period was exciting, and my hope is to make the book exciting too. About Reagan and Reaganism, I feel of course as you do, but I caution you not to write him off just yet, not because he's invulnerable but because the American electorate is stupid. It was knocked off balance by the news of the Iran-Contra affair, but that was four or five months back, and the blockheads have recovered their equilibrium: they feel the country has "had enough," and they want to get on to matters more urgent—like devising tax reforms that will stuff them still further while cutting welfare, food stamps, education, medical benefits, and wages—and spending more on Star Wars and nuclear bombs. Truly, if you want to succeed in American politics, you must never *over*estimate the voter's brains. The Contras put him in mind of our Founding Fathers, Reagan says, and Oliver North is a national hero. No wonder the world is laughing at us.

"The Land That Touches Mine," Cape edition, is possibly the hardest book of mine to obtain. I have, I think, only two copies.

You delighted my wife and me with this Norwegian/American Sanford Society. The only trouble is that the American branch is inactive. I do have some friends here, it would appear, for a couple of things recently arrived out of the blue. The University of Illinois Press put me up for a Senior Fellowship with the National Endowment for the Arts, and Boston University has nominated me for an award from the American Academy for the Arts. I'll win neither. People on my side of the fence don't get awards from the Establishment for trying to pull the Establishment down; they get what we call a swift kick in the ass. I think it was Alexander Pope who wrote "Whatever is is right," but whoever it was, I disagree: Reagan *is*, but he's wrong.

Thanks for the Samtiden, with the Olsen piece on "A Man Without Shoes." Would you, in a free moment, send me a translation?

I was touched by your gift of a rose to the purchaser of the last copy of "A Man Without Shoes." I hate to tell you this, but I still have 75 copies of the original (not the Black Sparrow) edition.

Volume 3 ought to be out during the summer.

My wife joins me in sending all good wishes to you and Mrs. Petterson.

Sincerely

155. To Cedric Belfrage

(Here, Bill K is William Kuntsler, Sanford's distant cousin by marriage and attorney for the defense in the court-martial of Marine Sgt. Clayton Lonetree. Galeano refers to the Uruguayan author Eduardo Galeano, who, in 1984, published a trilogy of books titled Memory of Fire, *translated by Cedric Belfrage; Galeano's Trilogy closely resembles Sanford's later work in that it offers interpretations of Latin American history.)*

28 August 1987

Dear Ced

Be sure that your warm letter was warmly received. We hear from few these days, and of those none carries us back as you do, to times of hope now so far away. I think of the Clipper, nearly fifty years dead, its pages yellowed but not its purpose, and I rejoice that, having worked for it then, we work for it yet.

Your invitation to Cuernavaca is one we'd gladly take advantage of if we were still the travelers of old. We're old, all right, but we travel no more; we too have our frailties, and they keep us on a short tether. It's a hard game we've all been playing for so long, but I hope some will say we've enriched it.

The Galeano was a stunner. I'd had no idea that anyone was working the same vein as I. Our manner is different, but there are remarkable parallels in what we see, balk at, try to change. I wish somebody would translate me into Spanish! I'd love to know what Galeano might say of the coincidence.

I haven't heard from Bill K since he sent the book, but of course he's been deep in the Lonetree case all along. It strikes me he has a good game on appeal. It was too much to expect, that a Marine Corps jury would acquit, as I think it should have; they're out to keep up the image—the fine North image! But the civil court, unless all the cards are stacked, ought to take the reasonable view that Lonetree did not have the combination to the safe. How preposterous, that he traded secrets for a roll in the hay. What secrets could a kid like that have been privy to? My guess is, he didn't even know how to screw. At the best, he's a fall guy for the guys upstairs.

Here's Black Sparrow's Fall/Winter catalogue. Vol 4 is about half complete, possibly for 1989.

Maggie joins me in sending much love and all good wishes to you and Mary—and do write if you can spare the time. The book and the letter were real treats.

Affectionately

156. To Lew Amster

13 October 1987

Dear Lew

I'm expecting Author's copies any day, so subscribers' copies shd not be far behind. Unless you have a behind.

This stumble-bum you mention, Young Kippur—he was well-known to us back in the Harlem days. His best fight, as we all know, was against a comer called Rush Hashonah. He lasted well into the second round.

Work on Vol 4 prigresses (that's close enough) daily. What a good thing it is to have a known publisher! My first ten books were put out by ten different houses, fuck'em all! I was 65 years old before I was published twice in a row. Shit! What a profession!

And a happy one to you. Next year, on dit, in Jerusalem!

Mag and I send love.

157. To Per Petterson

30 November 1987

Dear Per

I've been married for 49 years; I suppose that's why I regretted hearing of your divorce. I simply can't conceive what life would be separate from Maggie.

The book is a beautiful thing indeed—jacket, binding, type, and format. My compliments to the designer, Egil Haraldsen. And of course my compliments to you—you've done it! More than that, you've scored on your very first try. What you must do now is come up with other books, always trying to move forward from the last, bettering yourself every time. Never settle for a mere repetition of what you've done before; there's only one reason for continuing to write—continuing to improve. The saddest example in American letters was John O' Hara. *Appointment in Samarra* was a first novel, and a beauty. He must've written thirty books to follow, but never, never!, did he advance. All good luck to you. I only wish I could read Norwegian.

I hope something comes of the Danish connection. As to Galeano, someone in Mexico just sent me a copy of his *Memories of Fire* (Genesis), which in many ways is like my *A More Goodly Country.*

It would also be pleasant if Oktober did something with the book club.

As to selling you copies from my stock of Shoes, I dislike having to refuse you. These that I have are all that's left of the original printing of 2,000. Those sold by John Martin, though from the same printing, automatically became a reissue because of the introduction and the Black Sparrow title-page. So I simply would not be able to put a price on those I have, and in any case I'd rather not.

Vol 3 of the Autobiography has arrived. If Tronsmo ordered

any, they should soon arrive.

Best to you—and write again.

Cordially

158. To Per Petterson

29 December 1987

Dear Per

Well, Vol 3 is just out, and we're waiting for reviews. I don't know why they should be better (or worse) than reviews of Vols 1 and 2, but the devil knows what gets into these scriveners—or what runs out. I can say this, though, that from those individuals who've read the book, I have yet to hear a discouraging word. I could elaborate on that, but I'm not going to. *You* tell *me*.

I've heard from J Martin about paperback rights on *Shoes*, but he offers only the percentage he gives on anything else—no advance, no increased royalties, even though he surely means to photo-offset the original and not reset type. I told him he'd have to make a step upward, but so far he's staying where he is.

That'll leave matters just where they stand, and to be frank I don't much care. I hope you're sticking to your guns and writing your head off. If I can do it at 84, you can at 35. I don't mean writing fast; I mean writing well. There's a Hollywood story about a movie producer demanding more and more script, and the writer says "Do you want it good, or do you want it Thursday?" Make it good!

Here's wishing you all the best for 1988.

As ever

159. To George Lewis

3 June 1988

Dear Lewis

I don't get letters like yours—about one every couple of years would cover it—but however seldom they come, they're as vital as air. What critics say is nothing—that's their job, not their pleasure. But what the people say, those one writes for but never sees, that *is* the ultimate word. You say I inspire you? When you tell me that you stood for hours in a bookshop just to read me, *you* inspire *me!* Thanks.

But how in the world did you get my address?

All the Best to you, and it was good of you to note my birthday. My 84th, in case you're wondering.

Yrs etc

160. To Lew Amster

16 July 1988

Dear Lew

Damn it Amster (or Amster damn it), your book arrived after only 5 ½ wks on the road. You could've walked here and delvd it by hand in less time. That aside, it's a goodlooking job of book-making, and my congrats to Capra, which always puts out a decent book. Your stories, I know, of course, and you know I admire them, but be sure that Maggie and I will read them again, not only for themselves but also for the pleasure of seeing them in print. It's a shame, a shame, that the book wasn't the first in a long line of Amsters. You have a very real and fine talent, and you have no right to withhold it—and I'll keep on saying that until you put more of Joe Benjamin on the page. You lazy slob!

As threatened, Volume 4 of the Autobio is complete, and it's even now on its way to Black Sparrow for Spring issue. It goes from Nagasaki to the HUAC hearings of 1951, where Maggie and I got our come-downance. What next? Vas noch? I think they'll be no Vol 5—that's gone far enough. Maybe another book of historical commentary—I've still got some venom, though the fangs are questionable.

Maggie joins me in sending love to one of our favorite guys—youse.

As ever

161. To Lew Amster

10 Jan 1989

Dear Amsterdam it

I've sent you two Fidels. Your Super must be eating them. Here's a third, somewhat revised and incorporating the Hispanic's suggestions—at any rate, most of 'em. Throw the other versions away if the Super coughs them up. Re the K A Porter piece. Of course, it wasn't written from my point of view; I was never married to the woman. What I did was put myself in the position of someone who was, a guy half her age. It wasn't essential to the piece that he be named, but his identity is no secret from the world. I simply thought it didn't matter who the hell he was—if only I could get into his mind. If I failed, the fault is mine, not with the omission of a name.

This Saul Jarcho, I met him briefly through Pep West, whose cousin he was, first, I think. As a kid, he was brilliant, graduating from high school at about fourteen. And as a doctor, when connected with Mt. Sinai, he was held in high regard. I've known nothing about him during the fifty years last past.

My Queen of Nebraska was in the hospital again for eight days, right through the holidays and our 50th anniversary. I'd give all I have, which is eighteen books, if I could make her well.

Love to you and the Senora—guard her well.

Affectionately

162. To Bob Smith

(This is the first letter following the death of Sanford's beloved wife, Marguerite Roberts, who died in February, 1989.)

25 April 1989

Dear Bob Smith

Yes, I think I did further Maggie, but it was a small thing compared to her furthering of me. She'd've been among the best even if she never met me; without her, I'd've been nothing, another nobody talking on street-corners to scorning men. I'm the only one who knows the extent of her quality, and now I'm writing a book in the hope of conveying it to others. I don't believe I've got the talent for it, but I'm trying anyhow—and it's the only bearable part of the day.

Always best to Mrs. Smith and you.

As ever

163. To Bob Smith

("The Memoir" mentioned here is the book that would appear as Maggie: A Love Story, *published in 1993 by Barricade Books after John Martin of Black Sparrow Press turned down the manuscript after publishing Volume Five of Sanford's Autobiography.)*

14 October 1990

Dear Bob

Forgive me for not having answered your letters earlier. The truth is, I'd've had nothing good to report—only unrelieved sorrow. The Memoir does more, though. I must have close to 40,000 words of it now. I think it reads well, but it's too intimate a thing for me to judge. And frankly, I don't care much what anyone thinks: I'm writing it in honor of Maggie, and that's enough for me. As someone said of General Pope, I don't care for the public a pinch of owl-shit.

Martin informed me that he was almost clear of his Fall list and that soon Vol 5 would go to the typesetter. Hurrah for Octavio Paz! Better he than Mailer.

Best to you and the signora.

As Ever

164. To Aris Janigian

(This letter's recipient was once Sanford's literary executor. He is the author of the novels Bloodvine *and* Waiting for Lipchitz at Chateau Marmont.*)*

28 February 1991

Dear Aris

I've read each of the three stories twice, and here's what I think—along with a reminder that I'm not making a judgment; I'm merely giving an opinion, and opinions can be wrong, mine especially.

The first thing I'd like to say is you don't pay enough attention to form. You write in long paragraphs, great blocks of typing that daunt the eye. It's wrong to cram all your thoughts into packages like that. A few lines at a time, and then a break—and you'll find that the story builds far better.

Another weakness is your habit of introducing irrelevant material in the narration. In *Stalker*, for instance, the colleague you bring in adds nothing to the terror; in fact, he interferes with it. The same is true of the departmental intrigue and the facts you cite of the Genovese case. Your task in this story is to swell the sense of terror without a letup (a story of terror ought to terrify), and when the reader is treated to extraneous detail, you lose him. You lose him too (you lose *me*, anyway) with such words as *glitch*, *instinctual*, *ideation*, and *duplicitous*. In a story such as this one, don't try for effect with the big word, especially if it smells of your doctoral: knowledge is not literature. And finally, watch your living verbs: one does not *disembark* from a taxi—except in Venice.

Mosquito is greatly superior to *Stalker*; indeed, it's by far the best of the three. Here the obsession you deal with isn't the baseless terror of pursuit. We know very well that it's the need to quiet a sound, and you work it up to action very skillfully—and very plausibly.

There are almost no digressions of the kind you're partial to; an exception might be where you pause to chuck a stone or two at Porn's writing (and you must forgive me for calling it pornography). To offset any other objection, there are many felicities, chief of which are the fanciful references to sound: "the neutrality of sound," "a stupid sound," "the sound of something too small to think," "a thin weightless sound." These are very good things, indeed. *Mind-set!* Forget it, and for God's sake forget *Semiotics.* Whatever they are, forget them! Knowledge is not. . . .

As to *The Bridge*, it promised to be the best of the three because it seemed to have a social rather than an individual base. Its potential was allowed to ravel away. At the start, the reader is supposed to gather that the character's obsession is the safety of many, and you make it play so well against his wife's complacency that Chuck Morley is rendered excess baggage.

But time and again you bring in diversions, and what they do is divert, which in no way helps your story. The premonition about the space-shuttle does not add to the validity of the premonition about the bridge. The dissertation on "our elected leaders" belongs in New Masses. The engineering history of the bridge is a long piece of journalese. The woman who lives under the bridge is a red herring: she threatens the man's plans, and the threat turns out to be empty.

But there's worse. When the man's wife discovers the explosives, we learn that his intention was to destroy, not to save. Long too late do you reveal that you've been dealing with a lunatic. All those words in testimony of a social conscience—only to weaken and settle for melodrama. You had something that resembled *An Enemy of the People* when you began, but not when you ended. Ibsen's character was sane.

For as long as I've known you, you've had great respect for good writing—the good writing of others. You must learn to have the same respect for your own. Only too often do I find sentences, phrases, words that will *do.* That's not good enough. A high level of writing, seamless, rhythmical, original, and persuasive, is hard to reach, but it can never be reached by work that will *do.* Writing, as Dickens said of life, is a horrid grind, but the writer's only hope is in trying—and then trying some more.

To repeat what I said at the top: I don't know it all.

As Ever

165. To Joseph McBride

(McBride is the author of the biography Frank Capra: The Catastrophe of Success, *Simon & Shuster, 1992.)*

16 April 1991
Dear Mr. McBride

I have your Air Express letter of 13 April, and it gives me pleasure to learn that your Capra biography is about to be published. Of course you have my permission to quote from my Capra correspondence in the manner and to the extent you indicate.

I'm not proud of my style in the correspondence. A long way back, it began to strike me as fat, and I can only hope my later style is leaner. And one other thing: when I told Capra I was not a communist, I wasn't telling the truth, as anyone who has read my Autobiography must surely know. My only excuse for the lie, if a lie can ever be excused, is that Capra had no legal right to inquire. Nor did the House Committee later on.

I take the liberty of sending you the Black Sparrow catalogue, which lists Vol 5 of the Autobiography. The book ought to be off the press any day now.

All good luck with yours.

Sincerely

166. To Francis Irvin

8 September 1991

Dear Francis Irvin

Yours was the longest letter I ever received—the longest, I think, that anyone has. Thanks for the interest that put you to such labor. I wish I could reply in kind, but at 87, I'm a little pressed for time. It isn't necessary to comment on your positive points; I accept them gratefully. Certain negative ones, though, can't be allowed to pass.

I think I ought not to be taken to task for not having written the kind of books that others would've written were they I. What I write about, and what I put in and leave out—all of that is Sanford, and there's no use looking for someone who isn't there. My books are my books, and if they don't suit, or suit only in part, I'm willing to take the rap. But I will not write what others want me to write, nor will I write with any particular regard for what they may or may not understand. If they come to a book unprepared—as you were for the Melville piece—it's their fault, not mine. The solution: read Melville.

You coolly say anyone can write my kind of short historical commentary. If so, I've not yet seen it—and neither, I think, have you. Otherwise, you'd be writing long letters to them instead of me. I'm a modest enough guy, Irvin, and I don't blow my own horn—but nobody, *nobody*, writes that kind of piece, and nobody, *nobody*, could write it half as well.

Why wasn't I drafted in WW II? I was 36 years old and not draftable. My six tries at serving were voluntary.

My novels are my best work, you say. I disagree. My best, I think, are the historical quartet, and after that the autobiography.

It was hurtful to read that you skipped the "love-stuff," as you call it, in the Autobiography. The love between me and my wife was the great experience of a long life—the great accomplishment, I might say, and it was a far greater thing than my writing. Indeed, without that love, there'd've been no writing, for Maggie supported it all. I owe her a life, and it was unkind of you to slight her.

And finally, your rebukes about my Haymarket pieces. You seem to feel that I was flip in playing with the spelling of Louis Lingg's name, which is simply preposterous. You should know better without my telling you, and I can only set your error down to reading with a tin ear. I often speak in voices—dialect, slang, irony, scorn, and sometimes as a foreigner, and my "playing" with Lingg was the offhanded voice of the hangman, and it was meant to convey the utmost detestation of the legal proceedings. How could you miss that or should I say mis*read* that? And still write to praise me for other things?

But as I said at the start, thanks for liking so much of what I've done.

A word of advice. Better stop trying to put me forward. You will not succeed in making me known—and at 87, it doesn't matter.

Yours, etc.

167. To Per Petterson

29 Nov 1991

Dear Per

Thanks for your good letter—and your indignation.

I'm no warm friend of John Martin, but I think he was telling the truth about not being able to carry me any longer. I *do* lose, you know, and no other publisher would've stuck with me this long. What is also true is that he *did* say without reservation that he'd publish anything I wrote—and he went back on his word. And there's a further truth: he was not trying to squeeze paperback rights out of me; he could've had them for the asking. But, all truths being on the table, I might as well add one that has nothing to do with books. John has what my honored father used to warn me against: Beware, he said, of a man with a cold eye.

Please don't intervene. Men with a cold eye don't change their minds—and they just could turn the eye on you. Besides, the Memoir is being read by the Univ of Illinois Press. It will be rejected, I think, but as a result of submitting it, the Director of the press has asked for permission to reissue one of my old novels. I offered *The People From Heaven* (Harcourt 1943), and I have a strong feeling it'll be accepted.

The Memoir takes my Maggie's story all the way to her death in 1989. It'll be a heartbreaking thing if it doesn't see the light (it's really Vol 6 of the Autobiography). Is there anybody in Norway . . . ?

My best regards to your girl and to you.

All good things to both of you.

As soon as your letter came, I called Maxine DeB and read her your last paragraph. She was delighted and sends you greetings.

168. To Aris Janigian

3 March 1992

Dear Aris

I haven't read your book, but good or bad, it didn't deserve to be dismissed so imperiously. That agent must think pretty well of herself to risk such finality.

It's no good my telling you I've endured the same thing five hundred times; your headache gets no better because I have one too. I can only say this, that you've got to take the punishment or stop writing.

Get yourself another agent, let him/her handle the submissions, and turn to new work. That advice was given to me many times, and I never took it. Let's see whether you've got more sense than I had.

One more word. Pay scant heed to critics, whether they knock you or boost you. What the hell do they know? They sentenced Melville to sixteen years in the Custom House. That's what they know.

Yours, etc.

169. To Simone Dykmann

(Sanford met Dykmann in 1930 in Menton, France.)

6 April 1992

Dear Simone

You asked an important question in your recent letter, and I overlooked it at the time: you wanted to know how I was taking the changes in Eastern Europe. I deplore them: I regard them with disgust and dismay. Without doubt, terrible things had been happening in the Soviet Union for a long time—corruption, repression, discrimination, political murder, all of it under a smothering bureaucracy. The leadership was criminal, venal, ruthless, and the administration was as inept as if they had yet to discover the wheel. Granted, all that.

Still, I think that in junking Socialism because it hasn't run smoothly, they're throwing the baby out with the bath. This benevolent free society we live under here and in France and elsewhere is neither free nor benevolent—as the Russian idiots will soon discover to their sorrow. Once again, they'll find themselves on the outside looking in. It'll be dog-eat-dog again, a society of *mine*, *mine*, and to the strongest will go the meat and to the weakest the bone. What a pity! They had seventy years of living under Socialism, and it didn't take. What is man that he cares for no other man than himself? True, they ran the country as if it were a department store (My God, they had to buy wheat from Iowa!—and they had nine time-zones to grow it in), but while they mismanaged nearly everything, they oughtn't to punish themselves by jumping into Wall Street's bed. They should've found leaders that wouldn't sell them out for a car and caviar. They should've shot the leaders instead of those who complained.

My thoughts naturally turn to Maggie in this connection. After taking ten years on the Blacklist for refusing to betray her comrades, her comrades betray her! What irony! All the same, I know that even if she could've see this coming, she'd have done what she did. Another irony is that the capitalist world seems to be just as dismayed as I am, though for a different reason: we're going to have to support half a billion people—and we don't even want to support our own!

Love to the Three Sisters (Chekov).

170. To Joseph McBride

23 April 1992

Dear Joe

I just finished your biography of Frank Capra, and I want you to know without delay that I think it excellent. Over the past several years, in connection with my own writing, I've read biographies by the dozen, but none that I can recall did more than acquaint me with the story of a life. You made me feel that I was witnessing a tragedy made inevitable by reason of Capra's very nature. I'd known little of him before-hand, and it was your writing that made me perceive a man of great ability brought down by his innate fatal flaws. It wasn't the times, it wasn't the stars, it wasn't the ways of the world—

it was Capra himself that was Capra's undoing, and relentlessly and truly you chronicled his fall.

I say truly because I mean truly. I don't think you rejoiced in the fall; I think you deplored it. I think you deeply wished that there could've been a better second half to Capra's life, but knowing that it was otherwise, you chronicled it with sadness but with a clear eye. In doing so, you accomplished a wonder: you made me pity a man much of whose character I despised. That's art, Joe, and I congratulate you. It's a first-rate book, and I hope it's widely read.

With admiration

Miscellany:

Virginia Van Upp was a friend of my Maggie's, and she hated me. "What does he do when he's with you?" she asked. "Smash atoms?"

Howard Green, Claude Binyon, and Maggie raced horses together as Big Oak Stables.

My next-door neighbor is Ralph Riskin, son of Everett, and he's waiting for a crack at the book. He gets it today.

171. To Per Petterson

(The book of Harlem stories mentioned in this letter was eventually published with the title The View From Mt. Morris.*)*

15 May 1992

Dear Per

My father, best and wisest of men, told me to watch out for men with a cold eye; they had a cold heart to go with it. He must've had John Martin in mind. That guy had really put a crimp in me with his refusal to print the Memoir (actually Vol 6 of the Autobiography). It's a lost child. I can't get anybody to take it in. A couple of people are reading it, but my hopes are low, very low. And it's a pity too, because what the book really amounts to is a love-story, beginning with the day I met Maggie to the terrible day of her death. As in the other volume, there's a series of commentary to accompany it, all fifteen pieces new. Oddly enough, Maggie knew of them; they were written and read to her in her illness. You can easily understand, therefore, why the book is so dear to me—and Martin knew it! He picked a wicked time to cut me loose.

Of course I haven't been sitting on my ass and doing nothing. I've been sitting, all right, but at this machine, and I've finished the book of Harlem stories. I can't call them that, though, because in my time there (1904-1920) no blacks lived in my neighborhood, and the word Harlem connotes a black appearance, and the title would be misleading. So I'm calling it by the address of my birthplace: *2 West 120th St.* I've already been told that it's unappealing. You may tell me anything you like.

John Martin is a cold-hearted momser (Jewish for BASTARD).

I wish we weren't so far apart. We could talk straight stuff about those Los Angeles riots. Not a living soul yet has told the truth about them. There's all kinds of bullshit about lack of education, race prejudice, and the Rodney King beating—but the truth is, under Capitalism there's always *ALWAYS!* an underclass, and no amount of pious palaver will change it. You want to stop slums, discrimination, poverty? Get rid of the fucking system! Otherwise the next riot (and it'll come) will be worse. Hell, there was damn near a revolution *this* time!

But you aren't near; you're far away. However, you're near your girl, which is the best thing the world has to offer.

All the best to you and the kids and your Pia.

172. To Per Petterson

11 December 1992

Dear Per

Thanks for the new book, which I will read as soon as I learn Norwegian. But even without reading it, let me say this about its so-called "grey tone": tell your critics to go fuck themselves. If they want lighter books, let them write them. As for you, write as you God damn please, and piss on the bastards who think they know better. From this, you can easily see why I've been so successful.

Strange that you should steer me toward Greywolf Press. Many years back, they printed a book by a man I admired—Weldon Kees—and when Black Sparrow cut me loose, it was Greywolf I turned to first. Result: a form letter unsigned, saying they were swamped with manuscripts and couldn't etc.

Some weeks back, a friend engineered a submission to Lyle Stuart, which I made. I'm awaiting a verdict.

Here's one you'll like. As soon as Capra backed out, I had a letter from John Martin saying I was to resubmit the Memoir after the New Year, and *if he had the money*, he'd publish it. That's a big *if*, but it's better than a punch in the mouth.

I signed a contract with the Univ of Illinois Press for the republication of The People From Heaven, foreword by me, introduction by Prof Alan Wald, Univ of Michigan.

I grieve for you in your troubles. It must be very bad not to be able to live under the same roof with Pia—and almost as bad to give up Tronsmo. I wish I could say something helpful, but I don't have the words—except these. Get rid of the feeling of apathy! It'll kill whatever it touches.

All good luck with *Det er griet for meg.* It's a beautifully made book. May it win you prizes!

In friendship

173. To Lyle Stuart

(Stuart was the publisher of Barricade Books, which published Maggie: A Love Story *and* A View From Mt Morris.*)*

17 May 1993

Dear Lyle

This replies to your letter of 12 May.

Mt Morris is an account of the first sixteen years of my life. I'm not telling you anything you don't know when I say little of it resembles the usual autobiography. Its writing is unconventional—experimental, even—and rarely does it observe the general rules of form, time, and order.

You claim that after three more readings, you still find the ending defective for its failure to promise "a warm ongoing relationship." That's because you've been looking for the end at the end, which, in *Mt. Morris*, is the wrong place to look. In *Mt. Morris*, it's at the beginning, on p 11, in a scene called "Your Father."

What you believe is missing from the final scene (the promise of a warm ongoing etc) is revealed in the first. There, as clearly as I could state it, I set down that my Father was my lifelong idol; that my admiration for his character and my respect for his conduct were deep and lasting; that I longed for his approval and that, though often undeserving, I won it; that my love for him (and his for me) was undiminished when he died at the age of ninety-four—and that I kissed him in farewell after he was dead.

If more is needed, more is abundant in the scenes with him that follow. On several occasions, I use the phrase "in later years" to indicate a leapfrog in time, and my manner of speaking plainly shows that I'm far past the age of sixteen. Indeed, in a particular exchange with my father, he addresses me as "counselor," a title earned only after admission to the bar. Do not all these things suggest "a warm ongoing relationship"?

I think it fully established in the narrative that no lasting break, no break at all, occurred between me and my Father. For that reason, an explanatory tag pinned to the book would nearly belabor the obvious. Worse, it would ruin whatever art, whatever novelty of expression, whatever integrity *Mt. Morris* may possess. That's a fate I'd wish for no man's book, least of all for one of mine.

Mt. Morris is complete as it stands, and what is complete cannot be made more so; it can only be marred. I hope that on reflection you come around to my view.

Sincerely,

P S

Put aside for the moment all that I've written above and assume that there *was* no ongoing warm relationship.

What of it?

Not all relationships progress warmly until the cold universal end. I don't recall any such relationship in *Anna Karenina*; the woman threw herself under a train. Nor was there one in *The Great Gatsby*, or *An American Tragedy*, or *A Farewell to Arms*, or *The Scarlet Letter*, or *Moby-Dick* . . . . . . or the New Testament! There's a sweet warm note for you—Revelation!

All those good and some great—and not a one has a rosy ending.

174. To Per Petterson

1 September 1993

Dear Per

I hear from Barricade that printed and bound copies of *Maggie* have reached the N Y office. All I've seen so far is galleys, and I have only a hazy idea of what the complete book looks like. But from a rough sketch sent me by my publisher (himself!), I gather that the jacket will be a garish affair of yellow and azure, with a setting sun and a palm tree to make sure the reader knows that the locale is California. Of course suns set and palms grow in Egypt, a point that seems to have escaped my publisher (himself!)

(delay, letter put aside)

11 September

My fears have been realized: I have an author's copy. The design of the book apparently was entrusted to the local Pizza Man. It's quite the poorest work I've had since Boni's dentist designed *The Old Man's Place*. But what the hell—if the words don't score, the jacket won't hurt; and if they do, the jacket won't matter. I rather like the ones I've written, and I hope you do too.

I'm glad you found Weldon Kees a good writer. I valued him from an early day, and it was deplorable he could find no reason to live. He had a clean straightaway style, and he said what he meant without trying to convey the impression that he meant something else. I know too that he was responsive to my writing. When *The $300 Man* was published, the N Y Times assigned it to him for review. Somehow they also assigned it to someone named C D B Bryan. Bryan got it first and slaughtered the book. I was told that Kees' review, while not altogether favorable, was far better and would have put the work forward. Christ, a man must be king of the Shithouse to wear three initials!

I probably told you that Barricade took *The View From Mt Morris*, dealing with my first 16–20 years. I'm halfway into *The View From the Plains*, the story of Maggie's parallel years.

I don't like what's happening in the world, but that's nothing new; I haven't liked it since 1912. St. Petersburg! Can you beat that? Next thing you'll know, they'll find Anastasia's grandson, and he'll be Nicholas III. As for the accord (if accord is the word) in the Middle East, it remains to be seen whether it triumphs over discord.

Enough gloom. May you do well with Pia, your new book, your new home, and just plain living.

As Ever

175. To Joe Napora

23 November 1993

Dear Joe

Basically, your review of *Maggie* is philosophical, and as such, it wouldn't have a chance with the Times or the Nation. It shows too deep an understanding of the book's implication to appeal to that kind of trade. I agree with you—that it'd be better to try the more independent and therefore the more obscure journals with it. I wish you luck—and in today's market, you'll need it.

For some shithead reason, I'm in my publisher's doghouse. He hasn't written to me in four months, nor has any member of his staff, no doubt at his order. So I know absolutely zilch about how the book's faring. If you see any reviews, for Christ's sake send'em on!

I'm glad you liked *Maggie*. You're no pushover.

Best to you, kid.

176. To Jack Mearns

(Mearns is now Sanford's literary executor. He is Professor of Psychology and teaches in the graduate program at California State, Fullerton, and is author of the bibliography of Sanford's work, published by Oak Knoll Press.)

30 January 1994

Dear Jack

I have your two letters. Re the second, the answer to your question is: the correct title is *A Return to Pagany*, and the publisher Beacon Press (Boston) 1969.

Re the first, don't get worked up over the inequities of critical rejection: if it happened to Melville, it can happen to anybody. It troubled me once—though not to distraction, for I'm still shaming the devil at 90—but it troubles me no more. I don't care a pinch of shark shit for what the critics say. There was only one person I deeply desired to please, and she's gone and with her the pleasure of pleasing: I write now simply to speak, not to be heard.

Always a treat to see you—but that may be due to the Jewish lady you bring along.

Yours, etc

Someone tipped me that the subtitle of Henry Roth's new book is *A Star Shines Over Mt. Morris Park*. That made my own unusable.

177. To Joe Napora

(Wind Publications published 1917 *as* Sentences and Bills—1917 *in 2011.)*

4 May 1994

Dear Joe

Thanks for the 1917 poems and the poems on Central America.

I've read both with pleasure and admiration. One of the things that struck me was that you and I get outraged at the same national crimes—the Haymarket, the Bisbee Deportations, the Ludlow Massacre, the Haymarket [sic]. It's good to know that someone out there is fuming too. Now and again, I feel I haven't done a pinch of good—and then I wonder how in hell I know. Somebody may be getting it, I tell myself, and I keep on being sore.

You ask for a steer for the 1917 poems. I'd give you one if I could, but I can't. I'm out of touch. I was so long with Black Sparrow that I lost every other contact. I was lucky to get Barricade, but they'd be hopeless for 1917. They wouldn't know revolutionary poetry if it went off under their ass. You keep trying. 1917 deserves publication.

Best.

178. To Joe Napora

25 May 1994

Dear Joe

Didn't mean to depress you, fella. But when I said I was lucky to land with Barricade, lucky is what I meant. Black Sparrow had flung me out with a good book begging, and Barricade took me in. That's luck, and don't ever think it ain't. Barricade isn't Knopf or Harcourt (old style), but all I want these days is a hard cover on a book, and phrig prestige.

Just finished reading galleys on the new one, due in the Fall. I'll get Barricade to send you a copy. And—only today I completed my latest, this one on Maggie's childhood and first marriage (damn it, she didn't wait for me!) You'd've loved her; everybody did.

Best to you and Ms Schmidlapp.

Arriba the people!

179. To Jack Mearns

24 June 1994

Dear Jack

It took me all week to give the new Maggie book its last licks, and I didn't get to *King of the Dead Wood* till this morning. I read it in a sitting, and this is what I think.

It's far and away better than your Owen Tall story. In fact, it's a story, and the other is not. It's about a recognizable and fallible human being, such a one as you and I, and it begins and ends where it ought to: in short, it's complete. A good deal of felicitous writing has gone into the making of Dr Mandrel, and there's evidence of it everywhere (of Dr Williams on pp 164-5: "He was merely a passive conduit for the muse.") I give high marks to packed writing like that.

I wish it were the only kind of writing in *Dead Wood*, but it's not. There are paragraphs—pages, even—of classroom exposition that have no place whatever in a literary effort. More often than I cared to see, you slid into learned lecture, and your story slowed to a walk. Of course you know about psychology, and of course you know how to teach it, but that becomes art only when you write about it as of the figures on an urn. Drop into technical jargon, and art kisses you goodbye.

I don't suppose there's much objective criticism; most of it tells how the critic would do the thing. Bear that in mind when I say that I think you weaken Mandrel's story by the way you tell it. You have him pouring it out to a chance visitor in a long (an impossible) gush of orderly English. I'm uncomfortable with that, and you must be as well or you wouldn't try (transparently) to break the flow. A man can't be forever sucking a fucking pipe! The odd thing about the method you use is that so far from giving you scope, it cramps you; it makes Stansbury useless. All he can do is hear. If, though, you tell Mandrel's story in the third person, Stansbury can stand outside and inside at will: he can hear, and he can interpret. As much as anything else, that would get rid of the burden of the observer's knowledge of Mandrel's subject. The reader doesn't give a damn about the technical aspect of the subject he teaches; he does care, though, about the teacher. Surely you don't mean to write only for your confreres.

A few words about a bad habit you sometimes give in to—cramming stuff into the narrative that doesn't belong. Take Cooney. For all the good he does, he can be covered in a dozen lines and forgotten. His long (and for your purposes pointless) tale about ice-climb-ing simply knocks a hole in *Dead Wood*. And take Harold Frederic. You cannot stick a book report into the novella, however much you like the book. In addition, I don't believe in the parallel, because what you're telling me is that a psychologist needs a novelist to explain him. You're a psychologist; you explain him. That's what you get your name on a book for.

Pages 125-6-7—excellent writing, none better in the novella.

An odd point: I'm puzzled by your (Mandrel's) denigration of May. I'd been led to understand that she was bright, a good student. It's inconceivable that she has no grasp of his work; if so, you've destroyed her.

Still want to wash the windows?

180. To Joe Napora

(In letter 174 above, to Per Petterson, Sanford refers to this book by the title A View From the Plains. *In this next letter to Napora, the title has morphed into* The View From Afar Off. *It was eventually published by Capra Press as* We Have A Little Sister.*)*

12 August 1994

Dear Joe Napora

I offered to submit my new book, *The View From Afar Off*, to Barricade (Lyle Stuart), and he refused it, sight unseen. Seems he's still pissed because I let a magazine print (for free) a piece from *Maggie*. He must be *meshugeh*.

I need a publisher. I'm 90, and I need one soon. Have you any suggestions? Can you give me any leads?

The book, by the way, is about my beloved Maggie's early years in

Nebraska and Colorado, all of it leading to the moment we met in a Paramount hallway, and our lives really began.

Best.

181. To Jack Mearns

13 August 1994

My mood is not the best: Black Sparrow turned down *The View From Afar Off* on Monday. It was a surprise, because the reason given seemed specious: the book was about Maggie, not about me. It was useless to tell the guy that every book is about the writer, regardless of the subject, so I shut up and took the book to Capra the same day. Doubtless they'll reject it because it isn't about Apartheid.

If you know of any publishers, now's the time to speak.

A few points re your recent letter. The first is, don't start another project until you're sure you've gone as far as possible with Dead Wood. What's blocking you now will block you later, because the same writing problems are bound to arise no matter what you tackle. You won't leave them behind in Dead Wood.

Yes, no matter how you use the Theron Ware lesson, it'll belong to Frederic, not you. Advice? Find a new way (your own) of making the point, even if you make the snob say it straight out to Mandrell [sic]. In fact, that might be the very best way. No tricks, no borrowing. And the scene promises dramatic dialogue as an examination of character.

Forget your worries about being (how did you put it?) "a ponderous, wordy, non-dramatic writer." Secret: who isn't at the start? Most (may be all) the best writers were fumblefingered when they bought (stole) their first typewriter, and don't ever believe different. Tip: don't just write; listen to what you're writing. Without an ear, a writer must take up dentistry.

I know you want very much to become a writer. The only way to achieve that dubious ambition is to write, not by losing confidence, and not by letting errors defeat you. Defeat the errors! It doesn't come easy, and it may not come at all, but if it's there, it'll come.

Best to the Madel

182. To Jack Mearns

8 Feb 1995

Dear Jack

The only publishers I know are Black Sparrow, Capra, Barricade, and the U of Illinois. In my opinion, to submit to any of them would be a waste of time. Your best bet is the one you pass up—an agent. Agents know the ropes, and they cushion the anguish. If you have any kind of luck (literary, I mean), you'll have anguish aplenty. Why not let the agent absorb the punishment?

But if you're bound to go it on your own, hear this.

What to say, you ask? Little. As little as possible. Say that you have a book you'd like to submit for approval, give its title, offer only the briefest description, sign you name, and leave off. I think it would help to add you're a Professor of Psychology (full, assistant, or whatever), but crowding it on will only make an editor think you're selling your position rather than a book. What you're after is a reading. No letter, however detailed, will assure you of a publication. As for material, send it only on request. If the whole manuscript is called for, by all means send adequate postage for its return. Alas, there may be more than one. Brace yourself—Harcourt Brace yourself.

You ask, How would you describe me? Jack, my boy, never lead with your chin.

I haven't said anything cheerful in this letter—by choice. I want you to know you're getting into a bruising game. If you come out alive, there'll be no greater pleasure on earth. Except your wife. But surely you know that without being told.

I wish you good luck.

183. To the Editor of Calendar, *Los Angeles Times*

(This letter was published in the Los Angeles Times, *March 11, 1995.)*

2 March 1995

Dear Sir or Madam

Your issue of March 1 contained an article by one Kristine McKenna on women screenwriters of an earlier era. The piece is almost devoid of praise, possibly because Ms McKenna is almost devoid of understanding. The period she wrote about was governed by conditions far removed from those that obtain today: censorship guarded morals now quite extinct, rock-and-roll was only on the horizon, and the social drug was aspirin. The very up-to-date Ms McKenna regards that as quaint, forgetting that one day she too will be passé.

One of the writers scorned by her was my beloved wife Marguerite Roberts (1905–1989), but not for her alone do I resent Ms McKenna's heavy-metal prose. She also dismisses a corps of women who, within the restrictions of their time, wrote most admirably. Among those were Sonya Levien, Virginia Van Upp, Dorothy Kingsley, and Helen Deutsch, all of whom I knew and esteemed.

It will not do to dismiss their work, as Ms McKenna does, by saying, "If this extravaganza of unenlightened clichés is the best the gals can do, they should be permanently banished to wardrobe duties." My wife was on the M-G-M payroll for twenty years—twenty years straight!—and unless Ms McKenna can match that feat, I suggest it's she who belongs in Wardrobe.

Sincerely

184. To Lyle Stuart

(This letter represents the nadir of the Sanford/Stuart relationship. In the letter to Kuntsler that Sanford mentions, Stuart calls Sanford "one large pain in the ass" and recalls that Barricade lost "a great deal of money" publishing Sanford. Stuart was peeved that Sanford allowed The Santa Barbara Review *to publish work from* Maggie *without asking or telling Barricade, which the house considered "giving away rights." For his part, Sanford had trouble getting his manuscript of and original copyright certificate for* The View From Mt. Morris *from Barricade, and thus felt compelled to enlist Kunstler's help. What's more, Barricade seems to have intentionally left Sanford's name off the book's title page.)*

17 April 1995

Dear Stu

Bill Kuntsler has sent me your most recent outburst, and I note that the level of your abuse of me is as high as ever.

Until now, I've stood for it, thinking you merely a hot-headed and self-important fool. But I've come to realize that you're much more baneful. You're a vindictive and venomous tyrant, and it's high time that someone told you off. That someone is I, as you will discover in the next paragraph.

Go fuck yourself, Stu. But play it safe; wear a condom.

185. To Joe Napora

28 Sept 1995

Dear Joe

I'm glad you were pleased with that copy of *Shoes.* I prize the book myself, mainly because it finally saw light at Maggie's insistence: she paid for private publication. It still dazes me to think back on the book's history. On its appearance, it got nothing. On Black Sparrow's reissue thirty years later, it got eight columns in the N Y Times, with photo and sidebar.

You're generous to offer a review of the new *Maggie* book. I hope you like it as much as I do . . . but, hell, I like anything that deals with my baby. Baby, did I say? She'd be 90 if she'd lived.

Here's a review of the Memoir by Dan Giancola.

Best to you and Barbara. It'd be a pleasure to meet your son.

In friendship

186. To Jack Mearns

22 October 1995

Conrad:

I wrote about the writing of *David Holloway* in *The Waters of Darkness.* See scenes 57, 58, and 59.

Sisters is distributed from a center in Minneapolis, I'm told, or maybe it was Hong Kong. Depends on how long the book takes in transit. Don't hurry. There'll only be a line at the return counter.

You've gotten yourself into one hell of a profession. Get out before it closes in over you. If you don't, prepare to furnish your own (your only) satisfaction.

etc.

187. To Aris Janigian

7 November 1995

Dear Aris

For more than fifty years, Maggie ran my three initials together—J B S—and called me Jabez. Only the other day did I learn that Jabez is from the Hebrew and that it means *He will cause pain.*

I read "The Last Romantic" in two sittings. As I understand its plan, it deals with the relationship of twin brothers over a brief span, possibly no longer than two weeks. Layered into that period are scenes from their past, but except for a few casual contacts (father, mother, Cindy, Martha), the brothers carry the story. The plan and the story are good; the execution is not.

Some while ago, you showed me three or four of your short stories, and I faulted you for *stating* ideas instead of *dramatizing* them. The habit must be a strong one, because you still haven't shaken it. The pity is, that you *can* dramatize, but seem afraid to try the power consistently, with this result, that a few realized scenes are lost in a swamp of exposition. You're asking the reader to supply the drama; if he could do that, he'd write his own book.

I gather—rightly, I hope—that Alec is a diabetic, and Arthur, an anaesthesiologist, is about to give him shock treatment (and kill him, if "Critical" means what I take it to mean). The relationship is big with possibilities, but what the reader gets (this one, anyway) is stretch after stretch of heavy going impossible to slog through. The writer—and I mean you—is making a show of knowledge. He's a deep thinker, and he wants the reader—and I mean me—to be bowled over by his learning. Instead, mister, I'm bowled over by your assumption that I'm going to be bowled over. Do you really think you establish profundity with all that teutonic jargon? If so, guess again. Alec and his three-page speeches on What's-it-all-about?—who in the world can accept that in place of the deed? Here are twin brothers, complements of each other, halves (Death and Life, if you will), but they have no existence except in the past; during the two-week scope of the present, they're only language, precisely at the time that they must be people, for one of them is about to die. They talk, or rather one does and the other punctuates—and the words seem heavier than air. There are two "times" in the book, and you're using only one of them effectively. The past is faulty, but it's real, it's dimensional; the present is idea, philosophy, and if it's your own, I deplore it.

In the relationship of the twins, there's every possibility (which is why I say your story is a good one), but only here and there have the possibilities been exploited. . . .

> I stopped here to read over what I'd written, and it struck me that I'd been pretty rough on a guy I've long known and liked, and that maybe I ought to temper the wind to the shorn lamb. But then I thought this—phrig it! The guy's got strong opinions, strong enough to stand up against yours if you're wrong. So say what you have to say and forget about being mild. You may now proceed.

only here and there, as I've said, have the possibilities been exploited. The coyote episode, the pot-smoking scene, the scene at the lake with the girls, along with several others—all these are fine. But the scenes of the present, the vital scenes between the brothers, they lack, well, they lack vitality. They're used to give Alec the floor, where you seem to think he establishes character by spouting Weltschmerz. He doesn't—at least, not for me. I want to know why the twins have taken separate roads, why one is irresponsible and the other serious, in short, why the twins are twain. It won't do just to say they're different because they're different; you have to prove it. Five-hundred-word speeches prove nothing. The material from The Folder proves nothing (it's unreadable). The epigraphs and the italics prove nothing. My advice is to junk that stuff. You may think it's deep; if so, it's deep junk.

These boys were brought up in a cold household, but how do you account for their being colder? They have no compassion for a consumptive mother and a crippled father (through whose labors, by the way, they got a crack at culture), they have no gratitude, they have no love: their mother is a shadow, their father is The Oaf. You're the author, and you must speak of those lacks. It won't do to let them drink and screw and gaze at their navels; they've got to be human to make me care.

You're given to leading up to scenes and then skipping over them to the aftermath. Describe them, for Christ's sake! What're you scared of? See the fight in the bar; see the girl walking through fire.

You use a good deal of metaphor, much of it excellent:

> He rose, shackled with seaweed (p 148)
> The moon powdered the barn (p 160)
> Her limbs swept over things like an underwater plant (p 206)

Some of it is not:

> Eyes like stewed tomatoes (p 157)

Be on your guard against the kind of personification on p 157, where you speak of the sun:

> pitiless pain
> relentless violation
> merciless pummeling

That is not prose; in fact, it isn't even heat.

This isn't prose, either:

> The self is divided, and the division is endemic as it is immedicable.

Don't even ask me what it is!

Near the close, you reproduce a medical chart, and you give it without a break.

I think it would have far greater effect if you interlarded it with observations from the doctor, his fears, his feelings for Alec, his regrets, etc. Save two or three entries for the end, along with the stark "Critical."

Cindy is part of the final two weeks. Arthur treats her like a bedpan. If you make him cruel, know that you're doing so and say it.

Some of your paragraphs are written with great care, some with great carelessness. Aris, a writer has to care about every fucking word!

Quit flinging in "impressive" names—Rothko, Caravaggio, Heidegger. They don't impress me enough to find the correct spelling.

I could go on, but I've more than lived up to the meaning of my name, and it's time to sum up:

You've got a lot of talent, kid, but you've also got a lot . . . I was going to say a lot to learn, but it's more to the point to say a lot to *un*learn. You have a good eye and a good mind, you have experience, will, and all the machinery you need to get you far. But chuck away the non-literary baggage you're taking along. Who travels light travels fast.

Let me conclude with this. If I were an editor, and you'd shown me the book, I'd say: "go home and give 'The Last Romantic' a good hard look. Then rewrite it and *come back!*"

If my Maggie had lived she'd've been ninety years old on the 26th of this month. What a cute ninety she'd've made!

188. To Jack Mearns

10 November 1995

Jack

You worry me when you toy with the notion of quitting your teaching career to become a writer. You don't "become" a writer by chucking something else; it's a long hard road, and you meet few friendly faces on the way. I quit the law, true enough, but I didn't "become" a writer for a good twenty years—and there are some who think I haven't made it yet.

You haven't asked for advice, but I'll give it anyway. Do the research you need for tenure. It'll take time away from *La Brea*, but you're young (what? 35?), and *La Brea* just might be the better for the delay.

All the above from a nice guy who didn't listen to the same.

189. To Joe Napora

20 November 1995

Dear Joe

It pleases me greatly that you liked *Little Sister.* Writing it was the only way I had of enjoying the years before we met, knowing her before I knew her—a fancy I'd always had—and as you'll have seen, the book came from the heart. Thanks for being touched.

Your piece on my writing does me too much honor, I'm afraid, but, hell, it made good reading. A review of *Sister,* which you propose, would be equally good.

I'd very much have liked to see and hear *Scighte* when it was performed; it must've been an experience.

My respects to Barbara. Tell her what a treat it would be if the two of you came west.

Best.

190. To Aris Janigian

28 November 1995

Dear Aris

I've never set myself up as a critic of anyone's writing but my own, but when you ask for my opinion, my opinion is what you're going to get—without bullshit. I can be wrong—hell, I'm often wrong—but what I say is what I think, and you can take it or shove it, as you please.

Your defense of your novel is so spirited, but it fails to shake me loose from anything I said about the book. I'll go further: your explanation of it is lots clearer than the book itself. You had a worthy aim, no quarrel there, but your execution (which you set such store by) falls far short of what you say you had in mind. You have not dramatized the idea well enough to suit me, and the scenes between the brothers are too full of wool to allow more than a notion of them as people. They seem (to me, at any rate) to shred away in scholastic conversation that often becomes author's essay. Neither brother moves me, neither involves me: the doctor is more foil than character; the other is a long-winded pundit with high-flown spiel. Despite your forays into the past, you really say little about how they got to where they are.

You claim great depth for your theme, but if it's there, it's deeper than I was able to go. For my own writing, I make no such claim: whatever I have to say is on the page, not in some trench; it's there, I hope, with skill, but surely it's always clear. Your aim is not made clear by your execution of it (again, not to me), and your say-so doesn't make it so. Execution *is* important, and when I fault yours, maybe you ought to take another look. You might find out why, with the best of intentions, I could never find my way into the book.

I've made mistakes, many of them (Maggie could outthink me all day long), but there has to be some basis for my feeling shut out. It may be due to my lack of understanding, but it just could have been caused by the book. You're right when you defend your book—I'd do the same—but you ought to ask yourself why a long-time good friend with a real wish to admire it is simply unable to do so.

I remarked on your flair for metaphor, and you shook off the compliment as a sop. You miss the point, which is, when you turn to narrative and characterization, the flair leaves you. Heaviness then burdens the page, something I found in your early stories and tried to make you aware of. A measure of that language remains, and you seem to have no idea of what it does to pace, rhythm, and clarity. You've got to stop thinking (and writing) like an academician. You can't write a book by being one.

I began by saying that I'm no critic except of my own. If you're sure you're right, stand your ground and tell me to go to hell. That's what I'd do with your criticism (because I *am* sure), and you're free to do the same. Buena suerte.

Yours etc

191. To Joe Napora

6 Dec 1995

Dear Joe

I went to De Witt Clinton H S with Abel Meeropolsky back in 1917-21. I didn't know him to speak to, but I remember him as a *macher*, a big man in school politics. He was always running for office, and he usually made it. He was a progressive even then, but I knew nothing in those days (just like in these).

Thanks for the Eshelmon thing. I met the guy at the Black Sparrow offices when I was still on their list. I got kicked out for not making money.

Bad news re *Little Sister.* I was sure Elaine Kendall wd review it for the L A Times, especially after getting a card from her saying she was reading the book with "great delight." Yesterday my publisher called and sd she wd not be doing a review. No reason given. There goes my one hope of a big-city review. A nice little book is going to go unsung.

Best to you and the Signora.

As Ever

192. To Joe Napora

15 April 96

Good-guy Joe Napora

Thanks for the tip about the *Little Sister* review in American Book Review. Capra had gotten hold of copies and sent one along to me. They're broadcasting it to their reps in the hope of generating sales. Fat chance: Sanford doesn't sell.

I'm not bitter about it; I'm resigned. At no time in history has the world been more enslaved by pop-culture, and a man either writes for it or waits for good guys like you to come along and whistle for him—in the dark.

Tell Barbara I said she's gotten herself a prize. To both of you, always the best.

193. To Joe Napora

*(*The New World *mentioned here was published in 1997 as* Intruders in Paradise.*)*

19 April 1996

Dear Joe

What I like best about your review of *Little Sister* is your recognition of the fact that Maggie pervaded my writing life quite as much as my personal. To show how right you were:

We were not yet married in 1937, when I wrote *Seventy Times Seven* in her patio, with her Airedale Minnie the Moocher at my feet.

The People From Heaven, written in 1942, is full of the lingo of Maggie's family, which I'd married into in 1938.

Mary Homer, in *A Man Without Shoes*, is an early approximation of Maggie.

As for *The Land That Touches Mine*, all I knew about the El Centro locale, which I'd not as yet seen, I derived from Maggie, together with episodes out of her personal experience and a few attitudes that I bestowed on the character Jean.

The $300 Man was based on Maggie's screenplay *The Hero Suit*, which in turn was based on my novel *The Old Man's Place.*

Maggie is dominant in Vols 3, 4, and 5 of the *Autobiography*, appearing by name.

Maggie, of course, is the Maggie of *Maggie: a love story.*

Maggie is the little Sister in *We Have a Little Sister.*

Maggie appears in my latest, *The New World*.

Eight of my twenty-three books are dedicated to her, but she's entitled to all twenty-three.

Best to you and Barbara.

194. To Jack Mearns

21 July 1996

Dear Conrad

You've been worried, you say, about falling off in quality since your recent pit-stop. Don't be. I've read the latest batch of stuff from *La Brea*, and it seems to me to be up to your standard; you've picked up where you left off, which is all to the good.

You've also picked up on your ability to take two pages to say what one says better. At the rate you're going, you'll finish in the next millennium—or the next but one, depending on whether Malcolm is around. Conrad is still a long-suffering schmuck, and Malcolm is his seven-year itch. I wouldn't mind the guy if he weren't so answerable. He's as profound as a candy-wrapper, and Conrad lets him get away with his smartalecking till the reader wants to write the lines for him. I don't mind a pseudo wise guy, but he can't be shown as unanswerable; otherwise, you become liable to the suspicion that you take him seriously (you, not the Conrad in the book).

When you finish the book you'll have a cutting-job that'll require help. I foresee your reducing unemployment to 0, thereby raising interest rates and undermining Capitalism. You are a subversive.

I ought to be talking about Flight 800, but it's simply too terrible to dwell on.

195. To Stephen Cooper

(Cooper is another Nathanael West biographer. I've been unable to ascertain if he indeed published a biography of West. He did, however, publish Full of Life: A Biography of John Fante, *another Sanford contemporary and fellow California writer, mentioned in the following letter. The book was published by North Point Press in 2000.)*

23 October 1996

Dear Mr. Cooper

In his late years, I was on bad terms with Pep West, as I believe I told you, but I'd be doing a great disservice to the early ones if I let John Fante's appraisal of him stand. He seems to have based it on two sittings over almond duck, but on those occasions with Pep, he must've had the pip.

Pep dull? Never! He was one of the best-informed and informative people I've ever known, and many of [the] paths I walk were first pointed out by Pep. Nor was he, that I ever saw, a vain man or a truculent one. On the contrary, he was retiring and reasonable. And as for "exploiting the desolation of Hollywood culture," as Fante puts it, he could as well have scorned Balzac for exploiting the desolation of the bourgeoisie. What the hell does any good writer do? He exploits what he despises. My guess is that something else was bothering Fante. It might've been the almond duck.

Sincerely,

196. To Richard Wentworth

(The book whose title is under discussion in this letter would finally be called Intruders in Paradise, *published by the University of Illinois Press in 1997. Interestingly, one of Sanford's suggested titles,* The Trampled Vineyard, *he proposed as a title for his second novel,* The Old Man's Place, *in 1935.)*

19 November 1996

Dear Dick

No matter who suggests them, a title and a subtitle become the author's expression when used. I'd be making a false claim, therefore, if I said the book was about "fools and saints," because it isn't. As to the subtitle, I'd disgrace myself if I described my own work as "impassioned." That's a word for the publicity department or for a critic, if the book so moves him, but no author worth publishing may use it of himself.

I'll admit that my title *A Voyage Through Paradise* might lead a reader to think the book about travel—but why throw the baby out with the bath-water? The book has much to say about a paradise bloodied, desecrated, and paved by the white man, and the word (or its equivalent) would be most apt in the title. I offer

Trespassers in Paradise
A Farewell to Eden
The People of Paradise
The Trampled Vineyard
Intruders in Paradise

What say you?

Cordially

197. To Dan Giancola

(I had written to Sanford about my class's reaction to We Have a Little Sister, *which I was using in a section of Expository Writing that I organized as a class in memoir writing. In addition to Sanford's book, we were also using* Inventing the Truth, *edited by William Zinnser.)*

10 December 1996

I look forward to seeing you. The days you name for visits are fine with me. I wish I could invite you to stay at my house, but I'm not up to entertaining a guest; Maggie's death ended all that for me. Within moments of where I live, there are several good motels, some of them close to an excellent eatery called Tutti's, which you might try. But as to your two visits, be sure of a welcome.

I'm delighted by the response of your class to *Little Sister.* They may feel otherwise about my answers to the questions they raised.

What I know of Maggie's life before we met is based of course on what she and her family told me. They kept no records, and information came to me in snatches and often without any informing purpose: mostly it was family talk, reminiscence. It was up to me, in undertaking to write *Little Sister,* to fashion a continuity out of those scraps. The past presents a person and a personality; rarely does it present the person's story. I had, largely, to create Maggie's.

Nearly everything in the book is based on a fact; almost nothing is factual. Specifically, though Maggie did work for the Imperial Valley News, I wrote all the articles attributed to her; only two of them were founded on what she told me, the ice-house death and the Mexicali murder.

I never met Leonard Roberts, and, strange as it may seem, I never questioned Maggie about him; he was her past husband and irrelevant. But now and then she'd make a reference to him, and one of his letters is in existence, and out of such thin stuff, I tried to build a character. From what I've heard, I don't think I missed by much.

As you know, I've written a five-volume autobiography—fifteen hundred pages. What you surely do not know is that 97% of it is fiction. Not one conversation took place as written; all are written as they must've taken place. A date, a letter, a single remembered phrase—the scenes stand on little more. I'm not praising myself when I say that's the creative act; it's what any serious writer puts on the page, the product of nothing turned into something.

The bit about Pike's Peak was adapted from an account in Baedeker's *United States*, 1909. The trip made by Maggie and Leonard is a fiction.

Inventing the Truth—if your class applied that to *Little Sister*, nothing could be more apt.

Illinois looks at the book from the outside; they're thinking of attracting readers. I look at it from the inside; I'm thinking of what I'm trying to say. The two points of view clash. They always have; they always will.

Enough, save for regards to your class, along with my thanks for liking *Little Sister.*

Cordially

198. To the Editor, *Los Angeles Times*

(Martin Marty's article that Sanford responds to appears in the January 26th, 1997 "Opinion" section of the paper.)

28 January 1997

Sirs:

I have read Martin Marty's article on the director Elia Kazan, and I'm angered by his defense of a latter-day Judas and his plea for forgiveness of the unforgivable. Dr. Marty, a professor of religious history, has forgotten what justly befell the original Judas: "Now this man purchased a field with the reward of iniquity, and falling headlong, he burst asunder in the midst, and all his bowels gushed out." (Acts 1.18) Nothing has gushed out of Kazan but bitterness against the loathing he inspires in those he betrayed.

My wife was the screenwriter Marguerite Roberts, and she owes her ten years on the Blacklist to such sham patriots as Elia Kazan. In his testimony before the House Committee on UnAmerican [sic] Activities, he takes the pose of having chosen loyalty to his country over loyalty to his friends. The pose is false: the fink never lived who didn't invoke the flag. They're all patriots when their income is endangered—but God help the country that relies on such as he. They'd betray it for pieces of silver.

Kazan was an informer for gain, quite like the original on the field of blood. He whines, though, over being denied recognition by the Film Institute and the Film Critics Association. I applaud them for their view of him. It is in keeping with the world's view of his disemboweled mentor.

199. To Jack Mearns

(The Roth referred to here is Henry Roth, author of Call It Sleep, *published in 1934. After a 60-year absence from literary activity, he began publishing, in 1994, his four-volume work,* Mercy of a Rude Stream.*)*

9 March 1997

Dear Jocko Mearns

If you don't know that this guy Roth is shitting you, then I have just the suspension bridge you've been longing for—only hurry!

'Creative inanition' because he wasn't writing about the Jews?

Well, who in hell was blocking him? All he had to do was quit shoveling turkey-crap and dust off his typewriter. Instead, for sixty years, the fucker sat on his ass ruing the day he forsook the Jews. He could've rejoined the Tribes long before he got to be an old fart requiring—what does he call it?—redemption.

Now, about that bridge. . . .

200. To Jack Mearns

(Eric Foner, De Witt Clinton Professor of History at Columbia University, reviewed *Intruders in Paradise*, and the review appears in the Sunday *Los Angeles Times* "Book Review" section on October 19, 1997. Aris is, of course, Aris Janigian, Sanford's earlier Literary Executor and correspondent.)

22 October 1997

Dear Jack

All three of us—Aris, you, and I—have shown a shade of disappointment with the Foner review. I say now that we were wrong. It was bang-up, and we should've known it without being steered by others. True, Foner scarcely touched on "literary quality," but God damn it, it's high time somebody *did* get past my being a "superb stylist" and got to what I was doing with the style. Style is clothing, and without a body in it, it's simply finery on a hanger. Foner got to the body, and he did it proud. For once, a Leftie and his Leftist work haven't been cut to pieces by the Establishment. No wonder Illinois is ecstatic; I'm no longer a stain on their list. Read the review again; it's tremendous.

We ought to be ashamed of ourselves. Of course, I've always been ashamed of you and Aris.

Send a kiss to your Madel.

201. To Mel Fiske

(Jack Mearns believes "the new book" mentioned at this letter's end refers to Sanford's unfinished and ultimately abandoned Little Sister Spoken For.*)*

13 January 1998

Dear Mel

Thanks for the good wishes. Same to you and Diana.

What you said about *Every Island* led me to reread the book. I hadn't done that for maybe fifteen years, and I was stunned by its dark tone. I wrote the book during the year or so after Maggie's 10-year anguish on the Blacklist, and apparently my anger didn't end when her punishment did—and I let it out in the book. It's dark and dense, and its view of humanity is orrey-eyed. It beats me how you managed to like it. *Maggie*, now—that's another story.

The new book is at p 1140—and rolling. Ah, but so am I!

Love to you and Diana.

Yours

202. To Joe Napora

18 February 1998

Dear Joe

I'd long ago given up hope of hearing from you. It even occurred to me that Kentucky had seceded from the Union—and the planet.

Thanks for your attempt to make readers read me; it'll be fruitless. I'm against the Establishment, and of course it's against me. At no time in my career did I expect to be put forward by the very thing I was out to put down. Writers write to be read, as you say, but at this stage, I write only to write—and to those who will not read me, I say: May the Devil shit you flying!

The new book, which really is a resurrection of my beloved Maggie, grows by the day. It's meant to be the story of our fifty-year marriage, and at the moment, 1200 pages of manuscript have gotten me to the nineteenth year. Looks like the finished job will run to about 4000—if I live to get there, which at 94 I doubt.

Joe, my best to you always, and the same to Barbara.

203. To Francis Irvin

(In a letter dated 4 April 1998, Sanford apologizes to Ms. Irvin, writing he didn't "intend to rebuke" her. He says he was only expressing "surprise" because the book is "very close to my heart, largely because Maggie figures so vitally in it.")

22 March 1998

Dear Francis

I have your letter about *Intruders*, and I'm glad that the pieces you mention (except for the Cather) were to your liking. I have to say I found your choices surprising. Naturally, I like the entire book—I'd not have written it otherwise—but just as naturally I like some of the pieces best. Not one of those seems to have caught your eye. There are a dozen pieces on women in the book, but you mention the Cather only to say you don't like it. As I say, I'm surprised. The Kahlo, the Alonzo, the Jewett, and the Cather I regard as some of the best writing I've done in my life, and it's hard to account for their failure with you.

Another thing: you seem to regard my long piece on West as

'friendly." Far from it, very far. "*Un*friendly" is much more like it. I owe him only for having set me an example as a writer. Beyond that, nothing. He was for West all the way. Anyway, Thanks for having read the book. I'm sorry so much of it missed the mark with you.

Yours etc

204. To Dan Giancola

14 April 1998

Dan the Sleuth

When Grace Paulan tells Platt the story of "the pimple-faced man," she, the Widder of 70x7, becomes one with the Widder of The Old Man's Place. Clearly, therefore, her marriage to Paulhan was her second, but it may not have been clear when I was writing 70x7. I think, so far as I am able to think, that I got carried away by my own story, and I caused Grace to tell a story that established a connection earlier than the one with Paulhan. It's annoying—all lapses are annoying—but it's not the only one I've been guilty of. In The Water Wheel, I made a great to-do about a guy wandering around New York with only a dime in his pocket—and at day's end he's spent fifteen cents! Sanford the thinker.

I'm up to p 1313. I think.

As Ever

205. To Dan Giancola

12 June 1998

Dear Dan

No excuse for not answering sooner and thanking you for the new issue of the poems. Why did you put people off by quoting from that guy Sanford? You cost yourself readers. Whenever his name appears, even on his own books, people pale and turn away.

They'll have a lot to turn away from in my latest, now astounding me with the page-count: 1485! And think, only another 2,500 to go.

That's all I do—write the book for three-four hours and then try to pass somehow the other twenty. It's a wretched life without my lady, no life at all, really. People visit me, but even when they're here, I'm alone.

Throw this away; it's cheerless.

The best to you.

206. To Eli Jaffe

18 December 1998

Dear Eli

If your reported dialogue with Wilma is actual, my advice is—listen to the lady. She knows where and how you defeat yourself.

I said you tended to use the convenient word, and in reply you said that you looked up every word in the dictionary. Eli, Eli, that's just where *not* to look for the needed word. The only place it can be found is in your imagination, your sense of the poetic, your understanding that metaphor is often superior to the real. There are things for which precision will do—tree, hat, dog, brick—but where you want to convey a man's feeling for an Indian woman, you've got to let your fancy run free; you've got to do more than say her hair was black. In *Moccasin*, you set up the possibility of a vital and revealing relationship, and then you let it dwindle away at long distance. More than anywhere else, there was your chance to have your main character become one with his cause—and you threw the chance away.

Amigo, I'm sure you regard certain books as literature—Lord Jim, say, and The Return of the Native, and Huckleberry Finn—but have you ever asked yourself why, or have you merely read them? For fifty years now, you've wanted to be a writer, but you've paid no attention to *writing*. You've proposed, so to speak, in the dark. There's a gap between what you have in mind and what you put on the page, and you rely on the reader to supply the bridge. He can't, Eli; he won't even try.

You're wrong when you assert that I had nothing good to say of *Moccasin*; I said you had fine material and nobility of purpose. I'll go further and say that you oughn't to try the stage. Stick with the novel and cure its illnesses.

I wish you and your wise lady the best of the season.

With affection

1.—Find a way to tell the reader the meaning of the Indian language you use. In the book, without a glossary, it has none.
2.—*Litigate?* You use the word four-five times in the text, and it's one I left behind at law school. Forget it!
3.—Don't be mad at me.

207. To Dan Giancola

24 June 1999

Dear Dan

No, I haven't heard from Joe Napora—must be a couple of years now—and it finally dawned on me (to coin a phrase) that I must've said or done something to offend him. Accordingly, I just wrote apologizing in the dark (another beaut) and asking him to forgive the deed or omission.

No, Maggie and I were never in Key West. The only time I was in Florida was in 1923, when I quit law school to run away. But from what? Anyhow, I wound up in a Fort Lauderdale clink, a vagrant. Had to wire my long-suffering father for money to pay my fine. To this day, I can't figure how a vagrant can be expected to cough up $21.

A first in a 70-year writing career: Capra Press called to ask whether I had anything to show for possible publication. I have—A Palace of Silver, and if Capra likes it, Capra gets it.

I'm glad you and Rachelle had a fine time in Castroland. Give the lady my best.

All I can say is, I'm writing away.

Reflections on turning 95? Don't!

208. To Joe Napora

22 July 1999

Dear Joe

Your letter about Maggie and *Maggie* the book is a long way the most beautiful I've ever had from anyone about anything. I wept when I read it, and when I read it a second time, I wept again. Joe, what you said about my girl took me by the heart. It was a remarkable tribute, all the more so because you'd never met her. Somehow you seem to have sensed her, and what you had to say of her was deeply moving. I can't thank you enough.

About ten days ago, I sent off a manuscript to the U of Illinois—*A Palace of Silver.* My hopes are very low; it's a book with two characters, one of whom is in the grave.

And on the same day, I began another, to be called *With Boards of Cedar* (both titles from one of my ancestors: Solomon). I expect to have a good time with it, and this is why. Up to now, Maggie has appeared in eight books, always from my point-of-view. This time, *I'm* going to appear from *her* p-o-v. I intend to give myself a good going over.

Once again, Joe—thanks for your lovely letter. My best to you, Barbara, and the family.

With much affection

209. To Alan Wald

22 August 1999

I have no regard for the "critical commentaries" of this Kenneth Booker. In what he has to say of *People* and *Shoes*, I find no word whatever about literary quality. He goes on at length to establish their leftist orientation, but nowhere does he say whether I write well or ill. In short, he discusses my violin, but he doesn't seem to know I can play it. That isn't criticism; it isn't even reviewing.

Best to you

210. To Joe Napora

17 September 1999

Your latest letter was an eye-opener: I hadn't had the slightest notion that Crawford was Jewish. My first writing-partner in Hollywood back in 1936, was the playwright Lynn Riggs, a good friend of Crawford's and Tone's, and it was he who took me to their house. Thereafter, I was invited many times—for dinner, badminton, a swim in the pool. In addition, she introduced me to a producer, who later gave me a job. The only way to show my appreciation to someone who needed nothing was by giving her a book. I gave her *The Water Wheel* bound in morocco. At no time did she give any sign that the name Julian Shapiro stood for anything more than that of an author. I suppose she was pretending that I'd given her someone else's book. Those invites came to a sudden halt when, on being asked to dinner, I said I had a date with my girl—not *a* girl, *my* girl. I didn't see or hear from her for twenty years, until the episode with Maggie's screenplay. She was interested in it and asked me to set a price. She backed away hastily when her agent told her that Maggie was on the Blacklist.

She never said anything against the Jews, I must add. In fact, she was close friends with Ellin Mackey and Irving Berlin.

NEWS! Capra Press has accepted *A Palace of Silver*, probably for spring publication. When that happens, I'll have been published in two millennia!

As ever

211. To Dan Giancola

14 June 2000

Dear Dan

I've just written a query to Coffee House. Why not? I'll try any house but Out.

Children coming like comets—lovely figure, Dan. I still think of your Arabic on asphalt.

To your questions. Sun and Moon said it'd publish *Palace* in the fall. Unfortunately, I failed to ask *which* fall. I've written the guy, but he has yet to reply. As for the one about my father, it's past the halfway point. I call it *A Citizen of No Mean City*, a quote from the apostle Paul, with whom you are no doubt familiar. He was talking of Tarsus; my father's city was New York.

Give my regards to William Heyen. I've not forgotten his *Swastika*, a wonderful antitoxin for the venom of David Irving.

Keep me posted about your health, kid; you're valuable. Best to all the Giancolas, including Pepsi. As soon as Coffee House spurns me, I'll let you know.

212. To Dan Giancola

14 August 2000

Dear Dan

A belated report. Please forgive the old Yid: as his body grows feeble, so does his mind.

I got nowhere with Coffee House. They were willing to read the manuscript, but all they wanted to see were "sample chapters." I balked. *Little Sister* depends for whatever worth it has on the whole, not the parts. You wouldn't show a stanza, would you?

The memoir on my wonderful father is finished. Jack Mearns, my literary exec, will be offering it around to innocent victims. Which brings me

To a 50-page collection of mine called *The Sacco-Vanzetti Papers.* It comprises 14 pieces on the case, ranging from the arrest in 1920 to the vindication in 1977. All have appeared in one or another of my books, but I'd dearly love to see them side by side in a booklet. Do you know of a press that might be interested? If you'd care to see the sheaf, say so, and I'll send you a Xerox. Don't hesitate to say nay.

I got a laugh out of Mearns. He queried a press about *Little Sister*, and when it refused him, he said he felt a pang. Me, I'm pang-proof. I've had 500 refusals.

You ask about the title of the memoir. It's *A Citizen of No Mean City.* See Acts 29.

I hope your health is good, and the same for the Giancola family. By the way, what became of your threat to come to the state we stole from Mexico?

All best.

213. To Joe Napora

31 July 2001

Joe, what a generous letter! A touching one too, as anything is that mentions my beloved girl. It warms me to know that you've read *Maggie* so many times. I go back to the book myself, because, for me at least, it realizes Maggie better than I've done elsewhere; on some pages, I actually can hear her speak.

I'm still writing, of course. At 97, I'm no longer any good at bungee-jumping, so I put in my time at this 50-year-old Royal. You used the word "computer." What's a computer?

I've had the galleys of my new book for several weeks. It's called A Palace of Silver, and it's being brought out by Sun & Moon, a small outfit, in its Green Integer series. It'll give me pleasure to send you a copy. A couple of others are making the rounds, one of them about my Grade-A father, and I'm working on a book of short pieces. What the hell?

Joe, it's always great to hear from you. I only wish it were more often. I send my best to you and Barbara.

Love to you.

214. To Joe Napora

Rosh Hashonah 2001

I won't talk about the past week. I'm still unable to take it in. All I can do is stare stupefied at the TV.

The book you project is immensely attractive. As you describe it, it sounds like a new kind of literary criticism, the writer as autobiographer and interpreter. Far more than I, you're familiar with the ten you mean to use to exemplify your theme of alienation. Many of these I never ever heard of, and I can't comment on their aptness. As to the isolating effect of writing, I can comment, because in large part, it has kept me from living in my time. My mother died when I was ten, and it slowed me to a walk, and later, writing slowed the walk to a crawl.

It pleases me greatly to be one of your ten, and I wish I could be around to see what you have to say of me. It'll be otherwise, friend Joe. I have an aneurysm, and it won't be long before I'm in the ground beside my beloved Maggie.

Know this, Joe: I've always wished you well.

With much affection

215. To Joe Napora

20 October 2001

Dear Joe

You write a heady letter, my friend, but nothing will persuade me that I belong in the same league as W C Williams. He was an idol of mine, and as a reverential man, I belong at his feet. It happens that I've said so in print—in *W C Williams/John Sanford; A Correspondence.* If you're unfamiliar with it, please say so, and I'll send you a first edition (all my books are first editions).

My beloved Maggie's final few years were in poor health. Not long before her death, she said, "I'm not afraid to die, Johnny. I've had a wonderful life." To me, that was better than a Nobel, because I'd been part of that life for 52 of its 83 years, and I might've had something to do with its being wonderful. But if my part in her life was only contributory, her part in mine was all; she was life itself.

Your account of Barbara's father was fine. It ought to be expanded into a book.

My publisher promises copies of *A Palace of Silver* by Christmas. He failed to name the year.

Hearing from you is a great pleasure. My love to you and Barbara as always.

You ought to know of my literary Executor:

Dr. Jack Mearns

216. To Mel Fiske

26 December 2001

Dear Mel Fiske

I have your recent plea for a position paper from Sanford, him who possesses the Word.

In the Fifties, Maggie and I were "detained." Blacklisted and denied passports, we were confined in a big jail—the U.S.A. We were citizens, and though accused of no violence, we were denied our rights under the Constitution. It's hard for me to wring my hands over the present crop of detainees: they're *not* citizens, and they *are* from violent backgrounds. Many are illegals, and we have a right to know what they're up to.

We are at war only in the sense that we "war" against crime, against drunk driving, against poverty. What we are doing in

Afghanistan is justified; it's a police action against terrorism, and it's no different from what Israel is doing to put down Hamas and the Jihad.

If those actions are abandoned, we will also abandon every advance made by the world since the Renaissance and go back to the blackness of the Ninth century. If a stand isn't made now it'll have to be made later, when Islam begins its crusade in reverse. In fact, it's already begun, and the ACLU doesn't seem to know it.

I'd started worrying when you hadn't written for so long; I was worried that Diana hadn't been well. Give her my love. A happy New Year, and a better one.

Affectionately

217. To Classic Arts Showcase

22 January 2002

Dear Sirs

For many years, I listened to and watched ARTS on channel 21 (Santa Barbara), always with much enjoyment. For me, it was the finest program ever offered on Television. No where else was it possible to see and hear so much ballet, opera, and instrumental music. Mme Scuderi at 87 listening to herself sing *Tosca* at 28 was worth years of commercial television.

Of late, greatly to my disappointment, I find that ARTS has largely been supplanted by a dull program called usTV.

Please inform me whether this change is permanent. If so, I have no further use for channel 21.

Yours truly

218. To Mrs. Eli Jaffe

8 February 2002

Dear Wilma

As soon as I heard your voice, I knew that the news was going to be bad—and it could not have been worse: I've lost a friend, a long-time friend I'd loved and admired for sixty years. Eli was one of the best, Wilma, and everyone who had the luck to know him thought so. He was always to be found on the right side (which of course means the Left) of any issue, and there he stayed, because his heart was with the people. I'm moved by the knowledge that he kept my letters; it means that he regarded me as a comrade. There are only a handful of us left, and the loss of Eli is one we can't afford. I send you my love, and I urge you to keep in touch. All the best to you and family.

Affectionately

219. To Simone Dykmann

1 March 2002

Dear friend Simone

I was delighted by your call; it was a treat to hear your voice.

Long ago, when I was always broke, I'd rummage in Ruthie's purses for the forgotten nickel or dime. She called me a 'coin collector.' I'm not the one, however, that you found on the Net; numismatics is not one of my interests. I doubt that I'm even listed under literature.

Undeterred, I continue to work. A memoir called *A Palace of Silver* is in galleys, and will go to press, I'm confident, during this millennium. A memoir about my beloved father, *A Citizen of No Mean City,* is being offered around, and a collection of episodes, *Better Is A Dinner of Herbs,* is still incomplete and lying on my desk. It's the book I spoke of on the phone. Every episode is about a girl or a woman I've known, and so far the number is over a hundred. I hasten to assure you that my name is Julian, not Casanova. All these females are teachers, nurses, cousins, aunts, grandmas, secretaries, classmates, mothers, stepmothers, neighbors, etc. Each, I hope, reveals a facet of the female character, and there isn't a sensational page in the book. I admire women, and I hope the book shows it. The full quotation is *Better is a dinner of herbs where love is, than a stalled ox, and hatred therewith.*

I'm saddened by Jenny's plight; I wish she were still with you. When you see her next, please say that I send my love.

As for myself, what is there to say? At 98, no day passes without a bit of diminution, but as long as I can get to this old Royal, why complain? And to whom?

Be sure that when any book of mine appears, I'll send you a copy. Otherwise, my executor will send it. Meanwhile, my warmest love to you, to Olga, and to Jenny. Please write.

Always my best

220. To Neil Gordon

(The editor Sanford mentions near this letter's close is Eric Darton.)

19 April 20–2

Dear Neil Gordon

Thanks for sending me the collected issues of *Tambour.* It was Harold Salemson's magazine, and in it I made my first appearance in print; many must've hoped it would be my last. Three of my effusions were published by Salemson, and none of them frightened Henry James. It was years and years before I would make myself reread them, but they sure as life frightened *me*. For better or worse, though, they led to the writing of twenty-five books, and it was Harold who gave me the start.

I met him through his great-grandfather Leon Lait, an associate in my father's law office. It was he who told me of Harold, then in Paris and up to his eyeballs with *Tambour*. Had he been less occupied, he'd hardly have accepted my three blasts of bombast. They showed nothing but a will to write; they had no direction, no form, no cause to drive them, only an effort to get away from the law. And that's odd for this reason: it was precisely the law in which I'd one day find my cause.

In my *Tambour* years, I'd been graduated from Fordham Law School, I'd passed the bar, and I'd been admitted to practice in the State of New York—but (and this will be hard to believe) I had yet to hear of the Sacco and Vanzetti case, the most notorious example of prejudice and injustice in American jurisprudence. I was simply ignorant, and it took me long to learn where my course would lie. When I did, I began the custom of folding phases of the case into the books I was writing. A dozen or more of these phases, from the arrest of the two Italians on a Brockton streetcar to their vindication half a century after their execution, have been assembled by an editor, and all will appear together in next Fall's issue of *American Letters and Commentary*. It will be my atonement.

So as you can see, what Harold Salemson began resulted in a career—in obscurity, true enough, but none the less a career. Nor is it over yet. Also in the Fall, Capra Press will publish *A Palace of Silver*, a memoir of Maggie, my beloved wife.

My best to your class and to you.

Sincerely

221. To Dan Giancola

10 January 2003

Dear friend Dan

Your letter, written this last century, had been languishing, if letters do that sort of thing, in my desk, a nice place for it, for too long, and I must reply.

If only to say that my vision has grown so poor that I can barely see what I'm typing. Dan, I can no longer read even the large type used in your letter, which will have to wait on Jack Mearns, who'll be up in a few days. Meanwhile, I hope that what you wrote was all to the good and none to the bad.

A Palace will be out in March. Capra gave me an advance copy, a pretty nice job, with a photo of fatuous John standing behind his dame and encircling her with his arm. My oh my, but I did love that Indian girl (one-sixteenth Cree).

Forgive my tardiness, and give my love to Rachelle. I'll write again, if I can grope my way back to this Royal. An aside: after 75 years of it, writing has stopped. No one can read what I wrote yesterday.

Best

222. To Joe Napora

(John Sanford died on March 5th, 2003. This is certainly one of the last letters he ever wrote.)

25 February 2003

Dear Joe

If my typing is poor, it's because my vision is likewise, but I simply must say what ought to be said. In you, my writing has had a great good friend, none better, but hasn't it dawned on you that you've been working for a lost cause? After a lifetime of writing, I'm still obscure, and nothing is going to change that. My beloved Maggie wasn't troubled by my being unknown; with her, as eventually with me, it was only the writing that mattered, not the recognition—and write I did. *A Palace of Silver* is my 24th book, and it'll meet the same fate as the other 23, but she'd've said, "To hell with the public, Johnny. Hit 'em with #25." So spare yourself, Joe; you've done much more than your share for this old scrivener.

With much affection

John Sanford

AFTERWORD

My Conciliatory Tone
By Jack Mearns

This March will mark the 18th anniversary of the death of the writer John Sanford, at the age of 98—a long silence from a man who published 23 books during a 70-year career and was a sedulous correspondent. That is why it is such a pleasure to read Dan Giancola's selection of Sanford's letters, which breaks the silence and re-animates Sanford's voice. As I read through this volume, I was reminded of a line from Shelley's poem "Ozymandias"—"the hand that mocked them, and the heart that fed." For in Sanford's letters we see evidence of two warring sides of his personality: the generosity of spirit that praised and encouraged neophytes who sought his guidance, and the scourge of scorn for those who angered him. John Sanford was not one to hold back a singeing letter. On several occasions, I recall sitting in his office as he read to me, with an impish grin, a stinging screed pulled fresh from the typewriter, spearing someone who had offended him. In a shorthand reference to the unsparingness of these verbal lances that we'd developed, he would say archly, "You'll appreciate my conciliatory tone."

The roster of correspondents in this volume is full of well-meaning friends and fans who were friends no more after John bridled at some minor slight. Often, it appeared, John was spoiling for a fight; and, once he took offense, it was practically impossible to return to his good graces. Toward the end of his life—certainly for the fourteen long years after his beloved wife, Maggie's, death—John Sanford was a lonely man who craved both critical and personal attention. But he also detested dependency. In his final years, Sanford's behavior convinced me that his secret ambition was to die friendless and alone.

Evidence of the importance letter writing had for Sanford can be found in his thin volume *William Carlos Williams/John Sanford: A Correspondence.* In the commentary that accompanies the correspondence, Sanford—then a man of 80—empathizes with Williams's loneliness in his later years and rues his own callow selfishness: how infrequently he'd written his mentor, when a letter could have brightened the doctor/poet's later days.

My own relationship with Sanford began, appropriately enough, with an exchange of letters. I had been researching a project about a Lost Generation author and was seeking surviving contemporaries. Someone suggested I contact Sanford. I wrote and Sanford replied. It turned out the two had not known each other—Sanford was of the next literary generation—but Sanford had once sent this author a letter, admiring a piece he'd done. In researching Sanford, I discovered his autobiography, *Scenes from the Life of an American Jew*, and borrowed the first two volumes from the library with the idea that they could supply background material about New York City in the 1920s. I am embarrassed to admit that I started the first, *The Color of the Air*, in the middle. However, I was so taken with the beauty of the language that, when I got to the end, I went back to the beginning and re-read all the way through. After finishing the second volume, *The Waters of Darkness*, I wrote Sanford a note of appreciation to which he responded with a letter of his own. "Such expressions are rare," I recall his writing.

One of the aspects of the autobiography that captivated me the most was Sanford's description of overcoming a childhood marked by hardship, loss, and diffidence about his education—his mother died, after a long illness, when he was ten; his father had a series of crippling financial setbacks; he never graduated from high school because he flunked English his senior year—to make himself a writer of supreme erudition.

Several months later, I got up the nerve to write Sanford again, asking if I could come to Santa Barbara to visit. I can still hear the sound of his voice on the phone when he called to proffer an invitation. That visit was followed by many more—at first sporadically, then regularly. Those visits came to mark the passage of years for me. I think they did for Sanford, as well, for he once told me: "I write in the morning and then spend the rest of the day spending the rest of the day." An interlude with a friend broke the monotony of solitude.

John Sanford was born in Harlem, New York, in 1904. Aside from brief stints elsewhere, he lived in New York City until 1936, when he was brought to California by Paramount Studios to be a movie writer. At Paramount, he met the very successful screenwriter Marguerite "Maggie" Roberts, whom he married in 1939. After renting several homes, they bought a house during World War Two in Encino, an idyllic setting of several acres, including stables for the racehorses Maggie loved. She referred to the couple's time there as "the best years." The best years ended all too soon, though, when Roberts was blacklisted in 1951's HUAC hearings. In the hearings' wake, the couple sold their Encino home and, following a fruitless effort to find film work in Europe, moved to Carmel, in northern California. Sanford portrays this as a bleak period of exile.

In 1957, there were signs the blacklist was weakening; and Roberts hungered to return to her screenwriting career. That necessitated living closer to the studios. However, even though Roberts was eventually reinstated, the couple would never again feel part of the Hollywood that had banished them. They decided on a house in Montecito—about one hundred miles north of Los Angeles—that was one of two structures built for a planned estate that never came into being after the 1929 stock market crash. Their home was originally a gardeners' cottage. It was solid as a fortress: Sanford explained that it was double-hulled, with two sets of exterior walls. Its two stories were disconnected until the Sanfords installed a miniature elevator, which John never used after Maggie died, fearing being trapped should it malfunction. Thus, it was necessary to go from first to second floors by an outdoor staircase.

The ground floor had been a garage and laundry for the estate. The Sanfords turned the garage into their bedroom, adding a raised wooden floor and using the old garage doors to make closets. The sprawling laundry, with its slate-slab floor, became Sanford's writing room. In the corner was a small table with his manual typewriter, above it an articulated lamp clamped to a bookcase. Next to it was a phalanx of reference books—among them the *Dictionary of English Slang*, *American Dialect English*, *Modern English Usage*, and a 1908 set of the *Encyclopedia Britannica*. In the middle of the room, there was a somewhat sprung blue sofa that faced a high-backed green leather occasional chair. I can still picture Sanford lolling across that chair with his head on one arm and his knees crooked over the other. The south wall was lined with low, glass-fronted cases that had once held John's collection of first editions but now displayed author's copies of his own works. Above were large windows that brightened and warmed the room when the sun was out.

Often when I arrived, I would find Sanford hunched over his typewriter platen as—his eyesight failing—he struggled to make out what he had written that morning. He favored thick flannel shirts and a vest that appeared to be the sleeveless lining of a hunting jacket; he wore the same pair of moccasin-type loafers, sometimes without socks. His white hair was still thick. The skin of his hands showed his age, but his face remained mostly unlined. When I was lucky, Sanford would read me what he had written—a new passage from a book or a letter to an admirer or someone doomed to become a former friend. Other times, he held forth from his green chair.

After Maggie died, Sanford moved his living quarters upstairs. This had originally been the gardeners' residence; each of the little bedrooms had a lock on the door. There was a small kitchen, with an imposing copper stove and hood. At the kitchen table, John would host the rare visitor for coffee or a snack. I can still picture the ham sandwiches he served the first time my wife accompanied me—crusts trimmed off, each quarter wrapped individually in waxed paper. In a rear bedroom was a television on which I watched many a horse race with John. There was a living room and dining room that were rarely used. Off the living room was a loggia. When the Sanfords first moved there, they could see the ocean down the hill, over the treetops. And John recalled the two of them watching from there Sputnik flashing across the night sky.

When I think over what I have just written about Sanford and his house, I ask whether there is anything there that distinguishes him. And I must answer that it was not the house but what happened in it—the fever of brilliant creativity that re-invented times long gone—that sets this locale apart. The books are available to be read—those that are still in print. But they only show one side of the man, for they are eminently crafted. This new volume of letters, though not without craft, reveals a less guarded Sanford.

As Dan Giancola writes, the letters are telling of his relationships with others. Sometimes Sanford generously offered support and advice to aspiring writers. The three most important words he ever sent me were "You can write." Some of his acolytes went on to great success: witness Per Petterson. Others struggled for decades to get anything published. Through several letters to Eli Jaffe (#'s 96-98, 117, 118, 122, 206) we see an exasperated Sanford. However, when Jaffe finally had a short story, "The Snow Snake Game," accepted, Sanford was as elated as if it had been his own. In contrast, when Sanford's pride was threatened, the talons would come out. His letter to Lyle Stuart (#184), publisher of *Maggie: A Love Story* and *The View from Mt. Morris*, is one in a long string of pugnacious, bridge-burning letters to agents, editors and publishers. In the small world of publishing, such letters closed many a door. And Sanford knew, in moments of clarity, that his own rashness had sidelined him from early-career success with novels put out by the most prestigious houses of the day to books issued by university and boutique presses. In the end, there was no one willing to publish him at all. Even though Sanford acknowledged that spite had nearly fatally wounded his career, he averred on multiple occasions, "I wouldn't change a thing."

It was those closest to him who could suffer the most grievous wounds. In his autobiography, he has Maggie say to him, "You're not an easy man to get along with, Johnny. You can ask your friends . . . if you still have any." His letters to those dearest to him could be the most viciously cutting. Take his stunning 1949 letter to Melvin Friedman (#69), regarding his loyal cousin's efforts to help *A Man without Shoes* find a publisher. Sanford once admitted to me, regretfully, "I didn't treat him well." It was out of this regret that he dedicated *The Waters of Darkness* to Friedman.

Although Sanford claimed that he would not have changed a thing had he the chance, he was at times troubled by the wasteland of sundered friendships he left in his wake. The evidence of this, for me, is in the caustic letters whose carbon copies were not deposited at Boston University, proving a rueful hand shaped his archival legacy. I believe it is pure luck that the letter to Mel Friedman survived; I came across it, segregated from his correspondence, in a file related to his publishing. Other incendiary letters have disappeared. One vanished letter in particular stands out vividly in my mind.

Sanford had been rewriting his will and put a dear, young friend in charge of his health directives. However, Sanford later rethought this decision, feeling he had slighted Maggie's relatives; he maintained he owed everything he had to his wife. So, he wrote this friend, abrogating the new arrangement. The friend applied with a wounded letter whose sentimentality incited Sanford: he lashed out bitterly, "Come down off Mount Olympus!" When Sanford read me this composition, knowing his words were hurtful—intended to hurt—he asked me what I thought. I replied, risking that Sanford would be incensed by me, as well, "I like your conciliatory tone." Sanford paused a moment, then laughed. Thereafter, any harsh letter he read me he introduced with a delectating "You'll appreciate my conciliatory tone."

John Sanford was a complicated man with complicated relationships. The letters Dan Giancola has selected expose these complications—generosity mixed with flashes of the lash. This volume is a fine complement to Sanford's books, revealing the man behind his beautiful and polished prose.

INDEX OF RECIPIENTS

ACKNOWLEDGMENTS

I would like first to thank John Sanford's literary executor and my friend Jack Mearns for granting me permission to access and print these letters from Sanford's archive, and for his fine Afterword and his help with proofreading, fact-checking, and formatting. All errors that remain are my own. Thanks too to Suffolk County Community College for awarding me the half-year sabbatical for the time needed to do the work of completing this project. I am also indebted to the Howard Gottlieb Archival Center at Boston University and all the archivists who ran boxes of Sanford materials to and from my table, including Adriana, Claudia, Alex, and Nicole (whose last names I was too poor a researcher to record). Lastly, thanks to colleagues George Monahan, without whose technological acumen and assistance I would have been unable to apply for and complete my sabbatical, and Adam Penna, who offered his own sabbatical application as an example of doing it correctly. Of course, Thanks to John Sanford, who befriended me and wrote me so many great letters, providing the inspiration for this project.

D.G.

PUBLISHER'S ACKNOWLEDGMENTS

Profound thanks are extended to the following for their generous financial support which helped to defray some of this book's production costs:

Charles Agvent, Bulent & Olga Akman, Alkharraz, Geoffrey Arend, Thomas Young Barmore Jr, Robert E. Bason, Brian R. Boisvert, Chris Call, Bill Carroll, Sam Catanzaro, Scott Chiddister, Chelsea Clifton, Jangus C. Cooper, Sheri Costa, Malcolm & Parker Curtis, Robert Dallas, Curtis B. Edmundson, Isaac Ehrlich, Rodney David Falberg, Robert Patrick Frerich, Justin Gallant, GMarkC, Damian Gordon, Peter Graves, Aric Herzog, Jonathan Hope, Michael Hurley, Aris Janigian, Fred W Johnson, Kristiana Josifi, Haya .K., John J Kerecz, Dan E Kool, Paul Kuliev, Jim McElroy, Donald McGowan, Sam Mendlinger, Dr. Melvin "Steve" Mesophagus, William Messing, Lee & Jake Millen-Ouellette, Spencer F Montgomery, Joshua Y Montoya, Gregory Moses, Duncan Moss, Clyde Nads, Michael O'Shaughnessy, Sidney Orr, Adam Penna, Waylon M. Prince, Robert Price, Neil Ratna, Patrick M Regner, Jessica Rosen, Frank V. Saltarelli, Sharon M. Scarborough, Spike Schwab, Isabella Marie Skillin, Martin E Stein & Scott A Saxon, K.L. Stokes, Alan Wald, Rob Watt, Isaiah Whisner, Charles Wilkins, and T.R. Wolfe

www.ingramcontent.com/pod-product-compliance
Lightning Source LLC
Chambersburg PA
CBHW011508100726
47900CB00009B/2639

* 9 7 8 0 5 7 8 7 7 4 7 2 5 *